Indian English Fiction (2001-2020)

History and Reflections

Jagdish Batra

ATLANTIC
PUBLISHERS & DISTRIBUTORS (P) LTD

Published by

ATLANTIC

PUBLISHERS & DISTRIBUTORS (P) LTD

7/22, Ansari Road, Darya Ganj, New Delhi-110002
Phones : +91-11-40775252, 40775214, 23273880, 23275880
Fax: +91-11-23285873
Web: www.atlanticbooks.com
E-mail: orders@atlanticbooks.com

Printed & bound in India by Atlantic Print Services

For little Aryaveer

Preface

The present book is, I can humbly say, a labour of love, for I had been keeping record of all the books written in English by authors of Indian origin since the year 2000 AD, out of my interest rather than for any sort of gain or recognition. Even before that, I was given to the habit of religiously keeping notes on books that I studied or about which I got information. But, as we crossed over from the second decade of the present century, I thought it prudent to share this little storehouse of knowledge with the students and researchers of Indian English literature, or Indian Writing in English, as some still refer to this genre.

This habit was spurred by a certain observation. I have felt pained by the effort of western academy to which the Indian intellectuals have meekly acquiesced, in subsuming all Indian literature written in English under the rubric of South Asian Literature. I am not convinced by the reasons given to justify such an attempt at obliterating the Indian identity in literature when proud references are made to American Literature, Canadian Literature, and so on ('English Literature' as a term is always identified with British Literature).

After this brief submission, let me present the plan of this book. In the first part of the book, a survey or a brief history of the noticeable works coming from authors of Indian origin, whether staying here in India or residing abroad, has been taken up. These works have been classified into different categories. Such a survey involving assessment of works does involve a measure of subjectivity, howsoever hard one might try to adhere to strictly objective parameters. I have tried my best to balance my judgment with that of esteemed reviewers, readers' feedbacks, awards and recognition claimed by an author as also his/her precious record of literary output. I repeat here my words which I wrote with regard to such a study done previously for the first decade: "We know that what appears to be valuable today may be underrated by posterity; conversely, what is being discarded today might be celebrated tomorrow. Therefore, the disadvantage involved in judging things close by in terms of time is sought to be offset by the electronic-age advantage of being able to get feedback from readers and reviewers spread all over the globe."

With regard to the classification which is mainly done on the basis of theme, I shall like to submit that a novel is, by its very composition, a free-flowing narrative that encompasses many dimensions of life and world. When it comes to classifying it under a restricted category, all that we can do is to take up the most dominant aspect—be it a theme or style. There are always themes touched in a minor way or a stylistic variation that occurs on some pages, which have to be ignored. The other problem that I faced while classifying these novels was determining who could be accepted as an Indian author. The problem was resolved through resorting to reputed literary historian M.K. Naik's formula of taking up authors who are "Indian by birth, ancestry or nationality." Also, seeking information about the year of the base edition (in case of multiple editions) caused problem.

This survey is followed by enlistment of around 1400 Indian English novels published between 2001 and 2020. A caveat needs to be entered here however. I have focussed on novels only, leaving out story books as also translated works and to a certain extent, children's literature. I have worked hard to prepare a comprehensive list of all the novels produced during this period, but I humbly submit that there may be works which have been left out because I could not access information about them. As on date, there is no database which can give ready-made information about this kind of study and one has to be on one's guard to grab bits of information as and when a new novel is announced. The digital world provides stray references which have to be gleaned, sifted and verified for authenticity. Secondly, I had to restrict reference to long lists of publications of some authors by adding the words "and...more" to save space. This happened in the category of popular fiction.

In Section II, I have taken up the study of a novel each by some leading and a few promising authors. This study is done from a particular theoretical angle. The purpose is to give a deeper insight into an author through his or her work. Together with the bird's eye-view of literary output presented in the first section, this book, I hope, will be helpful to students, researchers and faculty members in colleges and universities as not much resource is available for the latest period of the two decades covered in it.

Finally, I shall like to submit that I have taken every care to note exact details like year of publication, etc., but considering the volume of the work, errors could creep in, for which I beg to be pardoned by discerning reader. I shall be grateful for your observations pointing out errors which would be set right in the following edition of the book. There could be disagreements regarding assignation of a particular category to a work. Your insightful comments in this respect will also be welcome.

I am thankful to my publisher Atlantic Publishers and Distributors Pvt. Ltd. for bringing out this volume on time.

Jagdish Batra

Contents

Section I: History

A Survey of Indian English Fiction (2001-2020)

There is no denying the fact that the genre of Indian English Fiction has shown remarkable growth since Salman Rushdie won the Booker for his *Midnight's Children* way back in 1981. His continued popularity with addition of more Bookers thereafter—Booker of Bookers in 2006 and Best of Booker in 2011 for the same novel—has been quite a phenomenon and indeed marks a watershed in Indian English literature (known previously as Indian Writing in English). Since then, there has been a gradual rise in the publication of novels written by Indian authors, whether staying in India or abroad. The pace quickened further with the other phenomenon heralded by Chetan Bhagat, who, did not win any Booker, but whose arrival was instrumental in establishing firmly the complimentary domain of popular fiction in India.

Background

Before we take up a brief survey of the literary production after the year 2001, it would be fruitful to remind ourselves of the literary scene prior to this time. Since the early days of Indian English Fiction and particularly from the days of the Great Trio, viz. R.K. Narayan, Mulk Raj Anand and Raja Rao, a number of prominent writers contributed to the progress of this genre. Among them can be counted Bhabani Bhattacharya, Manohar Malgonkar, Ruth Prawer Jhabvala, V.S. Naipaul, Kamala Markandaya, Arun Joshi, Shashi Deshpande, Nayantara Sahgal and Anita Desai. Also we should not forget the contribution of G.V. Desani, Khushwant Singh, Chaman Nahal, etc. Jhabvala was the first Indian author (India was her home till 1975) to bag the coveted Booker Prize for literature.

As the postmodern phase started with the arrival on the literary scene of Salman Rushdie, we note the presence of other authors of repute, viz. Amitav Ghosh, Rohinton Mistry, Shashi Tharoor, Vikram Seth, J. Allan Sealy, Vikram Chandra, and Upmanyu Chatterjee. While many among them won the Sahitya Akademi awards for their fiction, Arundhati Roy won the Booker in 1997 and Jhumpa Lahiri won the Pulitzer Prize in the year 2000.

For any spurt in literary activity, several factors—most of all a sizeable readership—are responsible. While the Booker award for Rushdie did raise the stock of Indian writers in the West, so that they were now welcomed with open arms by the publishers, within India too, readership increased gradually. At the same time, the winds of globalization impacted India in every field. The wave of economic liberalization that started in 1991 with the opening up of telephony and communication. Several multinational corporations started business in India which benefitted the educated youth belonging mostly to the middle class. We saw new IT hubs, BPO centres, etc. catering to their respective client companies abroad. The computer professionals formed the latest category of youth sought all over the world.

Also in place of the state-controlled Doordarshan, one witnessed huge proliferation of television channels. Burgeoning middle class with more purchasing power was a characteristic of the liberalized economy. More reforms were demanded and gradually allowed by the establishment. The rise of middle class engendered a measure of hope as also jealousy in the lower classes. Newer pressure groups and political parties as also newer configurations aimed at grabbing political power were seen to rise. However, overall it was a peaceful and progressive phase. India is now witnessing the reverse brain drain as also enlistment of foreigners as workers, mostly in the middle echelons of economy.

This pleasant state of affairs helped the growth of reading public. The English language capability of Indians was never in doubt. The biggest factor that inclined the people to learn English was its privileged status as the language of power even in postcolonial India. It helped the professional class in its success in career. At the same time, the growing popularity of English language fiction helped the spread of English language among youth. As a result, the reading public grew and more and more books in English got into circulation. It is in this context that the rise of popular novel in the wake of Chetan Bhagat's success can be appreciated. According to a report carried long back by *The Telegraph* (Sept. 15, 2012), the total titles published annually in Indian languages and English in India were 95000, the reading public 600 million and market size of ₹ 12000 crores growing annually at the rate of 30%! That also meant English gained more acceptability due to the rising executive class. Youth found in it a tool to realize the dream of global outreach and opportunities.

The remarkable growth in young readership has helped the rise of light fiction. The research undertaken by this writer suggests that the total number of novels published during these two decades should be way above 1400—the number accounted for in this book. Most of the novels relate to light fiction segment. Not only those who have studied literature and been trained in creative writing have produced fiction, but even professionals belonging to other sections like medical, banking, management, engineering, etc. areas have also published novels. It is like the Elizabethan times in England when it is stated that anyone who could write, wrote songs! The phenomenal growth in light fiction does not mean that all that is produced under this category is quality-wise laudable. Serious fiction, by implication, has taken the backseat. Let us now turn to the different categories into which the novels can be placed.

Individual/Relationship

Individual as a theme focusses on the protagonist who carves a niche for him/herself against the tide of time. The issue of identity is central to this category. Since identity is constructed in a society, the relationships that the individual forges with others in the world do reflect his/her personality. Family, as a microcosm of society, represents a network of relations that nature provides to humans to mould the personality and which culture transforms in time. When it comes to women, the traditional value system of the family and society pose a greater challenge than these would do to a male. Also, individuals with a challenged physical or mental state—regardless of gender—have also been subsumed under this category. There are historical figures and political icons who have towering stature but novels dealing with such characters have been taken up in history-based fiction. Major authors who have published individual-centric novels in the two decades under review include Shashi Deshpande, Chitra Banerjee Divakaruni, Jerry Pinto, Janice Pariat, etc.

Shashi Deshpande, a doyen in the field of woman-centric novels has written about different relationships like mother-daughter, father-daughter, husband-wife, etc. Over the years, one can mark a subtle change in her characters, so that the forward-looking Manjari of *Moving On* (2004) hardly resembles the submissive Jaya of *That Long Silence* (1989) in terms of liberated lifestyle of the former. A Padma awardee and a feminist in her own right, Deshpande has been known for weaving in great detail the web of family against which she marks the status of individual women bearing the burden of outdated traditions. In almost all her novels, in addition to the emotional aspects, women's sexuality—within and outside marriage bonds—have been taken up.

In *Small Remedies* (2000), Deshpande explores the lives of two women—Savitribai Indorekar, who is obsessed with music, and Leela, who is an ardent communist. Both strike a common chord as they break away from their families to seek fulfilment in public life. Her novel *Moving On* (2004) dwells on societal expectations from women which pay scant regard to their needs. The protagonist Manjari, aka Jiji is portrayed as an unconventional woman, who marries Shyam, the man of her choice against the wishes of her mother. Later, Shyam falls for Jiji's sister Malu and impregnates her before committing suicide. Raja, her childhood friend and a widower now proposes to her but she refuses. Instead, she develops physical relations with Rajan and she has the guts to reveal frankly to Raja: "It was just his body, nothing but his body."

Deshpande's novel *In the Country of Deceit* (2008) is the story of self-realization by the protagonist Devyani. She is a young, middle-class girl who decides to lead a solitary life in a small town after her parents' death. In this, she overlooks the advice of her family and friends. Then she meets Ashok, Rajnur's new police officer and they fall in love, even though Ashok is much older than her, is married, and has a 10-year-old daughter. Both of them realize from the very beginning that the relationship has no future. While her elder sister accuses her of stooping low for sex, Devyani believes she has found true love for the first time. The relationship ends as expected but Devyani cherishes happy memories. Deshpande delves deep into female psyche to bring forth the predicament of suppressed women. However, it would be right to say that her concern is not limited to female only as there are many male characters also.

Chitra Banerjee Divakaruni, though settled abroad and interested in immigrant issues, is basically a humanist who has actively taken part in rehabilitating battered married women in America. Her novel *The Mistress of Spices* (1997), which was made into a film that brought her into limelight in India, is a testimony to it. She aims at destroying stereotypes. Her *Vine of Desire* (2002) carries from her previous novel *Sister of My Heart* (1999) the life stories of Anju and Sudha, the childhood friends. They have relocated to America where their friendship is renewed. Anju has a miscarriage and this friendship provides her the strength to move on with her daughter Dayita, without the support of her husband. The twist comes when Anju's husband develops feelings for Sudha. Both young women enter into relationships with many other people which shake many of their cherished views about life. Divakaruni is a poet also whose elegant prose provides fitting vehicle to an emotional story.

Jerry Pinto's novel *Em and the Big Hoom* (2012) which won The Hindu Best Fiction award, explores the mind of a mentally sick woman, whose 10-year-old son is the narrator. Their conversation in a mental hospital reveals an interesting

12-year long courtship of their mother and father. In this, the novel indeed has struck new ground. Besides, it also throws light on Catholic community of Goa. **Amit Chadhuri's** *Odysseus Abroad* (2015) describes a day in the life of Anando and his uncle, on the lines of James Joyce's *Ulysses*. They are placed in London of 1980s. As it was in his earlier novel *A Strange and Sublime Address* (1991), the plot is quite thin, but Chaudhuri has the knack of spinning interesting yarn even without a central issue. The novel deals with an ordinary world rather than a spectacular one wherefrom he presents the snapshots of domestic and urban life in an impressionistic manner.

Manu Joseph's debut novel *Serious Men* (2010), winner of The Hindu Best Fiction award 2010 is also set in suburban Mumbai. It is a funny satire on the Mammon-worshipping mentality of the people. Love and revenge provide the motive for action which is handled in a very psychological manner. Ayyan Mani, a Dalit, has a boring job as P.A. to Arvind Acharya, a scientist. Moved by greed, Ayyan tries to promote his 10-year-old son Adi as a divine. Meanwhile, the scientist is accused of fudging data which gives a twist to the story. The writer's skill lies in portraying a conman Ayyan in a way that he wins the sympathy of the readers through his wit and intelligence. Joseph's second novel *The Illicit Happiness of Other People* (2012) brings out the pointlessness of life of an enlightened youth in an interesting manner.

Anita Nair in *Ladies Coupe* (2001) calls upon women to recognize their inherent powers and lead an authentic life. The story is set on the pattern of *The Canterbury Tales*. Akhila, the chief protagonist, buys a ticket to Kanyakumari and settles down in the ladies' coupe with co-passengers. She invites their opinions on whether she should and really could lead life as a single person—a question that had been haunting her for long. To this, there are varied responses, based upon individual life experiences. The discussion helps her realize the worth of search rather than of the goal. In her novel *Mistress* (2005), Anita Nair traces the delicate relationships that make and unmake Radha's life, who develops extra-marital relations with a travel writer as a result of her loveless marriage. Nair came up with *Lessons* *in Forgetting* (2010), which is a novel with an unlikely title. Meera, a well-groomed 'corporate wife' and a successful writer of cook-books, has to shoulder the responsibility of running her family. As chance would have it, she gets the companionship of a cyclone expert, who has also to nurse his 19-year-old comatose daughter. The struggle of the twosome brings them together in an interesting story full of twists and turns.

The Queer characters are taken up by the Assamese writer **Janice Pariat** whose novel *Seahorse* (2014) is a bildungsroman which has shades of the myth of Poseidon and Pelops. The male protagonist Nehmaih studying in Delhi falls for Nicholas Petrou, an art history professor from London. The seahorse is one of the creatures in the fish tank in Nicholas' house. There is a sudden disappearance of Nicholas and then, after finishing school, Nehmaih takes up a fellowship in London where he happens to meet Nicholas' sister. The ending remains ambiguous. Pariat has rich language to her credit. Her other novel *The Nine Chambered Heart* (2017) is the artist take on the woman protagonist. Her personality is assessed by nine different people, all of whom had loved her or were loved by her. The story is set in different locations and the objective seems to be to fix the identity of the protagonist in an impressionistic manner. LGBT issue is also at the centre of *A Married Woman* by Manju Kapur which has been taken up in the section on family here.

Preeti Shenoy who has appeared on the Forbes list of celebrities, has established herself as a fine story teller. Her novel *Tea for Two and a Piece of Cake* (2012) touches upon the life of an ordinary woman in a masterly manner. *The One You Cannot Have* (2013) deals with concentric lives of young people in search of true love. *It Happens for a Reason* (2014) focusses on a single woman's life. Her other novels too deal with the theme of love in its various mutations: innocent first love, extramarital affair, abandonment of wife many years later, search for love long lost, etc. **Rupa Bajwa's** Sahitya Akademi award-winning novel *The Sari Shop* (2002) deals with the life of Ramchand, a shop assistant at a saree shop in Amritsar. One day, he is sent to a client's house with a bundle of saris for selection for marriage. His trip to the Kapoor House is an eye-opener for him and motivates him to learn English and improve his personality to achieve his goal which, however, goes haywire. It is a realistic novel that combines sensitivity with humour. **Anees Salim's** fifth novel *The Small Town Sea* (2017) is the story of a teenager whose father shifts to a small hometown as the father wishes to breathe his last by the side of the sea. The father dies as he had wanted but then there are challenges to be met on his own by the son. The novel is written in the form of a letter to a London-based literary agent, which act resonates with the real life problems which the author had to face with his agents.

Avani Doshi's Booker shortlisted *Girl in White Cotton* (2020), published as *Burnt Sugar* in UK, deals with the dysfunctional relationship between a neurotic mother and her daughter. The unconventional mother who left husband for a guru but having fallen on bad days, she had to beg on streets along with her child and then went after an artist. She is now decrepit and amnesiac with age. Both mother and daughter are shown strong-headed characters. The novel *Tiger Hills* (2010) by **Sarita Mandanna** is high on passion. Set against the picturesque Coorg, it depicts a love triangle in which the orphan Devanna loves Devi who would rather have Machaiah, the single-handed slayer of a tiger. Machaiah seems to be from hoary past, what with his 12-year 'no-marriage' vow! However, circumstances compel Devi to marry Devanna and the focus shifts to the next generation of the protagonist. The botanical details overshadow the plot.

Jeet Thayil's *The Book of Chocolate Saints* (2017) portrays a Bohemian poet and painter living in New York flees the city in the aftermath of 9/11 to India for his final show. In between are thrown a host of incomparable characters—poets, artists, whores, journalists, murderers, drug-addicts, society ladies, and what not. The subjects discussed are art, love, sex, saints, God, etc., etc. It is a compendium of myriad voices in impressive prose. In *The Persecution of Madhav Tripathi* (2015), **Aditya Sudarshan** presents a leftist protagonist who is abducted by whodunit. As he tries to grapple with the identity and the mindset of his captors, the protagonist also reflects on the general psychology of educated elite.

Among others, mention may be made of **Dona Sarkar's** *How to Salsa in a Sari* (2008) which targets the adolescent reader and goes through the travails of high school life in a privileged American school. Clearly, the characters in such a diasporic work would be of mixed blood. **Mitali Perkins,** an American of Indian origin, has penned fiction for youngsters. Her *Extreme American Makeover* (2010) deals with the aspirations of a youngster whose father is fighting election for the presidency. **Ardashir Vakil's** *One Day* (2009) focusses on adultery in a narrative in an impressive interior monologue mode. Indian expatriate **Hari Kunzru** published three novels in the new millennium. *The Impressionist* (2002) is a hero-centric novel in which the protagonist changes places as well as identities. His novel *My Revolutions* (2007) studies identity against the background of a foreign milieu. **Khushwant Singh** too came up with his *The Sunset Club* (2010) which centres round the life of three senior citizens giving voice to their fancies and foibles, their family life and their physical problems.

Family

Indian family system has been considered all over the world as a model of loving relationships. However, modernization in the form of industrialization and urbanization has led to breaking up of joint families and creation of more and more nuclear families. Even so, rudiments of the old value system prevail under which the elders are given respect. There is also the flip side in that patriarchy rules the roost. The multiple roles of woman in a family present a fascinating area for exploration. Although family has deservedly been taken up for the study of feminist issues, it is by no means the only ground for such study, nor is woman the centre of every family-based novel. A number of novelists have, therefore, also been inspired to take up the workplace of the 21st-century Indian woman. The contemporary woman is depicted as a professionally qualified and politically conscious, and raring to prove her worth in a man's world. Most of the writers dealing with family as a background happen to be women.

Shashi Deshpande's novel *Ships that Pass* (2012) is the story of Tara and Shaan, who are surprisingly near strangers to each other even after fourteen years of married life. In contrast is Tara's sister, Radhika, who gets engaged to someone she hardly knows. Deshpande's novel *Shadow Play* (2013) is all about relationships. Three generations of a Brahmin family with extended relatives are described here but the focus is by far on women. Gopal, father of three daughters, walks out on his family one day as he wishes to meditate. The daughters are naturally frustrated, and when he comes back after many years, they have problem accepting him. However, things smoothen out slowly and love overcomes prejudices. Deshpande's forte is portrayal of life in its natural flow without seeking sensational twists and turns.

It is not only women writers but also the male writers who have dealt with the theme of family quite well. **Rohinton Mistry,** an Indian Parsi settled in Canada, whose novel *Such a Long Journey* (1991) was proscribed by the Maharashtra Government under political pressure, came out with his third novel *Family Matters* (2002), which was shortlisted for the Booker Prize. In it, Mistry takes up the cause of the aged but he cannot resist his penchant for linking private life to public events which invariably play havoc with ordinary individuals. Despite his nose for nauseating details of dirt and squalor, Mistry's is essentially a compassionate realism. This becomes evident when he deals with the life of a retired professor of English, Nariman Vakeel, who meets with an accident and is confined to bed. The financial problems of his step-children, coupled with low commitment to values, impels them to send the father to his daughter whose husband Yezad does not really like the idea but somehow keeps quiet. The story takes a turn when Yezad wishes to capitalize on the prevailing atmosphere of political blackmailing but does not have the good luck, with the result that the rest of his life becomes a saga of repentance. Mistry also came out with a 48-page long single-story book *The Scream* (2006), which was specially written for a charity in Canada. The shortest piece of fiction written by him, it gives a close-up of the mind of an old person who, though living with four generations of his family, is still an outcast, living as he does in a world of his own and watching the world go through a window.

A feminist to the core, **Manju Kapur** is known for challenging the traditional family values in her writings. In 1998, she published her debut novel *Difficult Daughters*. This was followed by *A Married Woman* (2003). Maladjustment in marriage finally leads the protagonist Aastha to revolt and establish lesbian relationship with another depressed woman Pipeelika, who had been married to a Muslim and is working for an N.G.O. Common to both the women is the distrust of marriage as an institution. In her third novel *Home* (2006), Kapur depicts an extended business family based in a suburb of Delhi. She covers a wide canvas and goes into the details of parents and grandparents of the protagonist. To her, these relationships are important in that they shape the choices of the characters.

Kapur's novel *Custody* (2011) focusses on the after-effects of divorce on a family. An ordinary boy, Raman has an arranged marriage with the charming Shagun whom he loves dearly. But Shagun is made of a different metal; she has an affair with Raman's boss Ashok. She is concerned only with her own happiness so much so that even the kids take secondary place in her life. She divorces her husband to settle down with Ashok. Now, the 10-year-old Arjun is sent to a boarding school. However, the other child Roohi remains with Raman who marries Ishita, a much better girl than Shagun. Thus, individualism has the better of family responsibility in this novel set in the 1990s when globalization started.

Amit Chaudhuri's Sahitya Akademi award winning novel *A New World* (2001) is the story of Jayojit Chatterjee, an ambitious professor and writer, working in America, who visits India after his ugly divorce, followed by two unsuccessful attempts to remarry. On his India visits, he stays with his old parents in Calcutta and during one of these trips, he has the occasion to connect with his seven-year-old son Bonny, who otherwise stays with his mother in America. Chaudhuri avoids focus on inner life; instead he takes up the minutiae like a round of table tennis with Bonny or Jayojit's mother's oily breakfasts, etc. His prose is rich and evocative and yet the emotional side is underplayed. Chaudhuri's *The Immortals* (2009) describes two families, one neck deep in corporate culture and the other steeped in music. His portrayal of the attractive but often hollow life of corporate executives in pre-IT boom India is masterly. As in the earlier work, the narrative comprises of petty events and the ending is abrupt but still the work is pregnant with insights.

Upamanyu Chatterjee's focus is on the westernized urban Indian class. In his *Way to Go* (2010), sequel to *The Last Burden* (1997), in which three generations of a family living under one roof are shown realistically in their love-hate relationship. In *Way to Go* (2010), eighty-five year old and half-paralyzed Shyamanand is on his death bed but he goes missing. His sons Jamun and Burfi reunite and in their quest to find out Shyamanand, they find a path out of desolation, even as Jamun's former beloved gets busy with rehashing Jamun's life history into a TV soap. In his usual powerful prose peppered with black humour, Chatterjee has produced a moving examination of family ties and the redemptive power of love. Another novel by Chatterjee during the period is *Weight Loss* (2006), which displays the writer's proclivity for the grotesque through the character of Bhola who is obsessed with sex from his school days to well after his marriage and believes he has attained his authentic existence.

Anita Rau Badami's *The Hero's Walk* (2001) is the story of Sripathi Rao who wants to lead an ordinary life and actually is able to with his spinster sister, mother, wife, and son, in a decrepit ancestral house. His only joy is his lively daughter Maya, but when she marries a fellow student Alan, Sripathi angrily severs relation with her, until the time when Maya and her husband meet their end in a car accident. All that he is left with now are regrets and Maya's seven-year-old daughter. **Amulya Mulladi,** an emigrant to Denmark, has written a number of novels. Her *A Breath of Fresh Air*, which appeared in 2003, probes the life of a twice-married school teacher Anjali with problems arising out of the arrival of her former husband. Her struggle to reconcile the roles of wife and ex-wife, working woman and mother is superbly delineated. Mulladi's second novel *Serving Crazy with Curry* (2004) tells the story of a woman's struggle for acceptance from her family and herself.

Andaleeb Wajid came out with a dozen novels including *When She Went Away* (2016) and *More than Just Biryani* (2014) during these two decades, all of which are devoted to the lives of Muslims in India. The hallmark of her narratives is a non-stereotypical stance with regard to choices the young Muslim women make. **Namita Devidayal's** *Aftertaste* (2010) is a long narrative of a business family that is naturally obsessed with money only. The matriarch of the family moots the idea of setting up a sweet shop in which the two sons and two daughters are involved. The plot being thin, the pages are filled with descriptions of black money in the country as also the methods of preparing various sweets. It is politics of the business family that comes to the fore.

Kankana Basu's *Cappuccino Dusk* (2007) describes the story of a Bengali family and its adjustment away from home in a multi-cultural ambience. In between are thrown a kidnap drama, a bomb blast before the story ends on a positive note. Witty dialogues and wacky rhymes vie with philosophical outpourings in accented Bengali. Such family contests happen at coffee time; hence the title. **Manpreet Sodhi Someshwar's** *The Long Walk Home* (2009) recounts the life story of an old person with comments on changes in society over a long period. Not many talk of values these days. Therefore, when a novel is titled *Family Values* by **Abha Dawesar** appears, it makes one sit up and take note. **Ruchir Joshi** came out with his *The Last Jet Engine Laugh* (2001), which deals with three generations of a Gujarati family who trace their Indian history back to 1930s. The conflict of generations is brought to the centre-stage. **Akhil Sharma's** debut work *An Obedient Father* (2000) takes up besides an incestuous and corrupt civil servant who seduces daughter, the corruption-ridden system in India. In the other novel *Family Life* (2014), he portrays an Indian family in US which makes sacrifices for the sake of an ailing son.

Socio-political

It is true that the milieu forms the backdrop of every novel, but if any particular socio-political problem has been focussed upon as a core element in a novel, that novel needs to be subsumed under this category. The single most lacuna is the author's own ideological inclination that might use the novel as propaganda rather than a literary tool to project his/her point of view, leaving the decision to the reader. Rational approach backed by credible storyline is needed. The writers have chosen problems like crime, terror, casteism, fundamentalism, corruption, poverty, realpolitik, etc. to base their narratives upon.

Salman Rushdie came up with a beautiful novel—very different from the magic-realism laced earlier fiction—*The Golden House* (2017) which deals with the underworld of Bombay and upholds classical humanism. Rushdie takes up the life of a Mumbai don who shuns the underworld in the aftermath of the terror attack on The Taj Hotel in which his wife is killed. He shifts to New York along with his three sons, but despite his riches, he and his children do not get a happy life to lead. His two sons meet violent death. He, along with his eldest son and second wife—a petite Russian girl—gets burnt up in the plot hatched by his mafia adversaries, and poetic justice is meted out to the family. Rushdie's style is interesting with his sharp wit and word play, and what's more, the language is not as complicated as in *Midnight's Children*.

V.S. Naipaul's *Magic Seeds* (2003), sequel to his last novel *Half-a-Life* (2001) appeared at a time when he had declared the 'demise' of novel as a form of literature. Naipaul's passion is to understand the forces of social change. Willie Chandran, the protagonist, is a listless wanderer in search of meaning in life which eludes him. His domineering sister Sarojini makes him join an underground movement in India. However, after seven years he is disillusioned and turns himself in to the police. In jail, he learns more about the caste-ridden society. Finally, he flees back to London, where he has a fling with another such activity. The writer wishes to bring home the message that there are actually no magic seeds, no short cuts to success in life. There is a surprise in store for the readers in the form of praise for Gandhi's autobiography.

Aravind Adiga upset quite a few veterans when he bagged the Man Booker Prize 2008 for his maiden novel *The White Tiger* (detail in the section on Dystopian Fiction). Prior to it, he had written short stories but he could not find any publisher. Adiga's second novel *Last Man in Tower* (2011) deals with the problem of precious land in the metropolis Mumbai. A realtor wants to buy out an apartment house. While the other occupants agree to vacate, a tenacious retired teacher 'Masterji' stays firm because of his sentimental association with the house, and takes on the powerful builder. Even though the Masterji had been rendering service to the fellow residents by teaching their children free, the residents are more after money than emotions and start conspiring against him. A powerful satire on human selfishness indeed!

Anurag Mathur, whose maiden novel *The Inscrutable Americans* (1991) created waves in literary circles, takes up the life of a marketing executive in a private company in his novel *Scenes from an Executive Life* (2000) and focusses on the travails of this competitive age. His second novel *Making the Minister Smile* (2002) places a fat American young man, coming from a business family, in post-liberalization India where he learns the most precious lesson of successful business (*a la* bureaucrats!) which is encapsulated in the title of the novel. In his *The Department of Denials* (2004), Mathur takes the reader into the murky world of Indian politics. The *piece de resistance* is a department created by a minister to deny numerous allegations levelled against him every other day! Being a bureaucrat, Mathur understands well the nitty-gritty of the system.

A brilliant novelist and screen-writer, **Kiran Nagarkar,** who was earlier awarded the Sahitya Akademi award for his novel *Cuckold* (1997), published his *God's Little Soldier* (2006) that touches upon the contemporary concern about growing fundamentalism and in taking up the psychological study of a newly-turned fanatic, disputes its stereotype. Here is a young student Zia who converts to Christianity and becomes Luceus but terrorism is his second nature, religious affiliation notwithstanding. Nagarkar's novel *Jasoda* (2017) deals with the poverty and oppressive traditions of the patriarchal society in the rural hinterland. His forceful narrative traces the journey of a woman of incomparable courage and resolve who has to move out of the arid country that has been in the throes of draught for long, to a city all on her own since her husband has to serve his master as a loyal servant. In the process, the journey becomes an epical one and the woman an epical hero(ine).

The poet **Jeet Thayil's** maiden novel *Narcopolis* (2012) which won the DSC award and which Thayil based upon his own experience as a former drug addict, is set in the 1970s. It talks of the drug world of Bombay, the hippies, communal riots, and the street life. Rashid, the owner of the opium house in Shuklaji Street is succeeded by his son in due course of time as drugs change from heroin to cocaine. **Vikram Chandra** came out with his third novel *Sacred Games* (2006). Like his earlier novels, this voluminous 900-page novel is also set in Mumbai with its underbelly given wide exposure, what with actresses selling their bodies to get to the top and gangsters manipulating politics. The 'sacred game' refers to the execution of the rival don which, according to the killer, is already destined. The novel has too much of known reality and too little of romance.

Journalist **Kishwar Desai**, known for *Darlingji* (2007), the biography of the film actors Sunil and Nargis Dutt, penned her novel *Witness the Night* (2009). The novel deals with the problem of female foeticide. All her novels have Simran Singh as the protagonist. Her other novel *Origins of Love* (2013) deals with the issue of surrogacy and adoption. Yet another novel *The Sea of Innocence* (2013) shows Simran Singh trying to find a British girl who went missing from Goa and featuring whom blue films turn up later. **Kota Neelima's** *Shoes of the Dead* (2013) is the third novel by the US-based writer of Indian origin. Devoid of digressions, the novel is a focused study of the problem of insolvency of farmers. In the fictional Mityala district Sudhakar Bhadra, a peasant, commits suicide because he cannot pay loan on land due to the draught. It is left to his brother Gangiri Bhadra, an educated government employee, to unravel the truth of the politician-moneylender nexus aimed at grabbing agricultural land for selling it at exorbitant rates to industrialists. Interestingly, Gangiri employs blackmail to trap the evil forces, and though he also commits suicide in the end, he is able to convert the villain to the right path.

Kancha Ilaiah's *Untouchable God* (2011) castigates the upper classes for their inhuman attitude towards the so-called lower classes. The novel presents images of fiendish Brahmin representatives from different states who come to celebrate the death by beating of a Dalit for the crime of thinking about God. It is a witty novel that presents the known views of the activist Ilaiah on caste discrimination. **Meena Kandasamy** too is devoted to bringing out the discrimination in society. Her novel *When I Hit You* (2017) brings out the hypocrisy of a professor who advocates revolutionary Naxalite ideals but beats his wife at home. Another novel *Gypsy Goddess* (2014) focusses on violence against Dalit community.

London-based **Neel Mukherjee** has used his pen to voice his concern for the slum dwellers in *A State of Freedom*. Usha K.R.'s third novel *Monkey-man* (2010) is, however, a serious work that charts the growth of Bangalore (now Bangaluru) from the city of pensioners to the present status of the Silicon Valley of India. **Malathi Rao** won the Sahitya Akademi award for her novel *Disorderly Women* (2005) in which she portrays the plight of four women who revolt against the traditional set-up as it was during pre-Partition days. In her novel *Afterwards* (2004), **Jaishree Misra** comes out as a brilliant novelist with her male point of view. Maya is trapped in an unhappy marriage in Kerala where Rahul shifts temporarily to learn music and so comes in contact with her. Later, taking her child along, she shifts to UK with him. The relationship between Maya and Rahul is platonic. Unfortunately, she dies in an accident and the custody of the child becomes an issue between Rahul, Maya's husband in Kerala and the British authorities. The topic is touched with female sensitivity and has emotional overtone.

The novel *Tell Her Everything* (2019) by **Mirza Waheed** is a confessional monologue by an aged Indian doctor who is reminiscing past and thinking of what to write to his daughter. The guilt of having performed the cruel surgical amputations of organs as ordained by the judicial system in a Middle East country sits heavy on his heart. The first sentence of Dr. K. (reminds one of Kafka's character with a similar name) "I did it for money," sets the tone of the narrative in which moral question becomes overwhelming. There are musings about whether lashing is better than solitary confinement or hanging is better than electric chair execution. In between come in for examination the coming-of-age of the doctor back in India and as a diasporic in Britain. It is a very thought-provoking novel.

Among others, mention may be made of **Anupam Srivastava's** *The Brown Sahebs* (2013) which is a kind of stock-taking of the post-independence era. **Bela Lal's** *For Honour* (2013) is about inter-caste love and its implications. **Tuhin Sinha** has written a number of novels. His *The Edge of Desire* (2012) links crime to politics. **A.M. Basheer's** *Riot Widows* (2013) is a poignant study of slum where majority of women wait for their husbands who are imprisoned on charges related to a riot. The novel, however, shows Nafsan, a girl who disputes the stereotype, through her socially uplifting moves. **Annie Zaidi** in her Tata Litfest 2020 award-winning novel *Prelude to a Riot* (2019) depicts a South Indian town where trouble is brewing between Hindus and Muslims. In monologues, multiple characters express frankly what they think of the other. The Bhopal Gas tragedy, which shook the conscience of the world, forms the subject of **Indra Sinha's** *Animal's People* (2008). It is a powerful voice raised in favour of the victims, though the element of grotesque puts off the reader. The novel *Coming Soon. The End* (2012) written by **Omkar Sane** is a satire on the working of the visual media in our country. **Mathew Vincent Menacherry's** debut *Arrack in the Afternoon* (2009) probes Mumbai's underbelly.

In the understatement-rich novel *Arzee the Dwarf* (2009), penned by **Chandrahas Choudhury**, the protagonist Arzee is shown working at a cinema hall as a projectionist who after losing his job takes the reader into the chaotic Mumbai. **Anand**

Mahadevan, a US based teacher of creative writing, has penned his maiden novel *The Strike* (2009), which describes the political scene of Chennai of the 1980s as it affects the 12-year-old Hari, whose sexuality also finds wide coverage. Some of the other notable novels covering social themes and published in the year 2010 are: *Blood Ties* by **Amita Rathore**, *Saraswati Park* by **Anjali Joseph**, *Come Before Evening Falls* by **Manjul Bajaj**, and *Lanterns on their Horns* by **Radhika Jha**.

Diasporic/Multicultural

It is a fact that most of the acclaimed writers belonging to Indian English Fiction are, in fact, diasporic. Now, the condition of the diasporic in the Indian context is such that they have strong family ties because of which they are emotionally linked to India. On the other hand, their bread and butter lies in the adopted land. This dilemma is slowly getting diluted because of the rise of materialism in life. It also depends on to which generation of diasporic Indians does the writer belong. Since within India, we have a number of sub-cultures with which we co-exist, Indians are adept at reconciliation of this nature and have, therefore, earned good reputation for adjusting easily in alien societies, but there are several other factors like the attitude of the host society and policies followed in the adopted land which give rise to anxiety, nostalgia, rootlessness, etc. These and other such concerns inform IEF produced by the diasporic writers even as they do write on a host of other themes. Several writers of standing belong to this domain—Salman Rushdie, Jhumpa Lahiri, Rohinton Mistry, Bharati Mukherjee, Chitra Banerjee Divakaruni, Kiran Desai, Aravind Adiga...the list is endless. Many of these writers have dealt with the situation in India and also touched upon Indian folklores and history. However, in this section, we take up only those novels that deal with diasporic experience or with multiculturalism.

Jhumpa Lahiri, the winner of the Pulitzer for her story collection *Interpreter of Maladies*, spins in her debut novel *The Namesake* (2003) a narrative covering three decades of the Ganguli household in USA and displays a fine-tuned sensibility along with psychological realism. The Ganguli couple's immigrant experience is contrasted with the acculturation of their America-born children. The naming of their son as Gogol and later as Nikhil represents a conflict between different identities. Lahiri also depicts Gogol's relations with his American girlfriends and his short-term marriage to a Bengali girl born of Indian immigrant parents. Through her tender narrative, Lahiri underlines the efforts needed to mediate between cultures.

Lahiri's second novel *The Lowland* (2013), which was also nominated for Booker, is devoted to the life of Gouri in India and as an immigrant in the US. It is an epical story covering sixty years in the lives of four generations of a Bengali family. In India, the story revolves around Maoist insurgency in the state of West Bengal. After her husband Udayan was killed by the police for his involvement in the Naxalite movement, Gouri migrates to the US to be a reluctant wife of her late husband's brother Subhash. While the story proceeds to cover the relationships of Subhash and Gauri, Gauri's daughter Bela and granddaughter Magna, in India, the novel traces the predicament of dashed hopes of parents left behind. In all, the novel presents troublesome relationships and a contrast between an idealist frame of mind and a practical one.

Kiran Desai, the prodigious daughter of the acclaimed novelist Anita Desai, created literary history, when she won the Man Booker Prize 2006 for her novel *The Inheritance of Loss*. At 35, she was the youngest woman to win this coveted prize. The press release marking the occasion described her book as "a radiant, funny, moving family saga." The novel portrays an old person—a former judge—who retires to a home in Kalimpong, in the Darjeeling district of India, in the company of his pet dog and a cook. The mantle for extricating him from this retirement falls on his orphaned granddaughter Sai, who falls in love with Gyan, her Maths tutor. The latter forsakes her to join the Gorkhaland agitation but returns towards the end of the novel. Apart from this picture of the regional unrest, there is focus also on the problems of the Asian immigrants in the US, as the cook's son Biju, who entered that country as illegal immigrant but failed to get citizenship or valid work permit. He returns home but not before he is deprived of his belongings by the indigenous agitationists. The snapshot-rich narrative that moves back and forth, rich imagery and beautiful language are the hallmarks of the novel besides the writer's awesome knack to compress a wide scenario in a sentence.

M.G. Vassanji is a respected name in the annals of Indian English literature, even though he has a tenuous connection with India as he was born to Indian parents in Kenya and raised in Tanzania before studying in America and settling down in Canada. His reputation grew with the publication of the novel *The Gunny Sack* in 1989. The novels dealing with the diasporic and multicultural life are *The In-Between World of Vikram Lall* (2003), *The Magic of Saida* (2012). The theme mostly concerns the condition of Indians in East Africa—Kenya, Tanzania, Uganda, etc. and also the re-migration of these people to the West. He also traces the history of host countries in Africa and the relationship of Indian diaspora with the native Africans. In *The Magic of Saida*, Vassanji is once again into exploring the history of East Africa from pre-colonial times to the present, and from social, political, and even personal angle. Vassanji believes that past is never dead and is always affecting present in shaping lives and cultures. Kamal, a Canadian doctor of Tanzanian origin, returns in his middle age to his native place in the fond hope of seeing his boyhood beloved Saida. He is the son of an Indian father from a well-to-do family who left early, and a Swahili mother of slave lineage. Through a series of flashbacks, Kamal's early life is resurrected.

Bharati Mukherjee deals with the predicament faced by the Indian immigrants to the West, in her novel *Desirable Daughters* (2002). Tara Chatterjee, the protagonist comes from the Bengali *bhadralok* family steeped in conservatism. Married to an Indian expatriate in the US, she is stung by the American cultural bug and goes in for a makeover, divorces her conservative husband, takes on an American lover, winks at the gay proclivities of her son but after sometime when she meets her ex-husband, the deep-rooted Indian sensibility asserts itself, hinting at the incompleteness of the cultural metamorphosis.

In her novel *The Immigrant* (2008), **Manju Kapur** tells the story of a thirty-year-old girl working as an English lecturer and looking after her widowed mother. Then, unexpectedly, a proposal arrives and she gets married to Ananda, a dentist in Halifax, Canada. She leaves her home and her country to build a new life with her husband. She now faces the reality about her husband that he is deficient in sexual power and so, he undergoes a therapy in which a Canadian female therapist acts as a live stimulator. Kapur boldly portrays action in titillating detail.

Anita Desai has stayed on in America for a long time now and her novel *The Zigzag Way* (2004) deals with multicultural scenario. Eric is an American who locates his roots in Mexico. Eric learns about the festival of the dead spirits and sets out to locate the grave of his grandfather but has a mystical meeting with his grandmother who recognizes him as Paul (Eric's father). The meeting appears as hallucination or a dream only. Desai brings into play the Indian humanist sensibility while describing the travails of Eric's grandparents who were miners destined to die toiling in pits.

Roswitha Joshi, a naturalized Indian of German origin, is settled in India after her marriage. In addition to short stories and humorous anecdotes, and her first novel *Once More* (2006), Joshi came out with *Indian Dreams* (2010) based partly on her own life experience. Norma, a German girl falls in love with an Indian research student who is studying in Germany. The plot thickens when it is known that Akash was already married but the marriage went wrong with his wife losing her mind due to loss of her child. The other focus in the novel is on the tourist destinations in India in which Norma has professional interest. That is why the novel turns into a tourist guide at times!

Tishani Doshi, a poet and novelist published her maiden novel *The Pleasure Seekers* (2010) that describes a reverse immigration and the plight of biracial children. The Patel family member Babo leaves for London for education and returns with an English wife Sian not because he wants to settle down in India but because the parents have put the condition of their staying with them for two years before Babo can be allowed to live where he likes. What happens is that the couple is firmly entrenched here for life but their younger daughter Bean goes to England develops multiple relationships there but finally is heartbroken and returns home. The novel has autobiographical touch as the writer is also child of Indian-British parents. Doshi's other novel *Fountainville* (2013) is based on the medieval Welsh tales of Mobinogian (story of youth) combining British history and legend. It re-invents one of the stories that is set in a town called Fountainville and has as its theme the surrogacy business in which pregnant women are shown cocooned in a house, much like hens waiting to lay eggs, till the time they are ready to give the gift of a baby to a stranger. Doshi's novel *Small Days and Nights* (2019) portrays a narrator of mixed origin who visits her dead mother's house in Pondicherry where she is called upon to deal with some family skeletons.

Another diasporic writer **Chitra Banerjee Divakaruni** has published fourteen novels including some for children, during this period. Her *One Amazing Thing* (2010) tells the story of nine persons gathered in the Indian embassy to get Visa. Suddenly, a quake demolishes the building and all of them are trapped. Without any hope of early escape, Uma suggests that they all share one amazing thing from their lives, to pass time. The characters are a mixed lot—Indian, Chinese, a Muslim American, English, etc. However, the ending is inconclusive. Divakaruni is committed to dissolving boundaries between people of different backgrounds, communities, ages, and even different worlds. Divakaruni's novel *Oleander Girl* (2014) presents a young girl who goes to the US where she finds love as also some secrets of the family.

Anita Rau Badami's *Can You Hear the Nightbird Call?* (2006) tells the stories of three women, who find comradery in love and loss over a span of fifty years. There is Bibiji, who steals her sister's fiancé and goes with him to Canada. Her neighbour Leela tries to get on with her life as an expatriate as another woman Nimmo tries to rebuild her life in Delhi. But all of them face conflict that are rooted in past. The diasporic experience interacts with the individual life histories in a mix of memory and myth, personal, and political.

Indian-American author **Kavita Daswani,** who published her first novel *For Matrimonial Purposes* in 2003 added *The Village Bride of Beverly Hills* (2005) and six more novels in this period. Most of these novels deal with the conflict between traditional Indian lifestyle and the Western one which a woman has to contend with. Her novel *Salaam Paris* (2007) centres around an Indian girl who is infatuated by the city of Paris and in order to live there accepts a match. Once there, she becomes a free bird and is even disowned by family. However, a turn comes when she finds that the match selected by her parents for her would have been perfect, but it is too late now. Daswani is adept at depicting love and its turmoils. In her novel, *Lovetorn* (2012), we find an Indian girl Shalini who leaves India with her fiancé Vikram to take up a job in USA. When she meets Toby, she is torn between her fiancé and her new find who has won her heart like never before. Her other novel *Bombay Girl* too follows the plot of *Lovetorn* to some extent whereas *Gifted* (2008) takes up the problems of the Indian immigrants in the US at the cultural level.

Amulya Mulladi has published eight novels during this period. Her *The Mango Season* (2004) is an accomplished novel, whose protagonist Priya Rao returns to her family after having spent 20 years in the US bringing along the unwelcome news of her engagement to an American. In India, her family would settle for nothing less than an arranged marriage with a nice Indian boy. The dilemma is further compounded with the revelation of a secret and Priya has hard time making a choice. Another novel by Mulladi *The Sound of Language* (2018) shows an Afghan girl Raihana shifting to Denmark to stay with her relatives. It is a country that is just opposite of Afghanistan in climate as also in many other things like the language which appeared to her as if they were mumbling with a potato in mouth. She comes close to Gunnar, an elderly widowed beekeeper and both develop a relationship that is soothing to both but not palatable to her relatives. It may be mentioned here that Mulladi, a software expert who worked in the Silicon valley has a Danish husband.

After his novel *Asylum, USA* (2000) dealing with a Parsi young man who goes in for a marriage of convenience with a lesbian girl in America in order to get the green card, **Boman Desai** came out with *A Woman Madly in Love* (2004). The novel is inspired by Desai's school days' teacher who fell for one of his classmates. Later, the woman is shown married in America, where her husband cheats on her explaining his liaison with the help of literary theories like deconstruction. There is the inevitable break-up and she returns to India only to go back to Chicago to lead an independent life. The novel ends on an optimistic note. Other novelists include **Mitali Parkins'** *You Bring the Distant Near* (2017) shows Indian parents in US worried about keeping girls Indian enough. **Sanjay Sahota's** *The Year of the Runaways* (2015) shows three Indian immigrants working in Sheffield and living together. There are insights into the politics that seems a common thread between India and UK.

History-based

The novels dealing with history have always been subject to questions like: how much is based on actual history and how much is pure imagination? Within historical detail too scope exists for applying the novelist's art, as for example, in delineating physical and mental traits of characters and in portraying dress, food, landscape, etc. of the historical period. There are also novels dealing with recent history which has politics embedded in it in a big way and with which the readers may be familiar. In that case, what scope exists for objectivity becomes another relevant question, particularly, where the novelist differs from official position. We come across various ways in which novels have been written in this period.

Amitav Ghosh's *Flood of Fire* (2015) completed his 1600-word long *Ibis* trilogy, creating a sensation in the literary world. Ghosh is an internationally acclaimed author who goes in for a lot of research before he puts pen to paper. This trilogy deals with the infamous opium trade which also led to the Anglo-Chinese Opium War of 1839-42. The first offering *Sea of Poppies* (2009) is an intensely humane work that fictionalizes the journey of the first wave of immigrants from India way back in the 1830s. At the heart of this epic saga is a ship, *The Ibis*, which carries the *girmitya* or the indentured labourers across the Indian Ocean to the Mauritian Islands. Besides, there are onboard sailors and stowaways, coolies and convicts, belonging to different countries. On the ship as *jahaj-bhais* now, their old family ties are forgotten and they look forward to building their future lives in the alien land. There is a mélange of languages spoken on the ship which alongside individual life histories of passengers are beautifully depicted. The second offering in the Ibis series, *River of Smoke* (2011) takes the reader to the opium market of Canton in China. Bahram, the Parsi opium trader from Bombay is the protagonist, but there are a large number of characters and incidents as is characteristic of Ghosh's other novels. One sympathizes with Bahram, who with his enterprise and intelligence, cannot cope with the forces against which he is pitted. It is a tragicomedy of sorts that celebrates in postmodern way, the loss of purity of language and culture.

The *Flood of Fire* shows the conflict between the state that wishes to resist the drug trade ruining the youth and Britain siding with its corporates in the name of free trade. Ghosh throws light on history through the four characters of his previous novel. There is Shireen Modi, the widow of an opium trader who goes all the way from Bombay to Canton to recover the dues of her dead husband; the bankrupt former raja Neel Rattan Halder, now working for the Chinese and carefully noting the advance of the East India Company on Chinese territory; and of course Zachary who is enticed by Mrs. Burnham. Needless to say, Ghosh brings out vividly the impact of global politics on ordinary people here.

Shashi Tharoor's *Riot* (2001) focusses on the background to the infamous riots in Gujarat in 2002. At the centre is an American girl Priscilla Hart who is a voluntary social worker. She is later involved in relationship with Laxman, the collector of the district named Zalilgarh. The love story makes the narrative interesting, but the high point is the views of different parties—RSS, Muslims, foreigners, media, and official ones which are given due space and thus present a 360 degree picture of the crisis. Tharoor uses different registers like diary, scrapbook, media report, interview script, etc. which makes it a truly postmodern work. There are also two poems mocking the politicians and the smug Indians!

India's premier poet and story writer **Keki N. Daruwalla** has also written some beautiful novels based on history. In his debut novel *Of Pepper and Christ* (2009), he takes up history of the time when Vasco de Gama led his expedition to India which event became the foundation of the medieval colonial project. As the title suggests, 'pepper' and 'Christ' actually symbolize the two planks—trade and Christianity, of the voyagers' motive. There is also a build-up on the Moor-Christian rivalry. Daruwalla has an unquestioned gift of words and ready wit. His second novel *Ancestral Affairs* (2015) dealing with the Partition times is divided in two parts. The first part takes up the well-known crisis created by the Nawab of Junagadh when he showed his inclination to join Pakistan but Sardar Patel, the then Home Minister of India, upset his plans. The second part is the story of growing up of Rohinton, son of the Parsi solicitor to the Nawab, Saam Bharucha, who was himself involved with a British woman. The novel sustains the interest of the reader through court intrigues and subtle humour that informs Daruwalla's writing.

In his third novel *Swerving to Solitude: Letters to Mama* (2018), Daruwalla takes up the nefarious Emergency era as the backdrop in which corruption thrived along with highhandedness of the Indira Gandhi Government. The protagonist Seema, the wife of a civil servant, is a journalist and is influenced by Leftist ideology. She gets involved unintentionally in an attempt to help an RSS activist and therefore is shadowed by the police. The later part of the novel introduces us to the World War II Mexico and the Indian revolutionary M.N. Roy who, according to the author, has not been given his due by the Comrades in India. The link is the diary of Seema's mother. The story has lot of drama and suspense in it.

Many novelists like **Shauna Singh Baldwin,** in her novel *What the Body Remembers* (2001) creates the pre-Partition family environment in a Sikh household besides portraying the political changes that occurred at the time of Partition.

It is patriarchal family in which a destitute girl comes as the second wife of a wealthy Oxford-educated anglophile and yet a conservative landowner and has to adjust with the first wife. India is partitioned and the family learns to adjust. **Madhulika Liddle** has published four novels which fit in the category of murder mysteries, but she recreates the 17th century like a historical novelist, and depicts a Mughal era detective, Muzaffar Jang, who features in all novels written by Liddle—*The Englishman's Cameo* (2009), *The Eighth Guest & Other Muzaffar Jang Mysteries* (2011), *Engraved in Stone* (2012), and *Crimson City* (2015). Needless to say that Liddle cannot be expected to be true to many of the historical facts of the period against which her stories are set.

Jaishree Misra, though adept at churning out romantic novels, has touched upon the life of Manikarnika aka *Rani of Jhansi* in her novel *Rani* (2004). That she is serious about touching history is corroborated by the Bibliography of history books appended to the novel. She has taken up the rumoured tale of romance between the queen and an English officer which infuriated people in Madhya Pradesh and led to banning of the book there. Another novel in which she has made use of history is *A Love Story for My Sister* (2015). Set in north India of our times, the young novelist Pia is figuring out the strange tale of Margaret, who, during the 1857 struggle in Kanpur, was abducted by a Muslim soldier whom she eventually married. When she is able to lay hands on Margaret's journals, she understands how it might have been for her sister Tara who was kidnapped in 1997 but later found murdered. It seems to be a case of Stockholm Syndrome because she did not opt to leave her captor even when there was a chance. The puzzling aspect is her murder which makes the novel an interesting piece of investigation.

Indu Sundaresan completed her trilogy on the famous historical monument Taj Mahal with the *The Shadow Princess* (2010). Earlier, she had brought out *The Twentieth Wife* (2002) and *The Feast of Roses* (2003). The novels are historical romances which deal with the lives of Mughal era princesses Meherunissa, Mumtaz Mahal and Jahan Ara, respectively.

Another novel *Splendor of Silence* (2007) is the love-story pertaining to the British era. Besides these, she published a novel *The Mountain of Light* (2013) which deals with the famous Kohinoor diamond and traces its history from the rise of Maharaja Ranjeet Singh to the adoption by the British of his son Dalip Singh and his acculturation in England. The writer describes in detail the smuggling out of India of the Kohinoor and its gifting to the Queen of England. The narratives are well-researched and succeed in transporting the reader to the bygone times.

Tanushree Podder has her fingers in many pies. Apart from her lifestyle books, she has penned several history-based novels and thrillers. In her novels *Nur Jahan's Daughter* (2005) and *Escape from Harem* (2013), she takes up the history of the Mughal era. In the former, as the title indicates, Podder rues that historians have not written about Ladli, the daughter of the most famous princess of the time. Ladli was born out of Nur Jahan's wedlock with Sher Afghan before she was widowed and re-married Emperor Jahangir. In the latter novel, Podder relates the goings on in harem. She takes up mostly the history of the period from Jehangir to Shah Jehan. In another novel *The Teenage Diary of Rani Laxmibai* (2020), Podder invents the diary of the famous Rani nee Manikarnika. As a young girl, she undergoes strenuous training in horse-riding and martial arts so that she surpasses boys. Her role as the queen and later after losing husband, her valiant fight against the British does full justice to history.

By her own admission, **Gita Hariharan's** main concern has been the study of power politics. Her novel *In Times of Siege* (2003) revolves around the life of a professor of history. Apart from focussing on the process of recording of history of Partition times, she also rakes up contemporary issues like religious fundamentalism, freedom of speech, etc. Her *Fugitive Histories* (2009) is woven around the Godhra carnage and has political overtones. The narrative relies on memory rather than history. In that sense, the approach may be called postmodern. **Kunal Basu** has written a number of novels dealing with different themes. His novel *The Yellow Emperor's Cure* is set in late 19th-century

China being ruled by the last queen of the Quing dynasty. The infamous Opium War is in the background. A Portuguese doctor Antonio comes searching for cure for syphilis, which leads to a love story involving many an erotic scene. His other novel *The Opium Clerk* (2008) deals with the period of the first war of independence with the nefarious opium trade encouraged by the British Government forming the main plank. Basu's *The Miniaturist* (2008) takes up the Mughal era history with Bihzad, the son of an artist at the court of king Akbar.

Shreyas Bhave is one of the young writers who have taken up history. He has touched upon an area that has been ignored so far. His Ashoka trilogy deals with the period when Emperor Ashoka ruled most of India and even part of Central Asia in 3rd century BC. The novels are: *Prince of Patliputra* (2017), *Storm from Taxila* (2018) and *Nemesis of Kalinga* (2019). Bhave has explored legends and folklores about Ashoka alongside Jataka tales and edicts as there is dearth of historical material. He has also taken up the mystery surrounding the death of the revolutionary Subhash Chandra Bose. While the Indian Government, after four commissions declared Bose dead in plane crash, in public discourse, Bose continues to live on and there are several stories of his life in disguise or in a foreign jail. In his novel *Prisoner of Yakutsk* (2019), Bhave has shown him as incarcerated in a Russian jail where he died forsaken by the successive Indian Governments due to political reasons.

Kiran Doshi's *Jinnah Often Came to Our House* (2016) also falls in the category of historical fiction. It deals with the life of the upper-class Muslim community of Bombay during at the turn of 19th century. The novel has sharp focus on history starting with the Partition of Bengal by the British rulers of India to the Independence. Against this background, after completing his law education from Britain, Sultan Kowaishi comes to settle in Bombay and has meetings with Jinnah. The novel shows how Jinnah was led into changing course from being a champion of Hindu-Muslim unity to being the creator of Pakistan.

The diasporic writer **Tabish Khair's** *Filming* (2007) describes Bollywood in its nascent stage at the time of Partition of the country. From there, the story moves forward to cover the progress of cinema through a series of stories against the background of rising communal hatred. It is a melodrama with several characters thrown in even though language and structural novelty are its high points. Khair's *The Thing about Thugs* (2010) is a period piece that links India with Victorian England in a mélange of literary styles in the true postmodern sense even though Khair is loath to affixing to himself any literary label. Another diasporic psychoanalyst **Sudhir Kakar's** *The Crimson Throne* (2010) is based upon the history of succession to Emperor Shah Jehan. His two sons—the spiritually inclined Dara Shikoh and the fanatic Aurangzeb. The writer has thrown in two foreign narrators, whose first-person accounts distinguish his narrative couched in simple language.

Amitabha Bagchi has published four novels, viz. *Above Average* (2007), *The Householder* (2013), *This Place* (2015), and the DSC award winning *Half the Night is Gone* (2019). The last one is set in pre-independence India, in which people looked forward to Gandhi's *Ram Rajya* to dawn and the protagonist, Lala Motichand, a businessman, is also a *kathavachak* who recites Ramcharitmanas and doles out romantic interpretation. The narrative is double layered with another character—Vishwanath, a writer, representing the opposite 'liberal' ideology. The saving grace is that the times in which these characters exist favour peaceful co-existence of opposite ideologies and present some lesson for our times.

Noted writer **Neelum Saran Gour** published four novels during the period under review. Her novel *Requiem in Raga Janki* which won her the Sahitya Akademi award in 2018 is essentially a period piece. The narrator is an unnamed nonagenarian female who relates the story of Jankibai Allahabadi, a singer-courtesan who actually lived around the turn of 19th century. Alongside her life story revolving around *thumri* and *gayaki,* the reader also learns about other contemporary people belonging like Akbar Ilahabadi, and events like the Coronation Darbar and the Maha Kumbha. An interesting read indeed.

Other notable writers include **Nayantara Sehgal** who published her *Lesser Breeds* (2003) which is based on the freedom movement and the leading figures dealt with in the style of a fable. **Basavaraj Naikar's** *The Sun behind the Cloud* (2001) deals with the rise and fall of Bhaskararao, the nineteenth-century king of Naragunda. His revolt against the British is the high point of the novel as it throws light on a not so-well-known chapter of the first Indian war of independence. An interesting fictional work touching upon recent history was **Jaspreet Singh's** *Helium* (2014). Singh is the son of a police officer who was instrumental in the perpetration of atrocities on Sikh people in Delhi in 1984 and the narrative lays bare what lay beneath the surface. As a young student, he had seen the burning alive of his teacher. Years later, he happened to meet the teacher's widow and the realization of the culpability of his father dawned upon him. The writer does not vindicate his father's actions in this political novel. As a scientist based in Canada, Singh draws upon science for metaphors.

A.K. Srikumar's *The Begum's Secret* (2010) is a novel based upon the history of eighteenth-century Awadh region. It is a tale of betrayal and greed as also of love and pride. The Nawab is shown starting a food-for-work programme as a famine hits the state. The title refers to the intelligent Bahu Begam's quest for a successor to the throne since her son the Nawab Asaf-ud-Daula is issueless. There is a lot of focus on the problems and intrigues going on in the harem. The novel seems well-researched and life of the period is effectively presented. **Suchita Malik** describes in *Women Extraordinaire: A Novel* (2014), a strong-willed woman who is widowed and left to face Partition time with her child. There are four more women from the family who look up to her as a model.

Among others, **Aijaz Ashraf's** *The Hour Before Dawn* (2014) is linked to Babri demolition. **Lakshmi Raj Sharma's** *The Tailor's Needle* (2012) is about a Bengali idealist belonging to the period of freedom struggle. **Neel Mukherjee's** *The Lives of Others* (2014) touches upon the history of Bengal from the time of draught to the Naxal era. **Jaina Sanga's** *Silk Fish Opium* (2012) relates to the pre-independence Hindu-Muslim alliance. **Sunanda Sikdar's** *A Life Long Ago* (2012) is based on Partition as it impacted Bengal. **Manju Jaidka** published in 2011 her first novel *Scandal Point*, which takes its title from a spot in Shimla where, during the Raj days, the then Maharaja of Patiala is said to have kidnapped the English Viceroy's daughter. The son born from this union grows unaware but as a youth, he launches on a search for his lineage.

Terrorism

Terror stalks the entire world today, therefore, it is natural for writers to take it up as a theme in novels. The clash of civilizations, whether imaginary or real, is getting manifest in acts of terror, and who would be better equipped to talk of it than **Salman Rushdie** who, even though a Muslim, was on the hit list of Ayatollah Khomeini for long. Those days of self-incarceration are at the back of this novel whose title *Two Years Eight Months and Twenty-eight Days* (2015) alludes to that period. Rushdie continues to hold aloft the banner of magic realism. He creates characters from this world and from another called Peristan. There are at least 1001 stories and sub-stories featuring male jinn and the female jinnia who cross over to earth through a hole in the wall, for the sake of facing a different world even as they enjoy life in Peristan and have sex a dozen-times-a-day! The central issue in the novel is a philosophical tussle between the rationalist Ibn Rushd and the theologian Ghazali of Iran. Both are historical figures from the 12th century, even though their intellectual positions have not been adhered to in the novel. One can easily guess the outcome of the fictional conflict: Ibn Rushd is exiled. Rushdie portrays a contented nation, only the people are denied dreams. Little wonder that the book advocates freedom of speech and decries Islamist terrorism, which is suggested to be partially due to the loveless lives of the terrorists.

Arundhati Roy came out, after 20 years, with her novel *The Ministry of Utmost Happiness* (2017) which is unwieldy tome covering at least three themes—neuters, violence in Kashmir, and the Naxalite movement. The writer's sympathy for the terrorists peeps through the chinks in the apparently neutral armour. While the amalgamation of the three themes is not quite appealing, Roy deserves kudos for her research into the life of the hijra community. Her craze for the postmodern style using rather overly, different registers—diary entries, police station FIR's, catalogues, Urdu poetry, etc. makes the novel appear like a patchwork. As compared to Roy's previous novel *The God of Small Things* (1997), this one is short on artistic merit and is more of propaganda material.

In contrast, published the same year, *The Infidel Next Door* (2017) by the psychologist-turned-novelist **Rajat Mitra** forcefully delineates the havoc caused by the terrorists in Kashmir. The novel focusses on the Kashmir situation in the 1990s when terrorists held sway over the valley. Lakhs of Kashmiri Pandits had to migrate out of Kashmir. They are now living like refugees in Jammu, Delhi and other places in their own country. In the novel, the writer vividly portrays the violent attacks on and murders of Pandits, rapes of Pandit women and confiscation of their properties. What the history will note is the number of people affected but Mitra, as a novelist is able to focus attention on the victims as human beings regardless of religion. What is more, the writer also brings out the effaced history of six earlier exoduses of Kashmiri Pandits from the valley brought about by Muslim rulers. The protagonist Aditya is a youth cast in Gandhian mould and trying Gandhian ways to win over the adversary in which he succeeds to a very limited extent.

Mukul Deva, a former army Major and presently chief of a private security organization, has been variously hailed by media as "India's literary storm trooper", "India's thrill machine," as also having "a Nostradamus touch" for a prescient writing. He has published a number of novels that fall in the category of spy thrillers dealing with terrorism. Known for his novels *Lashkar* (2008) and *Salim Must Die* (2009), *Tanzeem* (2011), *And Death Came Calling* (2014) and *Assassins* (2015), the writer has the benefit of intimate knowledge of spy operations which come in handy to make his thrillers realistic and interesting. There is focus at times on the conflict of interest between selfless patriotic youths and self-serving politicians but the former army man stands true to his salt. These are sagas of love, courage, and action against divisive and terrorist forces acting within the country as also being unleashed from across the borders.

The novel bearing an essay-type title *How to Fight Islamist Terror from the Missionary Position* (2014) by well-known writer **Tabish Khair** posits three Indian immigrants in Denmark—the Indian professor and unnamed narrator, a researcher named Ravi, and Karim, a taxi driver. The last named is a devout Muslim and is supposed (not proved) to have attacked the Danish cartoonist—an actual event that rocked the Muslim world. In between, the romantic episodes hog the narrative. The reader is informed at the beginning of the novel about the incident. The reality is revealed in the end and after many a twist. The novel is a satire on the gullible people who develop prejudices merely because others have such views even though there is no valid proof. In *Jihadi Jane* (2016), Khair takes up the case of a young girl Jamila who feels attracted towards the idea of radical Islam and along with her friend, the fanatic Ameena, joins ISIS in Syria but when the reality dawns on her and she comes across militant-brides, she rues her decision.

Among others, **Anees Salim's** *Vanity Bagh* (2013) which won The Hindu Best Fiction Award revolves around the issue of terrorism. It has an interesting cast of characters named after past Pakistani leaders who become unwitting participants in a bomb blast. **Joseph Sebastian's** *The Peacenik Swap* (2013) is a thriller deals with an escaped terrorist near the Wagah border whereas a terror group holds a batch of peaceniks as hostages to get Taufiq released.

Myth-based

Myth-based fiction achieved great popularity during this period. The ancient epics Ramayana and Mahabharata provide rich material for novels. It is up to the novelist to reproduce the story in original form, which is now a bygone thing, as more and more imagination is being used to create stories that appeal to the contemporary taste. A serious take is seen in the novels which re-tell the ancient stories applying current approaches like feminism. A large number of novels have been published. So great has been the response from readers that in a short span of time, the works based upon novels have been translated in many foreign languages apart from the Indian ones. Even foreign authors are re-telling stories of Indian epics. Among Indian authors, mention may be made of Ashok Banker, Amish Tripathi, Devdutt Pattanaik, Anand Neelkantan, Namita Gokhale, Sharath Komarraju, Anuja Chandramouli, etc. This tribe is ever on the increase.

The trend to write myth-based fiction with additions based on one's own imagination was started in a big way in our times by **Ashok Banker**, an Anglo-Indian by birth, who started his life as a journalist. He has more than fifty books to his credit which include thrillers, science fiction, love stories and adult novels. Since 2003, he has devoted his time mostly to churning out myth-based novels, some two dozen of which based upon Ramayana and Mahabharata have appeared till now. He brought out a series of nine books based on Ramayana which proved to be international best-sellers. These include *Siege of Mithila* (2003), *Prince of Ayodhya* (2003), *Demons of Chitrakoot* (2003), *Armies of Hanuman* (2005), *Bridge of Rama* (2005), *King of Ayodhya* (2006), *Gods of War* (2009), etc. Similarly, in the Mahabharata-based series, he has published around a dozen books including *The Seeds of War* (2011), *Flute of Vrindavan* (2011), *Fortress of Dwarka* (2015), *The Children of Midnight* (2015), *The Eclipse of Dharma* (2016), etc. Together with books on epical love stories like *Shakuntala and Dushyant* (2013) and *Satyavati and Shantanu* (2013), the re-tellings by Banker form a sizeable corpus.

In his novel *Sons of Sita* (2012) which is the last re-telling of the Ramayana series, we find that while Lav and Kush are being taught the Vedas and other books by Guru Vasishta, Sita and her Haryanvi female bodyguard Nakhudi train them in martial arts! Rama anoints himself emperor of Ayodhya and his soldiers perpetrate atrocities on people as they consider themselves 'dharmanators'! Rama even dubs his brothers Bharat and Shatruaghna traitors! Herein lies Banker's innovativeness, albeit in denigrating the image of revered idols of the Hindus. His Krishna series has eight books and Mahabharata series has six books. Banker's vivid and imaginative narrative is gripping, to say the least. Just as historical novel need not totally conform to the historical truth, Banker's treatment of myth also does not show much affinity with the accepted original texts. At the same time, it must be acceded that he displays a distinguishing literary style which makes him stand out.

Amish Tripathi started myth-based fiction later than Banker but stole a march over him. *The Immortals of Meluha* (2010), *The Secret of the Nagas* (2011), *The Oath of the Vayuputras* (2013), and *Scion of Ikshvaku* (2015) have all been block busters. In the last named, the characters—Ram, Ravana, Sita, Bharat and others are shown as real people with real lives, who get attracted to opposite sex, tease siblings and have daily quibbles. In fact, Bharat is the modern Casanova! In all these, as in the use of colloquial language, Tripathi seems to be following Banker. If Sita was a fighter in Banker, she is besides being a fighter, the Prime Minister of Mithila in Tripathi's *Sita: Warrior of Mithila* (2017).

In these feminist times, the mythical stories too have been interpreted from the feminist viewpoint. Sita has been almost the universal choice with the popular novelists. Thus, apart from Banker and Tripathi, a prolific writer **Chitra Banerjee Divakaruni** in her book *The Forest of Enchantment* (2019) relates the story of Ramayana from Sita's viewpoint. Besides, this novel also projects the sidelined characters, viz. Kaikeyi, Mandodari, and Surpanakha. Earlier, in her book *The Palace of Illusions* (2008), she related the ancient epic Mahabharata from the standpoint of Draupadi who is portrayed as an intelligent queen bound by conventions but she can rise above them and think about the status of women. Towards the end of the great war, she strives to help women who lost their kith and kin.

Devdutt Pattanaik, a physician-turned-author, who has to his credit some thirty books focusing on the relevance of ancient myths and legends for our times. As compared to Banker and Tripathi, Pattanaik is sincere towards the original versions of the epics Ramayana and Mahabharata. His earlier work *Jaya: An Illustrated Re-telling of Mahabharata* (2010) became hugely popular. The book is chapterized according to different episodes of the epic. In case of multiple versions available, he makes clear why he has taken up the one and left out the other, or at times, he juxtaposes some versions and authenticates them on the basis of folklores or even customs and traditions existing in our times in different parts of India. That shows a good bit of research. On the other hand, critics have faulted him for shoddy research with regard to the Sanskrit language. In his *Sita: An Illustrated Re-telling of Ramayana* (2013), he describes Sita's childhood, her coming of age, her sisters and other relations, and leads on to the Ashok Vatika days. In *The Girl Who Chose: A New Way of Retelling Ramayana* (2016), Pattanaik seems influenced by current theories and shows how the entire story can be interpreted as related to Sita's choices. The book also highlights Sita's role in making Rama a god. Besides retelling epics, Pattanaik has also written books throwing light on various mythical concepts.

Anand Neelakantan's debut novel *Asura: Tale of the Vanquished* (2012) which is based upon Ramayana but presents the story from the point of view of Ravan rather than Ram. Other novels written by him and based upon the Mahabharata are: *Ajaya: Roll of the Dice* (2013) and *Ajaya: Rise of Kali* (2018). In these two novels, Neelakantan has presented the story from the point of view of Duryodhana, the loser in the war and has therefore reversed the roles of the Pandavas and the Kauravas with the former being dubbed as the villains and the latter as the righteous ones. **Sundari Venkatraman** is another prolific writer. She started quite late, at the age of 53 to be precise, and has since churned out more than 50 novels. Most of these are romances, but she has written novels on many forms of Vishnu, better known as *Dashavatar* (ten avatars): *Matsya: The First Avatar* (2018), *Kurma: The Second Avatar* (2018), *Varaha: The Third Avatar* (2018), *Narsimha: The Fourth Avatar* (2018), *Vamana: The Fifth Avatar* (2018). The narratives are by and large loyal to the original stories.

Among other notable writers, **Anuja Chandramouli** is another novelist who has found myth an enchanting area and has published some ten books in a span of five years. Her first book was *Arjuna: Saga of a Pandava Warrior Prince* (2015). Since then, she has gone ahead with books on many historical and mythical figures like Yama, Kama, Durga, Kartikeya, Kamadeva and also historical ones like Prithviraj Chauhan and Padmavati. **Namita Gokhale** with her *Shakuntala* (2005) and *Lost in Time: Ghatokacha* (2017) has also dabbled in this genre. **Samhita Arni's** *The Missing Queen* (2014) is a myth-based thriller in which a contemporary journalist (if ever there was one in Ramayana days) starts his search for Sita who is missing. Similarly, **Kavita Kane** has taken to myth-based fiction from the standpoint of female characters. The titles of her novels tell it all: *Karna's Wife* (2013), *Sita's Sister* (2015), *Menaka's Choice* (2015), etc. **Anurag Anand's** *The Legend of Amrapali* (2012) is based on the legend of Amrapali. **Meenakshi Reddy Madhavan's** *The One Who Swam with the Fishes* (2017) is about the Mahabharata character Satyavati. **Usha Narayanan's** *Pradyumna: Son of Krishna* (2015) is an eponymous novel dealing with a neglected part of Mahabharata. **Krishna Udayasankar** has come out with Aryavarta Chronology comprising three novels *Govinda* (2012), *Kaurava* (2013), and *Kurukshetra* (2014).

Marginalized

Postcolonialism has given voice to the voiceless whether they were colonial subjects or are victims of suppression in independent countries. The suppression can be by state or society and rules as well as prejudices play a negative role there. We see bias against people belonging to other castes, creeds, and religion. Similarly, members of other races and also tribals bear the brunt of skewed thinking. Literature giving voice to such people continues to be written in this period also. It is another thing that those who give voice to the dispossessed do not themselves belong to those marginalized sections and they write in English language which is not understood by the large number of people including the tribals. In this, they prove Gayatri Spivak's averment. Regional literature scores over Indian English literature in this respect.

The Parsi community, however, is well-groomed in English culture. The Parsi playwright **Rohinton Mistry** published his *Family Matters* (2002) in this period which has focus on the Parsi community (detail in the section on Family). Similarly, Rohinton's brother **Cyrus Mistry** has also written about his community in the novels—*The Radiance of Ashes*—set in a Parsi colony and *Chronicle of a Corpse Bearer* (2014) whose title has reference to the Tower of Silence where dead bodies are taken to be devoured by vultures as per Parsi custom. **Esther David**, the winner of the Sahitya Akademi award, in her book *The Book of Rachel* (2006) touches upon the life of Ben Israel Jewish community in India. Similarly, **Jael Silliman** takes up the life of Baghdadi Jews community in her novel *The Man with Many Hats* (2013). It is a novel based on the life of writer's father. The focus on the miniscule Chinese-Assamese community is brought by **Rita Chowdhary** in her novel *Chinatown Days* (2018). **Nilendu Sen's** *Sonar Gaon* (2012) highlights tribal culture. This is an area woefully lacking in treatment in Indian English Fiction.

Veteran novelist **Kiran Nagarkar** published *The Extras* (2014) which advances the story of the characters Ravan and Eddie in the novel of the same title published way back in 1994. The novel makes interesting reading as the absurd is the watchword in it. Both the protagonists have grown into young men now and indulge in activities fit for them. Moreover, born and brought up in underprivileged environment in a Mumbai *chawl*, they aspire to be film actors one day, but end up being extras only. Some essays and poems interspersed in the novel dent its unity. The language laced with tickling humour reminds one of P.G. Wodehouse. Nagarkar's novel *Rest in Peace—Ravan and Eddie* (2015) completes the Ravan and Eddie trilogy.

Vikas Swarup's *Q&A* (2005) which was transformed into the movie *Slumdog Millionaire*, shows a young waiter's rise from rag to riches through participation in a quiz show though later, he is arrested and jailed on charge of cheating. A good addition to novels dealing with life in slums is by **Deepa Anappara's** *Djinn Patrol on the Purple Line* (2020) is the first-person narrative by a boy Jai who, inspired by a TV serial, acts a sleuth after disappearance of a friend. On the opposite end is a gated complex where his mother works. Jai's friend says the missing child must have been taken away by a djinn into a cave and eaten up. Missing boy's father—a labourer—gives a gold chain gifted to his wife by her 'madam', to a cop to expedite the search, but where the police fail, the boy succeeds. Narration may require gullibility but then the message is clear.

Also, professions which are looked down upon by society, even though these constitute important segments have been taken up by some novelists. **Kunal Basu's** *Kalkatta* (2017) deals with the life of Jami, who starts his career as a masseur and soon becomes a gigolo, offering services to rich women. Life at the margin in Indian society is touched by **Kavery Nambisan** in whose novel *A Town Like Ours* (2014) a prostitute talks about herself and others.

Regional

A number of novelists have written with strong focus on the topography and culture of their native places—areas that had been overlooked so far. The north-east India needed this attention. A votary of locale-centric narratives, **Amitav Ghosh** published his novel *The Hungry Tide* in 2005. It deals with the experiences of a scientist Piyali, who has come from America to study dolphins in the Sundarbans region of West Bengal. She meets Kanai, who acts as her interpreter. Both of them, along with Fokir, a local fisherman, who knows the area too well, go looking for the elusive dolphin. Apart from the binary of urban/rural to which his characters belong, Ghosh focusses on the havoc being caused by the MNCs to ecology of the picturesque Sundarbans region. Ghosh researches well for his books, even though the scientific and historical details test at times the patience of the reader.

Anjum Hasan, whose debut novel *Lunatic in My Head* (2007) was set in Shillong came up with her second offering *Neti, Neti* (2009) based on city life. It brings out the loneliness of the young protagonist Sophie Das in the city where she has her liberal-minded friends and her workplace, besides the pubs, concerts, malls, etc. Poet and award-winning novelist **Easterine Kire's** debut novel *A Naga Village Remembered* (2004) recounts the history of the battle between British forces and a Naga hamlet that took place in the 19th century. Her novel *When the River Sleeps* (2014) set in Nagaland, won the Hindu Best fiction award. Her second novel *Son of the Tundercloud* (2016) deals with Naga legends in lyrical prose. Her other novels include *A Terrible Matriarchy* (2007) and *Bitter Womanhood* (2011).

Poet and journalist **Mamang Dai's** Sahitya Akademi award winning novel *The Black Hill* (2017) is set in north-east India of the 1840s. It is the story of a young man from the Mishmi tribe who falls in love with a girl from the Abor tribe. The entry of a white missionary creates a love triangle. The portrayal of this historical period without reference to colonial rule and the accompanying proselytization project of the church is surprising, even though the novel presents a rich collage of characters, landscapes and events. Similarly, **Suravi Sharma Kumar's** novel *Voices in the Valley* (2012) highlights the topography, climate, flora and fauna of Assam in a big way. Besides, there is a sharp focus on local customs, food and dress habits, taboos, etc. However, the novel has a loose structure and references to too many problems take their toll on its unity.

Madhuri Vijay's debut novel *The Far Field*, for which she won the 2019 JCB Prize in Literature, focusses on the political situation in Kashmir where the protagonist, Bangalore-based, upper-class female Shalini goes after the death of her mother to pay tribute to her memory. What she witnessed as a child has now transformed into a conflict-ridden region where goodwill has been replaced by suspicion and hatred. This becomes the raison d'etre for tracing the history and examining the politics with a lot of compassion and sympathy. The novel has been hailed for its brilliance. **Nitasha Kaul's** *Residue* (2014) looks at Kashmir through the eyes of a diasporic.

Some other novelists who have dealt with particular regions are: **Janhavi Acharekar**: *Wanderers, All* (2015) set in Goa; and **Malathi Ramchandran**: *The Legend of Kuldhara* (2017) portraying life in Jaisalmer. Similarly, **Aruni Kashyap's** *The House with a Thousand Stories* (2013) focusses on Assam. **Charu Singh's** *Path of the Swan* (2014) is about Sikkim and Tibet region. *The To-let House* (2010) by **Daisy Hasan** is a coming-of-age novel for four characters based in Shillong, in which the region's own search for identity contributes a lot. **Dhruv Hazarika's** *Sons of Bramha* (2014) as also **Mitra Phukan's** *A Monsoon of Music*

(2011) are set in Assam. **Anand Ranganathan's** *For Love and Honour* (2015) focusses on Mizoram.

Travel and Adventure

Travel has become far more common in this globalized age. Primarily because of commerce, but also due to curiosity to see the world that has always been there in human beings but made more accessible now, travel across the world has picked up. However, what is taking shape is not the type of travel narrative of yore. It has elements of thriller with musings on almost everything under the sun.

Salman Rushdie's *Quichotte* (2019) is his fourteenth novel. The title is the French spelling of "Quixote". The protagonist, Sam DuChamp, an Indian immigrant in America is depicted as an author. He is besotted with Salma R, a former Bollywood star who hosts a talk show now in New York. He keeps on sending her love letters under the pen name Quichotte—the title of the novel and then launches on an adventurous trip across various cities of the US in pursuit of her. He is accompanied by no real person but his "imaginary son", Sancho, named after the squire in the old classic *Don Quixote*. Sam's sister is named Trampoline! Rushdie's penchant for queer names and magic realist mode of narration are back in use, after he dropped it in his earlier novel *The Golden House*. The contemporary issues of drugs, racism and political wrangling are also dealt with in the novel. Style-wise, it can be called metafictional, for the characters know they are being written about in the novel! The novel is, as in most of Rushdie's novels, rich in imagery and cerebral matter in his signature "chutnified" language.

Amitav Ghosh's novel *The Gun Island* (2019) gives expression to his favourite theme of journey. It presents an aging protagonist Deen, who is a dealer of rare books in the US, and who, even though he loves a quiet life, inspired by a family folklore, launches himself on a long journey from India to Los Angeles and Venice. The story has link with the Sunderbans legend connected with a shrine dedicated to Mansa Devi and her curse on a Bonduki Saudagar or the gun merchant, just as *The Hungry Tide* (2005) was to a goddess Bon Bibi. The characters

Piya, Moyna, and Nilima of *The Hungry Tide* return here, but there are other characters also to support the plot: Tipu, Rafi, and Cinta. This journey is also of self-discovery as much as it is about the Bengali legends. Ghosh's other concerns regarding environment and the refugee crisis with their background history find space here along with lots of philosophical musings. Style-wise the real and the fantastic are interwoven.

Karan Bajaj's debut novel *Keep off the Grass* (2008) shows Samrat, an American of Indian descent leave job to join MBA in India. His restless soul, however, tries to find solace in friends, Vipassana sessions, sex, etc. In the end, Ruskin Bond advises him to lead life in a holistic manner and to keep "off the grass", i.e. marijuana. He realizes that he belongs to India and in the West, he is living someone else's life. His second novel *Johnny Gone Down* (2010) also portrays Nikhil Arya, an MIT graduate with a restive spirit that takes him places in Asia. The journey enables to become a drug lord, then take part in a civil war in which he loses his arm, then become a Buddhist monk and finally rises above the common rut of humanity to give the gift of life to a friend. The plot is complex which retains reader's interest till the end, even though events unfold at a hectic pace.

Pico Iyer, in his novel, *Abandon* (2003) has made a foray into the world of Sufism against the backdrop of a world riven by conflicts. An English student Johan Macmillan is studying Sufism in California. When he lands in Damascus, he learns about certain secret manuscripts taken away to Iran. A neurotic character Camilla is connected to the manuscripts but then suddenly, the manuscripts appear and Camilla disappears. The high point is the depiction in a masterly manner of the various locations in India. Also there are mystical musings in it which give some food for thought to the reader. **Rahul Bhattacharya's** debut novel *The Sly Company of People Who Care* (2011) is based on the life of an Indian immigrant in the Caribbean region. The unnamed Indian narrator is driven to that region due to his love of cricket. The reader is treated to the blend of white, brown, and black cultures here born of colonization, slavery, and indentured labour. The writer's impressionistic take on the life and manners of the numerous characters that populate his novel haunt the reader. The book is more of a fictional travelogue.

Amitabha Chatterjee whose novel *Of Wooing, Woes and Wanderings* (2009) takes for its location the far-off Venezuela besides Syria and Qatar—places where the protagonist Rajarshi travels in connection with his job, which is working on the oil-rigs. His exotic, though hardly convincing, live-in relationship with Marisel brings out the multicultural aspect of contemporary society. **Anjali Joseph's** *Another Country* (2012) takes the hero from one country to another in the world in search of peace. The narrative is fractured even as the images are vividly described.

Popular Fiction

Chetan Bhagat's publication of his novel *Five Point Someone* in 2004 initiated a revolution in the field of popular fiction. The novels sold in the range of lakhs whereas earlier, the serious or light fiction had touched sales volumes in thousands only. This encouraged a breed of young writers who started writing fiction and also got good response from readers. We saw young professionals belonging to different areas like teaching, medicine, engineering, management, journalism, etc. come out with their stories.

The domain of popular novel known by different names like Metro Reads or Quick-Reads is well-established now. Other divisions of this broad popular category are—Chick-lit, Lad-lit, Tech-lit, Campus-lit, Career-lit, etc. Major themes in this fast-emerging genre are campus and office comedies, professional life, live-in and extra-marital relationships, and practically anything that could be of interest to youth—all couched in chirpy, colloquial language. This fiction also encompasses stories of crime, murder mysteries, racy thrillers, etc. Popular fiction or light fiction targets the young readers with little time but with plenty of penchant for reading. It touches upon all types of themes but the treatment is not very deep as it is in serious fiction, and this is the major distinguishing factor between the two. This fiction is amenable to Bollywood masala movies as the stories mostly follow formulae of popular cinema, whether in Hindi or in any regional language.

During these two decades of 21st century, Bhagat published nine novels beginning with *Five Points Someone* (2004). Almost all of his novels achieved popularity and many of these were transmuted into Hindi movies. That is proof enough of the correspondence between light fiction and the Bollywood movies. A striking feature can be noted in the titles all of which have a numeric contained in them—something that reminds one of such fads entertained by people in the Bollywood. Apart from the first novel mentioned here, others are: *One Night @ Call Centre* (2005), *The 3 Mistakes of My Life* (2008), *2 States: The Story of My Marriage* (2009), *Revolution 2020* (2011), *Half Girlfriend* (2014), *One Indian Girl* (2016), *The Girl in Room 105* (2018), and *One Arranged Murder* (2020).

Bhagat's *Five Point Someone* (2004) belongs to the then nascent breed of Campus Novel whose early practitioners include Prema Nandkumar, Rita Joshi, etc. Bhagat makes fun of the education system which looks down upon mediocrity. His novel *The 3 Mistakes of My Life* (2008) cashes in on the craze for cricket in India besides roping in the Gujarat earthquake and the riots. Unlike his previous offerings, Bhagat's *2 States: The Story of My Marriage* (2009), a semi-autobiographical piece, focusses on the cultural divide between north and south India. More than this novel, however, the movie version became more popular. His novel *Revolution 2020: Love, Corruption, Ambition* was published in 2011. Besides the themes alluded to in the title, the focus is also on the private coaching industry that has become so popular. The novel has a love triangle also to appeal to the young readers.

Half Girlfriend (2014) is the story of love between Madhav, a Bihari boy who is rather weak in English and Riya, a sophisticated Delhi-ite girl. Their common passion is sports that brings them near, but as emotions bloom, a rustic remark by Madhav upsets the girl who leaves him for an NRI boy. Chance is a valuable element in romance and so, while Madhav leaves his studies mid-way to look after his mother's school in a backward village of Bihar, he happens to get a largesse from Microsoft founder Bill Gates who also visits his school. Also the long lost girl Riya appears in Patna, though after a short fling, she leaves him with the note saying she was suffering from terminal cancer. The woe-struck Madhav gets hold of Riya's journals which he hands over to who else—Chetan Bhagat—to decipher. And then hey presto! Madhav gets the hint that the girl is hale and hearty singing somewhere in New York. So, he takes the next flight to New York and after the reader is given some anxious moments, there occurs finally the union between the two at Riya's music show.

One of the best-selling Indian authors, **Durjoy Datta** has penned 19 novels during the two decades, out of which at least eight have co-authors, mainly centering on love and romance. His first novel, *Of Course I Love You! Till I Find Someone Better* (co-authored with Maanvi Ahuja) was released in 2008 while he was still a student. The book was based on his experiences at Delhi College of Engineering. The book was a bildungsroman of a young, overprotected boy and how his life changes during the four years he spends at college. During the second decade of this century, the publications include *She Broke Up I Didn't! ... I Just Kissed Someone Else!* (2010), *You were My Crush! Till You said You Loved Me* (co-authored with Orvana Ghai, 2011), *If It's not Forever! It's not Love* (co-authored with Nikita Singh 2012), *World's Wóŕśt´* Best Boyfriend (2015) and *Wish I could Tell You* (2019). The startling titles are again the hallmark of popular fiction. There are, of course, contemporary events which provide the context like the bomb blasts, drug abuse, but mainly it is youthful love suffused with sexual overtones that takes the cake.

Beginning her writing career in 2011 at the age of nineteen, **Nikita Singh** had penned 13 novels. Dealing with love, romance, social media, and topics of interest to young people, the novels have catchy titles like *Love @ Facebook* (2011), *Accidentally in Love... With Him? Again?* (2011), *Right Here Right Now* (2014), and *After All This Time* (2015). The novels written in racy language also relate to contemporary events. **Ravinder Singh**, having worked as a software professional, took to full-time writing after his novel *I too had a Love Story* (2009) became a hit. Based upon his own loss of beloved, the intensely passionate novel won him his present wife. During the period under study here, he has published seven novels including *Can Love Happen Twice?* (2011), *Like it Happened Yesterday* (2013), and *Your Dreams are Mine No* (2014). The sincerity of feelings appeals to readers in his novels.

Sundari Venkatraman, fed on Mills and Boon as a youth, has been publishing mostly romances that conclude with "happily lived thereafter" ending. Some of her works are *The Malhotra Bride* (2014), *An Autograph for Anjali* (2016), *Scorpio Superstar* (2017), *The Marriage Predicament* (2018), *The Runaway Bridegroom* (2019), *The Drunken Wife* (2019), and *The Taurus Temptation* (2020). **Rana Dasgupta's** debut novel *Tokyo Cancelled* (2005) in which eleven international passengers stranded at an airport tell their tales to pass time *a la The Canterbury Tales*, except that there is no promise of a feast—is a popular novel which has won international readership.

Chick-lit

While most fiction in the popular segment deals with romantic relationships on or off-campus, it would be fruitful to take up separately, the category of Chick-lit in which young women are at the centre of romantic or friendly relationships. This is supposed to be a novel by a woman writer and talks of women even as it is meant for the female readers. The themes generally include love, romance, workplace, fashion, etc. The women characters are mostly liberal-minded, fun loving ones, language colloquial and chatty as in most popular fiction, and the tone more intimate. Rather than mushiness, the narrative has a lighter touch about it.

In **Advaita Kala's** *Almost Single* (2007), the protagonist in Kala's novel is Aisha, a modern 29-year-old Guest Relations Manager at a hotel who professes that she is better off as a single person what with her freedom, fun-loving company and all that even though she is seeking a perfect partner and her mother is counting her years. But then heart has its own inclinations and when a charming young man comes her way, she has to contend with the reality of traditions, superstitions, and so on. The first person account reminds one of the diary of the protagonist in Helen Fielding's novel *Bridget Jones' Diary*.

This category subsumes many of **Jaishree Misra's** novels like *Secrets and Lies* (2009), *Secrets and Sins* (2010) and *A Scandalous Secret* (2011). The first-named narrates the story of four girls who developed friendship at school but now they are married and tasting life in different ways in either India or UK. A mystery murder in the past comes up as the common problem and as a twist in the tail of the story which they have to contend with. Misra's other two novels can be put under the category of Young Adult Fiction as these relate to school time affairs. **Anuja Chauhan's** *The Zoya Factor* (2008) which is high on romance between an advertising executive and a cricket player. The story-line includes female bonding and booze parties. **Swati Kaushal's** *Piece of Cake* (2004) has an Indian working girl as the central character in an interesting plot that is imbued with humour.

Shivangi Ramsay, a self-proclaimed Mills and Boon fan, has written novels dealing with romance and with women at the centre. Her *Addicted to Love* (2020) portrays three young women experimenting with relationships with males who do not have single allegiance. Her other novel *Passionate Love* (2015) has a strong-willed woman as its protagonist and *Mine for Tonight* (2020) is based on the concept of one-night stand as the title indicates. *Right Fit Wrong Shoe* (2009) by **Varsha Dixit** is a racy thriller of contemporary liberated lifestyle. **Mayank Anand's** novel *Love from the Sidelines* (2010) is written in the first-person. It is described by a critic as a 'girlie novel' produced by a man. The novel also has illustrations done by the writer himself. The protagonist Samira, an artist, tells her story in the first person. **Anita Jain's** *Marrying Anita* (2008) centre on search for the right guy by female protagonists.

Campus-lit

Campus novel has indeed attracted many young writers. Chetan Bhagat's *Five Point Someone* set the pace for this category in 2004. **Suman Hossain's** *A Guy Thing* (2010) is a campus novel, in which an IITian Sahil shows the courage to follow his dreams. References in such novels to SMS-ing,

Orkut-ing, mobile-dating and online-chatting are bound to be commonly used here. Hostel life, romance, and studies weave the warp and woof of the novel. Another campus novel by **Daman Singh** appeared under the title *Nine by Nine*. This one concerns the students of a girls college with focus on a relaxed pace of life. **Anirban Bose's** *Bombay Rains, Bombay Girls* (2008), celebrates success and not mediocrity. **Anurag Anand's** *Reality Bites* (2012) explores the girls' hostel of a school and the bizarre as also passionate goings-on there.

Leena Walawalkar's *You've Got To Be Kidding* (2002) is a campus novel but the students are not teenagers; they having left jobs to join the London School of Business. **Neeraj Chhibba's** *Zero Percentile* (2009) is the story is of an IIT-entrance exam failed young man who goes over to Russia to study engineering. **Debaline Haldar's** *The Female Ward* (2013) focusses on the menace of ragging in college. **M.N. Krish's** *The Steradian Trail* (2013) is about life at IIT even as it involves a murder mystery. Other writers and their works belonging to the campus genre are: **Abhijit Bhaduri's** *Mediocre but Arrogant* (2012) and **Harish Sharma's** *Prankzz* (2012).

Career-lit

Although the title is Career-lit, i.e. fiction focused on career, it does not mean that a novel will only deal with the hassles or privileges of a career; it could as well make a foray into romance in the office or out of it. *Nothing can be as Crazy* (2009), maiden novel by **Ajay Mohan Jain**, an IIT-ian, falls in the category of career novels. It focuses on love and vocational life of Suresh, a bank probationary officer. *Married but Available* (2008) by **Abhijit Bhaduri**, an HR professional, follows the life of friends who have passed out of B-school and embark on a journey through the corporate world. *Call Me Dan* (2010)—a maiden piece by former banker **Anish Trivedi** is another call-centre-based novel. **Sujita Nair**, a former army officer-turned-writer has come out with her debut novel *She's a Jolly Good Fellow* (2010) which is a story of two women army officers who take on adversities, learning their lessons the hard way. There can be no two opinions about the fact that her description of life in the army should be authentic. **Tanushree Podder's** set of two books *Boots, Belts, Berets* (2011) and the other with its long-titled and self-explaining title *On the Double: Drill, Drama and Dare-Devilry at the IMA* (2015) situates four young trainees who find the rigmarole quite tough but brave it out forming a lasting relationship, love fun and play pranks at the expense of the company commander.

Quite a few fictional works have been produced by people working with the media. One such novel is *If I could Tell You* (2009) by **Soumya Bhattacharya,** who is an editor with a leading daily. The market crash undoes the protagonist. The novel is in the form of confessional letters written to the narrator's daughter Oishi or the divine one, who is the only character by name in the novel. **Bhavna Chauhan's** *Where Girls Dare* (2010) which is about girl cadets at Chennai's Officers' Training Academy. The novel *S.O.A.R.* (2015) by **Abir Mukerjee,** who has written many thrillers, deals with four friends who start a business that unfortunately runs aground.

Erotica

In this age of unbridled freedom, there is upsurge of new value system based upon freedom of individual choice. The great experiment underway is to find out if life in a social set-up could really be devoid of any socio-cultural norms. An increasing tendency in the popular novels written by those on the high circuit of corporate or advertising world is that their novels have a sort of bitchiness and irreverent style. The subject of sex was a taboo for women novelists the world over. No longer now.

The trend setter is **Shobhaa De,** the popular columnist and writer of *Sultry Days* (1994) and *Starry Nights* (1989). Incidentally, all her novels begin with the letter 's'! Her novel *Sethji* (2012) depicts an important politician whose party called ABSP is a coalition partner in the government. A thoroughly despicable and lascivious character, he has a daughter Amrita also thirsting for power and sex. Her husband creates a problem for his father-in-law which the daughter is called upon to set right. The book is a racy narrative with a new sleazy character added in each new chapter. Sex and violence provide the bulwark for this novel. Other novels published by De during this period are *Second Thoughts* (2013), *Sandhya's Secret* (2009), *Snapshots* (2006), *Sisters* (2014), and *Srilaaji* (2020).

Namita Gokhale's protagonist Paro of her earlier social comedy *Paro: The Dreams of Passion* (1984), who as a butterfly or temptress hopped from bed to bed, had her friend Priya who becomes the protagonist in Gokhale's novel *Priya in Incredible Indyaa* (2011). There is the gap of some 25 years and she is a middle-aged woman with two sons of marriageable age. She can watch Poonam do what Priya did in the earlier novel. Some new characters are added. The novel gives the reader a glimpse into the artificial life of the high society in Delhi. **Siddharth Shanghvi's** *The Last Song of Dusk* (2004) graphically describes the lesbian ways of physical relationship. Similarly, **Tarun Tejpal** of the Tehalka fame came up with his *Alchemy* of Desire (2005) which, true to its name, deals with characters high on sex. The novel *Of Course I Love You..! Till I find Someone Better* (2008) written by **Durjoy Datta** and **Maanvi Ahuja,** which is said to have run into thirteen impressions, has the shades of soft porn.

Crime

Thrillers based on crime form an important segment of popular fiction. **Rajkamal Jha,** a celebrated journalist, not only uses his acumen in investigative journalism but also garnishes the language of the narrative with a poetic touch. His novel *The City and the Sea* (2019) is based upon the 2012 Nirbhaya gangrape that brought shame to the country and saw Delhi and other parts of the country boil with rage. Jha's other novel *Fireproof* (2007) is an old style murder mystery with a slight twist in that the victim's ghost appears *a la* Shakespeare's *Hamlet.* **Vikas Swarup's** second novel *Six Suspects* (2010) is based on Bollywood actor Salman Khan's shooting of black bucks and the infamous killing of a model-cum-bar-girl in Delhi. Besides, *The Last Flamingoes of Bombay* (2009) written by **Siddharth Dhanvant Shanghvi** is based on the famous Jessica Lal murder case that took place in Delhi and involved children of important politicians.

Irwin Allan Sealy of *The Trotter-Nama* (1988) fame came up with *The Brainfever Bird* (2003), which deviates from his usual backdrop of nature and instead places his characters in the overcrowded Delhi as also in far-off Moscow. It is the story of a spy falling in love with a liberated woman and runs along the lines of a thriller. **Manreet Sodhi Someshwar** has created a female protagonist Mehrunisa Khosa in her thrillers—The *Taj Conspiracy* (2012) and *The Hunt for Kohinoor* (2014) published by her. A management professional as also a self-acclaimed history buff, Someshwar has the knack of tying the reader down to her book. **Aditya Sudarshan,** who started out as a law intern, turned to fiction writing. He has four novels to his credit including *A Nice Quiet Holiday* (2009) and *Show Me a Hero* (2012). Other popular writers of romance novels include **Sachin Garg** and **Sudeep Nagarkar.**

EMERGING CATEGORIES

Reflective Thrillers

Even though a writer of thrillers, **Ashwin Sanghi,** following Dan Brown's lead, has dabbled in a postmodern mélange through a mix of myth, science, history, politics, etc. in his works. Sanghi goes off the historical tangent in *Chanakya's Chant* (2012) as Chanakya is shown re-born as a wily pundit who successfully makes a woman powerful. *The Krishna Key* (2012) is not exactly a re-telling of the Mahabharata story. In this thriller, a murderer executes his meticulously planned murders, believing he is the reincarnation of Krishna! His latest work *Keepers of the Kalachakra* (2018) has the Buddhist myth of Kalachakra or wheel of time as the motif. The story relates to our times and begins with the search of the cause of some disease that has struck dead leading figures of the world. The intelligence agencies of the US, Russia, China, and India come together for this sake. As the work proceeds in a lab in India, we come across several discussions on the philosophies, myths, legends of different civilizations. All this is interspersed with references to contemporary events and personages. So, there are shifts of time and space, but the story is rivetting. This type of fiction demands a different categorization and the title 'Reflective Thriller' should, according to the writer of these lines, do justice here. **Karan Bajaj's** novels too show this tendency of taking a swipe at the ontology, though in an embryonic form. **Salman Rushdie's** novel *Quichotte*, though placed in the Travel and Adventure section here for its overarching motif of journey can also be viewed as a reflective thriller. In fact, all his novels have a heavy dose of intellectualism.

Corporate Fiction

The newly inaugurated genre of Corporate Fiction is a reflection of the postmodern world where MNCs mould not only the economy of the host country but also the mindset of employees with regard to questions of nation and nationality. It is not that novels based on corporate culture were not written earlier. Writers like Amit Chaudhuri and Anita Nair have written such fiction. For one, if fiction of this type discusses scams and frauds, such fiction should belong to the theme of crime. Besides, the Career-lit also takes up aspects of corporate life. But what corporate fiction is claimed to unravel is the corporate environment which fosters a culture that bears the imprint of the Western MNCs. The neo-liberal ambience strikes a chord with the youth. So far as the women are concerned, they are still seen as objects of desire, what with stress on immaculate dressing in modern attire, acquiring latest gadgets and cars and going abroad without so much as a murmur on the advances of male bosses.

Chetan Bhagat's second novel *One Night @ Call Centre* (2005) is taken as the reference point wherein he describes the goings-on in the lives of characters working in the call centre. As the title indicates, within the span of a single night, the characters undergo experiences as varied as dancing at a disco and then listening to God's voice on the mobile phone. The novel weaves a high romantic tale in simple language peppered with slang. **P.G. Bhaskar**, a banker, published five novels of which *Jack Patel's Dubai Dreams* (2011) and *Jack is back in Corporate Carnival* (2012) are based on banking operations in Dubai and Africa. Humour is his forte which makes his novels interesting and readable. **Ravi Subramanian**, a banker by profession, who started out with catchy titles like *If God was a Banker* (2007) and *I Bought the Monk's Ferrari* (2008), produced novels based upon corporate politics as played out in an MNC. These include *The Incredible Banker* (2011), *The Bankster* (2012), and *God is a Gamer* (2014). Also, novels like **Nishant Kaushik's** *A Romance with Chaos* (2009) and **Amrita Tripathi's** *Broken News* (2018) fall in this category.

Biographical Fiction

This category, also called Bio-fiction, includes both novels based on the writer's own life (also called auto-fiction) as also on the lives of others. Vikram Seth's *Two Lives* (2005) can be called a biographical novel, as it tells of the writer's uncle Shanti and German aunt Henny. Seth came in contact with them while he studied in England. Many letters written by Henny to the author are quoted. The details of historical events during the world war come with a bit of sermonizing by the author. In a similar vein is Ved Mehta's *The Red Letters* (2004) the eleventh and the last volume (No. XI) of his autobiography entitled *Continent of Exile* (2005). Surprisingly, it focusses on the life of his father and his beloved. Mehta has carved out a niche for himself in the world of letters with his spruce and elegant style of prose. The genre of fact-cum-fiction has always had its loyal readership. Suhdir Kakar's *Mira and the Mahatma* (2004) which deals with Miraben, nee Madeline Salade, the English disciple of Mahatma Gandhi, also belongs to this category.

Other novelists who have tried this mode of writing include **Reema Moudgil**, who in an emotional journey into past, touching on partition, travels to different places, separation from loved ones and ultimate acceptance of fait accompli. It is a fine piece providing glimpse into a woman's heart and life. Also **Boman Desai's** *Trio: A Novel about the Schumanns and Brahms* (2004) deals with the lives of the German classical musicians Schummans and Brahms. It is a well-researched book. **Farookh Dhondy's** *London Company* (2012) is a collection of fictionalized memoirs.

Science/Fantasy Fiction

Fictions based upon science and fantasy have been put under a single rubric for the simple reason that science throws open newer worlds for a novelist just like imagination. There are improbable scenarios which science is ever trying to understand and invent tools to turn the impossible into possible. A dash of scientific jargon or references to scientific ways brings an element of legitimacy to the rational mind of a novelist or a reader infatuated by science. Hence, most science fiction lands in the realm of fantasy too. Such fiction was written earlier also by writers like Jayant Narlikar and Chaman Nahal, but still it is at a nascent stage. It does not have deep roots in Indian English literature.

Jayant Narlikar, a famous scientist himself, wrote *The Return of Vaman* in 1989 and it is considered to be an interesting piece of work, particularly for the children. **Amitav Ghosh** supplied this genre in his *The Calcutta Chromosome* (1996) with what was found lacking in Narlikar's work, namely a literary style. **Andleeb Wajid's** *Tamanna* trilogy (2014) consists of three novels—*No Time for Goodbyes*, *Back in Time*, and *Time will Tell.* A touch of magic realism is reflected in the time travel of the young girl Tamanna who watches the times when her mother was a teenager. However, she ends up falling for Manoj who was her mother's neighbour. **Samit Basu's** *The Simoqin Prophecies* (2004), part of his Game World trilogy—*Turbulence* (2012) and *Resistance* (2013) are his other fantasy novels. The story revolves around two prophecies made before a great war that took place 200 years before. One of these predicted the return of the great *rakshas* (demon) Danh-Gem, and the other told about his antidote, a hero. Another young man is then drafted in to save the world from the *rakshas*.

Chitra Banerjee Divakaruni has also dabbled in fantasy as in a trilogy based on the 'Brotherhood of the Conch'. In *Shadowland* (2009), the last offering of this trilogy, fantasy, and time travel combine in a thrilling adventure. The novel portrays a dystopian world with polluted air and water and sequestered and hermetically sealed domes as residences of the rich while the poor struggle to survive as ever. **Kunal Basu's** *Racists* (2006) delves into the experiment of bringing up children without any cultural nurturing. Two scientists bring up two young children with the help of a dumb nurse on a barren island to find out the surprising result that love survives. **Aayushi Pandey's** *Okozbo* trilogy starting with the first book *Okozbo: The Fights* (2015) is about other worlds and a potential war that involves the entire universe. **Bhalindra Singh's** *A Three Faced Coin* (2017) focusses on paranormal activities and parallel universes. However, human feelings are universal. **M.G. Vassanji's** *Nostalgia* (2017) is a sci-fi thriller of a period when science has controlled age leading thereby to population explosion. **Indra Das's** *The Devourers* (2015) also falls in this category.

Dystopic Fiction

Envisioning future has been mostly along dystopic lines and is becoming popular lately. The writers are tempted to imagine a world where the normal rules of the world have been suspended or changed. We find world mostly as black or white. **Aravind Adiga's** *The White Tiger* (2008) is a dystopian novel. The novel dispels the set notions about canonical literature and has been criticized by many as a specimen of India-bashing which is popular in some Western circles. Balram Halwai, the orphan protagonist of this novel hails from a poor family of a backward Indian village. Hard times moulded him into a worldly-wise, shrewd, and sycophant chauffeur who is jealous of the rich people. His employer is a typical corrupt businessman who, under pressure of his cunning elder brother, even thinks of foisting the blame for a road accident on the chauffeur. Eventually, Balram murders his master for money, steals his identity and starts a taxi business in Bangalore. The novel is in the form of several mails written to the Chinese Premier Wen Jiabao to impress him with his business acumen and to lambast India for poverty, violence, injustice, and indiscipline, in a language real enough for a semi-literate chauffeur and therefore devoid of literary grace. However, the writer fails to convince the reader of the *raison d'etre* for the murder of an otherwise kind master.

Hari Kunzru's *Transmission* (2005) is quite interesting as it tells of an Indian software expert Arjun who gets laid off in America and in a revengeful mood releases a deadly virus that shakes the entire world, reaching finally the protagonist's favourite Bollywood star. Playwright and cartoonist **Manjula Padmanabhan's** twin novels *Escape* and *The Island of Lost Girls* (both 2015 publications) depict a New Dark Age in which the entire female population, excepting one—Meiji—is savaged and exterminated. She has three 'uncles'—Eldest, Middle, and Youngest to look after her. As she grows into an adolescent girl, they are worried about her safety. She is confined to an island meant for wounded girls. Thereafter, it becomes a kind of adventure with her guardian trying against all odds to reach her. **Prayag Akbar's** *Leila* (2017) envisages human settlement in the form of residential colonies on the bases of communities only. While it could be termed a reflection of myopic vision, some might find it a cautionary tale.

Graphic Fiction

What started as comic strips in newspapers and journals has now grown into full-fledged category of fiction which is of primary interest to children. **Sarnath Banerjee's** *Corridor* (2004) was hailed as the first graphic novel in India. His *The Barn Owl's Wonderous Capers* (2007) based on the legend of the Wandering Jew is an eccentric, though interesting account of life in 18th-century Calcutta with international linkages. **Amruta Patil** came out with her *Adi Parva: Churning of the Ocean* (2012). In this graphic novel, Patil depicts events like the gods and the demons competing with each other in churning the ocean. Other events mentioned are the king Janmejaya's yajna and queen Gandhari's willing sacrifice of eyesight. As can be expected, the number and variety of characters is large. Apart from myths, well-known legends have also been taken up for retelling. **Vishwajyoti Ghosh's** *Delhi Calm* (2010) mocks the role of the Marxists during the infamous Emergency era in India.

Conclusion

This survey leads us to certain conclusions. The volume of output in the genre of Indian English Fiction in these two decades has been tremendous, considering the past record of a limited production. It can be observed that the majority of novels fall in the category of light fiction. The young breed of writers, once it hits the road, churns out novels quite fast so that most of them have written upward of a dozen novels each!

Apart from the factors pointed out in the Introduction, the replacement of the previously rigid and tortuous publication process by a far more convenient one has revolutionized it. The electronic publishing in the form of Kindle or an e-book is so much faster. It is not the wily publisher who rules the roost, one could go in for Self-publishing at virtually no cost and there are platforms which would disseminate the work for a little cut. Writers have gone the whole hog, so to say, to make a killing. The example of the novelist Sundari Venkatraman, who has published more than fifty books in digital format is a shining example. This trend is going to make the future task of documenting all such works and assessing them for their worth quite challenging.

Coming now to the assessment aspect, one finds that serious fiction, though small in number, is contributing to literature in a valuable manner, touching upon all types of themes as discussed earlier in this essay. The only theme that is conspicuous by its absence is the more serious philosophical concepts. Popular fiction is marked by a superficial treatment of social and individual issues. Secondly, a large number of acclaimed authors are part of the Indian diaspora settled in western Europe, USA or other advanced countries. Diasporic literature has its own plus and minus points. While diasporic novelists have created a niche for Indian English literature on the world stage, the projection of India is subordinated to the lure of lucre. A Neo-Orientalist approach seems to find favour with many of diasporic novelists for this very reason.

It is not only the diasporic writers but the home-based category of writers too that is dominated by, what is normally referred to, as the public-school graduate, English-speaking, metropolis-based elite class which does not have the real connect with the ordinary people. Their model of language is the Yankee

English, their depiction of life is superficial and sensibility far from intense. They are particularly not aware of the problems or lifestyle in rural India. Literature written in regional languages is, therefore, more in tune with the Indian sensibility and reality.

Apart from these features, one finds excessive fascination for Western theories. At times, literature seems to have been produced merely to conform to such theoretical concepts even if these do not apply to the Indian situation. This calls for search of own identity of Indian English literature. One finds growing Indianisms in language as also the use of Indian narrative styles. But is it sufficient to reflect Indian ethos—is debatable.

Winners of Major Literary Awards

Award Winning Novels

Booker/Man Booker Award		
2006	Kiran Desai	*The Inheritance of Loss*
2008	Aravind Adiga	*The White Tiger*
DSC Prize for South Asian Literature		
2013	Jeet Thayil	*Narcopolis*
2014	Cyrus Mistry	*Chronicles of Corpse Bearer*
2015	Jhumpa Lahiri	*The Lowland*
2016	Anuradha Roy	*Sleeping on Jupiter*
2018	Jayanth Kaikini	*No Presents Please (stories)*
2019	Amitabha Bagchi	*Half the Night is Gone*
The Hindu Best Fiction Award		
2010	Manu Joseph	*Serious Men*
2011	Rahul Bhattacharya	*The Sly Company of Men Who Care*
2012	Jerry Pinto	*Em and the Big Hoom*
2013	Anees Salim	*Vanity Bagh*
2014	Ashok Srinivasan	*The Book of Common Signs (stories)*
2015	Easterine Kire	*When the River Sleeps*
2016	Kiran Doshi	*Jinnah Often Came to Our House*

2017	Deepak Unnikrishnan	*Temporary People (linked stories)*
2018	Neelum Saran Gour	*Requiem in Raga Janki*
2019	Mirza Waheed	*Tell Her Everything*
JCB Prize for Literature		
2019	Madhuri Vijay	*The Far Field*
2020	S. Hareesh	*Moustache (translated)*
Sahitya Akademi Award		
2002	Amit Chaudhuri	*A New World*
2004	Upamanyu Chatterjee	*The Mammaries of the Welfare State*
2006	Rupa Bajwa	*The Sari Shop*
2007	Malathi Rao	*Disorderly Women*
2010	Esther David	*The Book of Rachel*
2015	Cyrus Mistry	*Chronicle of a Corpse Bearer*
2016	Jerry Pinto	*Em and the Big Hoom*
2017	Mamang Dai	*The Black Hill*
2018	Anees Salim	*The Blind Lady's Descendants*

Novels Published During the Two Decades

Novels Published Between 2001 and 2020 AD

Author	*Titles*
A.M. Basheer	*Riot Widows*
A.K. Srikumar	*The Begum's Secret*
Aatish Taseer	*The Way Things Were*
Aayushi Pandey	*Okozbo: The Fights*
Abbyshek Chandra	*Love You Forever*
Abha Dawesar	*Babyji, This Summer in Paris, Family Values, Miniplanner*
Abhay Narayan Sapru	*The Valley of Shadows*
Abhijit Bhaduri	*Mediocre but Arrogant, Married but Available*
Abhimanyu Jha	*A Dilli Mumbai Love Story*
Abir Mukherjee	*S.O.A.R., A Rising Man, Smoke and Ashes, A Necessary Evil, Death in the East*
Adirath Sethi	*Where the Hills Hide Their Secrets*
Aditya Mukherjee	*Boomtown*
Aditya Sharma	*Champs of Devgarh*
Aditya Sudarshan	*The Persecution of Madhav Tripathi, A Nice Quiet Holiday, Show Me a Hero, The Outraged: Times of Ferment*

Aditya Wig	*King's Fall*
Advaita Kala	*Almost Single, Almost There*
Aijaz Ashraf	*The Hour Before Dawn*
Ajay Mohan Jain	*Nothing can be as Crazy*
Akash Kapur	*India Becoming*
Akash Verma	*Three Times Loser...Love Never Dies, A Broken Man*
Akhand Singh	*The Slip of Me*
Akhil Sharma	*An Obedient Father, Family Life*
Ali Ansari	*Dear Prophet: A Women's Story*
Aliyyah Enaiath	*The Yard*
Amandeep Sandhu	*Roll of Honour*
Ameeta Rathore	*Blood Ties*
Amish Tripathi	*The Immortals of Meluha, The Secret of the Nagas, The Oath of the Vayuputras, Ram: Scion of Ishvaku, Sita-Warrior of Mithila, Raavan*
Amit Chaudhuri	*A Strange and Sublime Address, Odysseus Abroad, Friends of My Youth, A New World, The Immortals*
Amit Dasgupta	*The Lost Fragrance, Indian by Choice*
Amit Majumdar	*Soar*
Amita Trasi	*The Colour of Our Sky*
Amitabh Pandey	*Himalayan White*
Amitabha Bagchi	*Above Average, The Householder, This Place, Half the Night is Gone*
Amitabha Chatterjee	*Of Wooing, Woes and Wanderings*
Amitav Ghosh	*The Glass Palace, The Hungry Tide, The Sea of Poppies, River of Smoke, Flood of Fire*

Amitava Chaudhari	*A Thing called Love in an Utterly Rotten World*
Amrendera Narayan	*Fragrance Beyond Borders*
Amrit Raj Shetty	*Love Over Coffee*
Amrita Mahale	*Milk Teeth*
Amritha Srikanth	*Heart on the Sleeve*
Amruta Patil	*Adi Parva: Churning of the Ocean, Kari*
Amulya Mulladi	*A House for Happy Mothers, The Copenhagen Affair, The Nearest Exist May be Behind You, A Breath of Fresh Air, The Mango Season, Song of the Cuckoo Bird, The Sound of Language, Serving Crazy with Curry*
Amulya Mulladi	*The Copenhagen Affair*
Anand Mahadevan	*The Strike*
Anand Neelakantan	*Ajay: Rise of Kali, Asura: The Tale of the Vanquished, Ajaya: The Role of the Dice, Ajaya: Rise of Kali, The Rise of Shivagmi, Mahishmathi, Chaturanga*
Anand Ranganathan	*For Love and Honour*
Anand Suspi	*Half Pants Full Pants*
Anand, Mani Ganesh	*If God Went to B-School...Would Love Follow Him There?*
Ananda Devi	*Indian Tango*
Ananda Mukerji	*A House in the Old Style*
Ananth	*Play With Me*
Andaleeb Wajid	*Blinkers Off, Back in Time, My Brother's Wedding, More than Just Biryani, No Time for Goodbyes, Time will Tell, When She Went Away* (+ 11 others)

Anees Salim	*The Vicks Mango Tree, The Blind Lady's Descendants, Tales from a Vending Machine, Vanity Bagh, The Small Town Sea, Fly Hasina Fly*
Anees ul Haq	*Firdaus*
Aneesh Pradhan	*Chasing the Raag Dream*
Anil Menon	*Half of What I Say, The Beast with Nine Billion Feet*
Anil Menon & Vandana Singh	*Breaking the Bow*
Animesh Verma	*I am Broke...! Love Me*
Animesh Verma	*Love, Life and Dream*
Anirban Bose	*Bombay Rains Bombay Girls, The Mysterious E-mail, Mice in Men*
Anirudha Bahal	*Bunker 13*
Anis Shivani	*Karachi Raj*
Anish Sarkar	*Benaami*
Anish Trivedi	*Call Me Dan*
Anita Desai	*The Artist of Disappearance, The Zigzag Way*
Anita Jain	*Marrying Anita*
Anita Krishanan	*Despite Stolen Dreams, Tears of Jhelum*
Anita Nair	*Mistress, Cut Like Wound, Idris: Keeper of the Light, Alphabet Soup for Lovers, Chain of Custody, The Better Man, Eating Wasps, Ladies Coupe, Mistress, Lessons in Forgetting*
Anita Rau Badami	*The Hero's Walk, Can You Hear the Nightbird Call?*
Anita Shirodkar	*Aryavir (Guardians of the Blue Lotus)*

Anjali Banerjee	*Imaginary Men, Bringing Back Grandfather, Looking for Bapur, Seaglass Summer, Invisible Lives*
Anjali Joseph	*Another Country, Saraswati Park, Difficult Pleasures, The Living*
Anjum Hasan	*Neti, Neti, Lunatic in My Head, Difficult Pleasures, The Cosmopolitans*
Ankush Saikia	*The Girl from Nongrim Hills, More Bodies will Fall*
Anne Cherian	*The Invitation*
Annie Zaidi	*Sleep Tight, Gulab, Prelude to a Riot*
Anshu Pathak	*Serendipity, Fate & Karma*
Antara Ganguli	*Tanya Tania*
Anu Kumar	*It Takes a Murder*
Anuja Chandramouli	*Arjuna: Saga of Pandava Warrior-Prince, Shakti: The Divine Feminne, Yama's Lieutenant and the Stone Witch, Prithviraj Chauhan: The Emperor of Hearts, Karitkeya: The Destroyer's Son, Kamadeva: The God of Desire, Ganga: The Constant Goddess, Rani Padmavati: The Burning Queen, Muhammad Bin Tughlaq, Monini: The Enchantress*
Anuja Chauhan	*The Zoya Factor, Battle for Bittora, Those Pricey Thakur Girls, The House that BJ Built, Baaz, Club You to Death*
Anukriti Upadhyay	*Kintsugi: A Novel*
Anupa Mehta	*The Waiting Room*
Anupam Srivastava	*The Brown Sahebs*
Anupama Garg	*The Tantric Curse*

Anuradha Roy	*The Folded Earth, Sleeping on Jupiter, All the Lives We Never Lived, An Atlas of Impossible Longing*
Anurag Anand	*Birth of the Bastard Prince, To Hell and Back, Reality Bites, A not Innocent Love Story, The Legend of Amrapali, The Quest for Nothing, The Assassination of Rajat Gandy, Where the Rainbow Ends, Love on 3 Wheels*
Anurag Garg	*Love not for Sale*
Anurag Mathur	*The Department of Denials, The Country is Going to the Dogs, Making the Minister Smile*
Aravind Adiga	*The White Tiger, Last Man in Tower, The Selection Day, Amnesty*
Ardashir Vakil	*One Day*
Arefa Tehsin	*Iora and the Quest of Five*
Arjun Dutt	*The Last Seen Romantic*
Arjun Nath	*White Magic: A Story of Heartbreak, Hard Drugs & Hope*
Arjun Raj Gaind	*Death at the Durbar*
Arjun Roy	*Third Best*
Arnab Ray	*The Mahabharata Murders*
Aroon Raman	*The Shadow Throne*
Arun Mirchandani	*You Are Not Alone*
Aruna Chakravarti	*Jorasanko*
Aruna Chakravarti	*Daughters of Jorasanko, Suralakshmi Villa, The Inheritors*
Aruna Jethwani	*Dance O' Peacock*
Arunava Sinha Shankar	*Chowringhee, The Middleman*

Arundhati Roy	*The Ministry of Utmost Happiness*
Aruni Kashyap	*The House with a Thousand Stories*
Arup Kumar Dutta	*The Bag: A Novel*
Arvin Chawla	*Deadly Recall*
Arvind Parashar	*All you need is Love*
Ashim Choudhury	*The Sergeant's Son*
Ashish Ranjan	*Love Will Find Its Way*
Ashish Vikram	*The House With the Green Roof*
Ashok Banker	*Vengeance of Ravana, Sons of Sita, Blood Red Sari, Siege of Mithila, Prince of Ayodhya, Demons of Chitrakoot, Armies of Hanuman, King of Ayodhya, Gods of War, The Slayer of Kansa, The Seeds of War, Bridge of Rama, Vortal Shockwave, Dance of Govinda, Lord of Mathura, Rage of Jarasandha (and 14 more)*
Ashok Chopra	*Memories of Fire: A Novel*
Ashok Shrinivasan	*Once Upon a Time*
Ashwin Kumar Mishra	*Feet in the Valley*
Ashwin Sanghi	*The Rozabal Line, Chanakya's Chant, The Krishna Key, The Sialkot Saga, Keepers of the Kalachakra, The Vault of Vishnu*
Avani Doshi	*Girl in White Cotton*
Avijit Chakraborty	*The Unhealthy Love*
Avijit Ghosh	*Bandicoots in the Moonlight*
Avtar Engill	*City of Unrest*
Ayush Ansal	*Into the Abyss*
Azhan Ahsan	*Love, Lust and Life*

Azharuddin	*Ten Days*
B.P.S. Mander	*Shades of Olive Green*
Balli Kaur Jaswal	*The Unlikely Adventures of the Shergill Sisters*
Bani Basu	*The Enemy Within*
Basavraj Naikar	*The Queen of Kittur, The Sun of Freedom, The Sun Behind the Clouds, Light in the House*
Basharat Peer	*The Collaborator, The Curfewed Night*
Bela Lal	*For Honour*
Bhalindra Singh	*A Three Faced Coin*
Bharati Mukerjee	*Desirable Daughters, The Tree Bride, Miss New India*
Bhaskar Chattopadhyay	*Here Falls the Shadow, Patang*
Bhavna	*The Diary of a Reluctant Feminist*
Bhavna Chauhan	*Where Girls Dare*
Bidisha Ghoshal	*The Rape Trial*
Biman Nath	*The Tattooed Fakir*
Boman Desai	*Trio, A Woman Madly in Love, Servant Master Mistress, Trio 2*
C.K. Meena	*Seven Days to Somewhere*
C.M. Nimbalkar	*Fast Forward*
C.P. Belliappa	*Victoria Gowramma: The Lost Princess of Coorg*
C.P. Surendran	*Lost and Found*
C.V. Murali	*Dreams Die Young, Prisoners of Hate*
Chaman Nahal	*Akela and the Blue Monster*
Chanchal Sanyal	*The Glass House: A Year of Our Days*

Chandrahas Chaudhury	*Clouds, Arzee the Dwarf*
Chandraprakash Mohata	*The Dev-D Syndrome*
Charu Singh	*Path of the Swan*
Chatur Rao	*Currents of Life*
Chetan Bhagat	*Five Point Someone, One Night @ Call Centre, The Three Mistakes of Lie, 2 States: The Story of My Marriage, Revolution 2020, Half Girlfriend, One Indian Girl, The Girl in Room 105, One Arranged Murder*
Chital Mehta	*Are You the One for Me?*
Chitra Banerjee Divakaruni	*Oleander Girl, Before We Visit the Goddess, Sitayan, Neela: Victory Song, The Vine of Desire, The Conch Bearer, Queen of Dreams, The Mirror of Fire and Dreaming, The Palace of Illusions, Shadowland, One Amazing Thing, The Forest of Enchantments*
Chitralekha Paul	*Delayed Monsoon (2011)*
Cyrus Mistry	*Chronicle of a Corpse Bearer, The Radiance of Ashes*
Daisy Hasan	*The To-Let House*
Dakshita Das	*Myself Meena, IAS*
Daman Singh	*Kitty's War, Nine by Nine, The Sacred Grove*
David Davidar	*Ithaca, The House of Blue Mangoes, The Solitude of Emperors*
Debalina Haldar	*The Female Ward*
Debashish Irengbam	*Ma, Mia, Multiple, Charlie Next Door*
Deep Ghatak	*Fish in Paneer Soup*

Deepak Chopra	*The Daughters of Joy and Soulmate*
Deepak Kaul	*Corpokshetra: Mahabharata in the MBA Yug*
Deepak Srivastava	*A Love So Special*
Deepika Shetty	*The Red Helmet*
Deepti Kapoor	*A Bad Character*
Dev Prasad	*The Curse of the Surya*
Devapriya Roy	*The Weight Loss Club*
Devdutt Pattanaik	*Hanuman, The Pregnant King, Lakshmi, Jaya: An Illustrated Retelling of the Mahabharata, Sita: An Illustrated Reading of Ramayana, Shyam: Retelling of Bhagwat*
Devi Yasdharan	*Empire*
Dharampal	*Twilight*
Dharini Bhaskar	*These Our Bodies Possessed by Light*
Dhruba Hazarika	*Sons of Bramha*
Dibyendu Palit & Arunava Sinha	*Illicit*
Diksha Basu	*The Windfall, Destination Wedding*
Dina Mehta	*Mila in Love*
Divya Kumar	*The Shrine of Death*
Dona Sarkar	*How to do Salsa in a Sari*
Durjoy Datta	*Our Impossible Love, The Girl of My Dreams, Our Impossible Love, Till the Last Breath, Hold my Hand, When Only Love Remains, World's Best Boyfriend, The Perfect Us, She Broke Up, I didn't...I Just Kissed Someone else! (and 11 more including some with co-authors)*

Durjoy Datta & Maanvi Ahuja	*Of Course I Love You..! Till I find Someone Better...*
Durjoy Datta & Nikita Singh	*If it's not Forever, it's not Love, Someone Like You*
Durjoy Datta & Orvana Ghai	*You were My Crush! Till you said you love me*
Easterine Kire	*Bitter Wormwood, When the River Sleeps, Son of the Thundercloud, Don't Run My Love, A Respectable Woman*
Eliyaah Eniath	*The Yard*
Eshwar Sundaresan	*Behind the Silicon Mask*
Esther David	*Book of Rachel, The Man with Enormous Wings*
Eunice de Souza	*Dangerlok*
Fahad Samar	*Flash Point*
Farhad Zama	*Mrs. Ali's Road to Happiness, The Marriage Bureau for Rich People, The Many Conditions of Love*
Farrukh Dhondy	*London Company, The Bikini Murders, Poona Company, Stealing Nasreen, Six Metres of Pavement*
Fatima Ahmed	*In Haleema's Words*
Feroz Rather	*The Night of Broken Glass*
G.B. Prabhat	*Early Indications*
Gajra Kottary	*Broken Melodies, Once Upon a Star, Girls Don't Cry, The Last Laugh*
Gaurav Suri & Hartosh Singh Bal	*A Certain Ambiguity: A Mathematical Novel*
Gautam Malkani	*Londonstani*
Geeta Abraham Jose	*By the River Pampa I Stood*
Girvani Dhyani	*S.T.A.L.K.E.D.*

Giselle Mehta	*Blossom Showers*
Gita Hariharan	*I Have Become The Tide, In Times of Siege, When Dreams Travel, Fugitive Histories*
Gitanshu Garg	*The Second Breath I took*
Gopal Gandhi	*Refuge*
Gopalkrishnan Kottoor	*Hill House*
H.S. Risam	*The Scalpel*
Hansda Sowvendra Shekhar	*The Mysterious Ailment of Rupi Baskey, My Father's Garden*
Hardik Dhamija	*Love in the Reality*
Hari Kunzru	*White Tears, The Impressionist, Transmission, My Revolution*
Harish Sharma	*Prankzz*
Harsh Snehanshu	*Ouch! That 'Hearts', Oops! I Fell in Love*
Harsha V. Dehejia	*Parul*
Harsho Mohan Chattoraj	*Ghosts of Kingdom Past*
Hemangi Gawand	*Love or Arranged...Just Marry me!*
Hetal Adesara	*Matrimonial Mocktales*
Himanjali Sankar	*Mrs C Remembers*
Himanshu Modi	*Mom days 'Get Married'*
Huma R. Kidwai	*The Hussaini Alam House, Meer*
I. Allan Sealy	*The Brainfever Bird, Red*
Inderjit Badhwar	*The Chamber of Perfumes*
Indra Sinha	*Animal's People*
Indu Balachandran	*Runaway Writers*
Indu Muralidharan	*The Re-engineers*

Indu Sundaresan	*The Twentieth Wife, The Feast of Roses, Splendor of Silence, The Shadow Princess, The Re-engineers, Atria*
Iqbal Ramoowalia	*The Death of a Postcard*
Ira Trivedi	*There is No Love on the Wall Street, What Would You Do To Save The World, The Great Indian Love Story*
Irwin Allan Sealy	*The Small Wild Goose Pagoda*
Ismita Tandon Dhankar	*Love on the Rocks*
Jagmohan Bhanveer	*The Curse of Bramha*
Jahnavi Barua	*Rebirth*
Jaina Sanga	*Silk Fish Opium*
Jaishree Misra	*A Scandalous Secret, Secrets and Lies, Secrets and Sins, Accidents like Love and Marriage, A Love Story for My Sister, Ancient Promises, Afterwards, Rani*
James Joseph	*God's Own Office*
Janhavi Achrekar	*Wanderers, All*
Janice Pariat	*The Nine-Chambered Heart, Seahorse*
Jaskiran Chopra	*Autumn Raga*
Jaspreet Singh	*Helium, Chef*
Jatinder Parmar	*Lost once, found forever*
Jayant Kulkarni	*No Presents Please*
Jaysinh Birjepatil	*Chinnery's Hotel*
Jeet Thayil	*Narcopolis, The Book of Chocolate Saints*
Jerry Pinto	*Em and the Big Hoom*
Jhangir Kerawala	*JFK*

Jhoomur Bose	*Confessionally Yours*
Jhumpa Lahiri	*The Namesake, The Lowland*
Joseph Sebastian	*The Peacenik Swap*
Joygopal	*Chief Minister's Mistress*
Judy Balan	*Sophie Days, Half Boyfriend, I have a Theory About That*
Juggi Bhasin	*Bollywood Deception, Blood Song, The Terrorist, The Avenger, Blood Song*
K.R. Meera	*The Unseeing Idol of Light*
K.B. Trehan	*Illusion of Love*
K.R. Meera	*The Poison of Love*
K.R. Usha	*Girl and a River, The Chosen*
Kaka Vidhate	*Duryodhan*
Kalpana Swaminathan	*The Secret Gardener, Venus Crossing*
Kalpesh Ratna	*Room 000: Narratives of the Bombay Plague, The Quarantine Papers*
Kalyan C. Kankanala	*Road Humps and Sidewalks*
Kalyan Ray	*No Country, Eastwards*
Kamesh Ramakrishna	*The Last Kaurava*
Kamilini Sengupta	*The Top of the Raintree*
Kancha Ilaiah	*Untouchable God*
Kanchana Banerjee	*A Forgotten Affair*
Kanika Dhillon	*Bombay Duck is a Fish, The Dance of Durga*
Kanishka Gupta	*The History of Hate*
Kankana Basu	*Cappuccino Dusk*
Kanwaljit Deol	*The Year of the Hawks*

Karan Bajaj	*Keep off the grass, Johny Gone Down, The Seeker*
Karan Mahajan	*The Association of Small Bombs*
Karan Puri	*Shit Happens*
Karuna Ezara Parikh	*The heart asks pleasures first*
Kaushik Barua	*Windhorse, No Direction Rome*
Kaveri Nambisan	*The Story that Must Not be Told, A Town Like Ours*
Kavita Daswani	*Bombay Girl, Betrayed, Lovetorn, Kingping: Made in Singapore Destroyed in Dubai, Everything Happens for a Reason, Salaam Paris, The Village Girl of Beverly Hills, Indie Girl, For Matrimonial Purposes*
Kavita Daswani	*Betrayed*
Kavita Kane	*Karna's Wife, Sita's Sister, Lanka's Princess, Manaka's Choice, Fisher Queen's Dynasty, Ahalya's Awakening*
Keki N. Daruwalla	*For Pepper and Christ, Ancestral Affairs, Swerving to Solitude: Letters to Mama*
Kesava Reddy	*Ballad of Ontillu*
Keshava Guha	*Accidental Magic*
Khayaal Patel	*Tarishir: The Awakening*
Khushwant Singh	*Mahraja in Denims, Burial at Sea, The Sunset Club*
Kiran Desai	*The Inheritance of Loss*
Kiran Doshi	*Jinnah Often came to Our House*
Kiran Khalap	*Two Pronouns and a Verb*
Kiran Nagarkar	*The Extras, Rest in Peace—Ravan and Eddie, God's Little Soldier, Jasoda, The Arsonist*

Kishor Thukral	*The Chronicler's Daughter*
Kishore Pillai	*Ambition's Curs*
Kishwar Desai	*Origins of Love, The Sea of Innocence, Witness the Night, Darlingji*
Komal Mehta	*Nick of Time*
Konkana Basu	*Lamplight*
Kota Neelima	*The Honest Season, Riverstones, Death of a Moneylender*
Krishan Pratap Singh	*Delhi Durbar*
Krishna Dutta	*Walking from the Gallows*
Krishna Shastri Devulapali	*Jump Cut*
Krishna Udayshankar	*Govinda, Kaurava, Kurukshetra, Immortal, Beast*
Kritika Malhotra	*It's always been you*
Kuldip Singh Saini	*Her Flight to the Love Nest*
Kulpreet Yadav	*Murder in Paharganj*
Kunal Basu	*The Yellow Emperors' Cure, Kalkatta, Intimacies, The Endgame, Sarojini's Mother, The Miniaturist, The Opium Clerk, The Japanese Wife, The Racists*
Kunal Bhardwaj	*Love was never mine*
Kunal Mukherjee	*My magical palace*
Lakshmi Raj Sharma	*The Tailor's Needle*
Lalita Das	*Dancing with Kali*
Lata Gwalani	*Incognito*
Lavanya Sankaran	*The Hope Factory*
Leena Verghese	*A Silver Dawn*
Leena Walawalker	*You've Got to be Kidding*
M. Koteswara Rao	*The Game, The Future*
M. Ramesh	*Silence of the Cicadas*

M.G. Wassanji	*The In-between World of Vikram Lall, The Assassin's Song, The Magic of Saida, Nostalgia, A Delhi Obsession*
M.N. Krish	*The Steradian Trail*
Madan Das	*Story of Harry Singh & Sophie Kaur*
Madhu Gurung	*The Keeper of Memories*
Madhulika Liddle	*Engraved in Stone, Crimson City, The Englishman's Cameo*
Madhumita Bhattacharya	*The Masala Murder, Goa Undercover*
Madhumita Mukherjee	*The Other Side of the Table*
Madhuri Banerjee	*Losing my Virginity & Other Dumb Ideas*
Madhuri Vijay	*The Far Field*
Maha Khan Philips	*Beautiful from this Angle*
Mahendra Jakhar	*The Butcher of Benaras*
Mahesh Bhatt & Suhrita Sengupta	*All That Could Have been*
Mahesh Rao	*Polite Society*
Mahtab Narsimhan	*The Tiffin*
Makrand Paranjape	*Body Offerings*
Malathi Ramchandran	*Edge of all the light, The Legend of Kuldhara, Mandu, The Wheel Turned*
Malathi Rao	*Disorderly Women*
Mallikarjun Patil	*Two Generations*
Mamang Dai	*The Black Hill*
Mamta Alva	*Some Chilli Snakes*
Manasi Vaidya	*No Deadline for Love*
Mandar Kokate	*Oh Shit, Not Again*

Mandar Kokate	*Oh Shit, Not Again*
Manik Dhar	*Funda of Mix-ology*
Manika Lal	*Chasing New Rainbows*
Manil Suri	*The City of Devi, The Death of Vishnu, The Age of Shiva*
Manjiri Prabhu	*The Cavansite Conspiracy, Voice of the Runes*
Manju Jaidka	*Scandal Point, Amaltas Avenue, The Next Milestone: A Mother's Journal*
Manju Kapur	*Custody, Brothers, A Married Woman, Home, The Immigrant*
Manjul Bajaj	*Come Before Evening Falls, Another man's wife*
Manjula Padmanabhan	*The Island of Lost Girls, Escape*
Manjushree Thapa	*Seasons of Flight*
Manoranjan Byapari	*There's Gunpowder in the Air*
Manreet Sodhi Someshwar	*The Taj Conspiracy, The Hunt for Kohinoor, The Radiance of a Thousand Suns, Earning the Laundry Stripes, The Long Walk Home*
Manu Bhattathiri	*The Town that Laughed*
Manu Joseph	*The Illicit Happiness of Other People, Miss Laila Ahmed and Dangerous, Serious Men*
Manveen S. Anand	*The High Sea Conspiracy*
Mariam Karim	*My Little Boat*
Mary John Williams	*Aryaveer: The Guardian of Dakshin Durgh*
Mayank Anand	*Love from the Sidelines*
Mayur Patel	*Vivek and I*

Mayuresh Pokharankar	*The Comical Saga*
Medha Deshmukh	*Frotiers*
Meena Arora Nayak	*Endless Rain, The Kathasaritsagar of Somadeva*
Meena Kandasamy	*When I Hit You, The Gypsy Goddess*
Meenakshi Reddy Madhavan	*Cold Feet, Split, The One Who Swam with the Fishes, You are Here*
Meenu Mehrotra	*Lilacs Bloom in My Backyard*
Meera Godbole-Krishnamurthy	*Gardens of Love: Stories of a Marriage*
Megha Majumdar	*A Burning*
Meghnad Desai	*Anamika*
Melvin Durai	*Bala takes the Plunge*
Menacherry Mathew	*Arrack in the Afternoon*
Mihir Raj	*Plz. Kiss Me or Kill Me*
Milan Vohra	*Tick-tock, We're 30*
Minakshi Thakur	*Lovers like you and I*
Minty Tejpal	*The Last Love Letter*
Mira Jacob	*The Sleepwalker's Guide to Dancing*
Mirza Waheed	*The book of gold leaves, Tell Her Everything, The Collaborators, the Book of Gold Leaves*
Mishana Khot	*Welcome to the Zoo*
Mitali Perkins	*You bring the distant near, Extreme American Makeover*
Mitra Phukan	*A Monsoon of Music*
Mohit Parikh	*Manan*
Mohit Uppal	*Here Be Dragons*
Mohyna Sirinivasan	*The House on Mall Road*

Mona Verma	*God is a River*
Monabi Mitra	*FIR, The Final Report*
Monideepa Sahu	*Riddle of the Seventh Stone*
Monika Pradhan	*The Hindi Bindi Club*
Mridula Garg	*The Last Email*
Mridula Koshy	*Not only the things that have happened*
Mukul Deva	*And Death Came Calling, Assassins, R.I.P., The Dust Will Never Settle, Weapon of Vengeance, The Garud Strikes, Pound of Flesh, Lashkar, Salim Must Die, Blowback*
Munaf Shaikh	*The Journey*
N. Sampath Kumar	*Campus Cola*
Nachhatar Singh Brar	*Paper Marriage*
Nadia Hashmi	*The Sky at Our Feet*
Nadim Ali	*Maps for Lost Lovers*
Nalini Rajan	*Love and Death in the Middle Kingdom; Sinking, Not Swimming*
Namita Devidayal	*Aftertaste*
Namita Gokhale	*Book of Shadows, Priya in Incredible Indiyaa, Lost in Time: Ghatokacha, Of Graves and Godmother, The Book of Shadows, A Himalayan Love Story*
Nandhika Nambi	*Unbroken*
Nandini	*A House of Butterflies*
Nandita Puri	*Nine on Nine*
Narayan	*Saptarshi*
Naresh Fernandes	*City Adrift*
Nargis Dalal	*The Nude*
Narhari Das	*The Reluctant Nun*

Naveen B.C.	*What Goes Around Comes Around*
Navtej Sarna	*The Exile*
Nayanika Mahtani	*The Gory Story of Genghis Khan*
Nayantara Sahgal	*When the Moon Shines by Day, The Fate of the Butterflies, Lesser Breeds*
Neel Kamal Puri	*Remember to Forget*
Neel Mukherjee	*The Lives of Others, A State of Freedom, Past Continuous, A Life Apart*
Neelum Saran Gour	*Sikandar Chowk Park, Messrs Dickens Doyle & Wodehouse Pvt. Ltd., Requiem in Raga Janaki, Invisible Ink*
Neelima Dalmia	*Merchants of Death*
Neerja Gaurie	*The Harbinger*
Neeru Iyer	*Of Bridges Among Us*
Nihshanka Debroy	*Checkmate*
Nikhil Mahajan	*My Love Never Faked*
Nikhil Pradhan	*Cold Truth*
Nikita Achanta	*A Beautiful Catastrophe, Wrecked Souls*
Nikita Lalwani	*The village, The Gifted*
Nikita Singh	*Accidentally in Love... With Him? Again?, If It's Not Foever...It's Not Love, The Promise, Someone Like You, The Unreasonable Fellows, Right Here Right Now, Like a Love Song, After All This time, Love @ Facebook*
Nilanjan Choudhury	*Shillong Times*
Nilanjan P. Chowdhary	*Bali and the Ocean of Milk*

Nilanjana Roy	*The Wildings*
Nilanjana Sanyal	*Jesus in our time*
Nilendu Sen	*Sonar Gaaon*
Nilima Kota	*Shoes of the Dead, The Honest Season, Riverstones, Death of a Moneylender*
Nipun Ranjan	*The Lost Scraps of Love*
Niraj Chhibba	*Zero Percentile 2.0*
Nirupam Kumar Reddy	*One Day*
Nirupama Subramanian)	*Keep the Change*
Nisha Amarnath	*Victims for Sale*
Nishant Kaushik	*A Romance with Chess*
Nitasha Kaul	*Residue*
Niven govinden	*Black Bread White Beer*
Novaneel Chakraborty	*Forever is a Lie, How About a Sin Tonight?, Forget Me Not Stranger, That Kiss in the Rain, The best Couple Ever, Roses are Blood Red, Cross Your Heart; Take My Name*
NS Inamdar	*Shahanshah: The Life of Aurangzeb*
Omar Shahid	*The Spinner's Tale*
Omkar Sane	*Coming Soon The End*
Oswald Pereira	*The Newsroom Mafia*
P.G. Bhaskar	*Jack Patel's Dubai Dreams, Jack is Back in Corporate Carnival, So Who Says I'm Middle Aged, I Stole Her Story, Mad in Heaven*
P.J. Sindu	*Marriage of a Thousand Lies*
Palash Krishan Mehrotra	*The Butterfly Generation, Eunuch Park*

Pallavi Aiyar	*Chinese Whiskers*
Pankaj Dubey	*What a Loser*
Pankaj Sekhsaria	*The Last Wave*
Parinda Joshi	*Live from London*
Parismita Singh	*Peace Has Come*
Paritosh Uttam	*Dreams in Prussian Blue*
Parkash Sohal	*At Night You Sleep Alone*
Parth Sarathi Basu	*With or Without You*
Parul A. Mittal	*Arranged Love*
Parul Mittal	*Heartbreaks and Dreams: The Girls @ IIT*
Parul Sharma	*By the Water Cooler*
PCK Prem	*A Handsome Man, A Heart for the Man, Not Their Lives*
Pepita Seth	*The Edge of Another World*
Phukan Mitra	*Collector's Wife*
Pia Padukone	*Where Earth Meets Water*
Pico Aiyer	*Abandon*
Pinki Virani	*Deaf*
Piyush Jha	*Mumbaistan, Compass Box Killer, Raakshas- India's No. 1 Serial Killer*
Poile Sengupta	*Inga*
Poomani Kalyan Raman	*Heat*
Pradeep Sebestian	*The Bok Hunters of Katpadi*
Prayaag Akbar	*Leila*
Preethi Nair	*One Hundred Shades of White, The Colour of Love, Gypsy Masala*

Preeti Shenoy	*Tea for Two and a Piece of Cake, Love a Little Stronger, Life is what you make it, Wake Up Life is Calling, The One You Cannot Have, Love Kisses and All Things Warm, A Hudred Little Flames, 34 Bubblegums and Candies, The Secret Wishlist*
Preeti Singh	*Circles of Silence*
Preeti Taneja	*We That Are Young*
Prerna Wadhawan	*The Word Keeper*
Preti Taneja	*We That Are Young*
Priya Parmar	*Venesa and Her Sister*
Priya Sarukkai Chabria	*Generation 14*
Puja Borker	*Masterji*
Qurratulain Hyder	*Fireflies in the Mist, River of Fire, Ship of Sorrows, Chandni Begum*
R. Chandrasekar	*The Goat, The Sofa and Mr Swami*
R. Raj Rao	*Boyfriend, Hotel Room 131*
R.S. Sudarshanam	*The Tree of Life*
Radha Viswanath	*Ravana Leela*
Radhika Jha	*Smell, Lanterns on Their Horns*
Radhika Oberoi	*Stillborn Season*
Radhika Vaz	*Unlady Like a Memoir*
Rahul Bhattacharya	*The Sly Company of People Who Care*
Rahul Mehta	*No Other World*
Rahul Saini	*Those Small Lil Things...*
Raj Doctor	*Melancholy of Innocence*
Rajal Pitroda	*Starstruck*
Rajashree	*Trust Me- A Romantic Comedy*

Rajat Chaudhuri	*The Butterfly Effect*
Rajat Mitra	*The Infidel Next Door*
Rajeev Balasubramanyam	*The Dreamer*
Rajeev Jhaveri	*I, Romantic*
Rajeev Singh	*The Erotic Muse*
Rajendra Chenni	*Mud Town*
Rajesh Devraj & Meren Imchen	*Sudarshan Chimpanzee*
Rajesh Khullar	*Viral Watch*
Rajesh Singh	*That hardly happens to someone*
Rajesh Talwar	*An Afghan Winter*
Rajinder Singh	*When a Jilted Lover Hits Back*
Rajiv G. Menon	*Thundergod: The Ascendance of Indra*
Rajiv Rajendra	*Doosra, The League*
Rajiv Seth Srishti	*Neverr say goodbye*
Rajkamal Jha	*If You Are Afraid of Heights, Fireproof, The City and the Sea, She Will Build Him a City*
Rajorshi Chakraborti	*Roller Coaster, Derangements*
Rakesh Kaul	*The Last Queen of Kashmir*
Raksha Bharadia	*All and Nothing*
Ram Vignesh	*The Book*
Raman Chopra	*The Last Rain of the Winter*
Rana Dasgupta	*Tokyo Cancelled, Solo*
Ranjan Kaul	*Through the Forest Darkly*
Ranjit Lal	*Bambi, Chops and Wag*
Rashmi Bansal	*I have a Dream*
Rasleen Syal	*Happily Murdered...*

Ratika Kapur	*The Overwriter, The Private Life of Mrs Sharma*
Ratna Vira	*Daughter by Court Order, It's Not About You*
Ravi Dhar	*Orphans of the Storm*
Ravi Subramanian	*The Bankster, God is a Gamer, The Bestseller She Wrote, In the Name of God, Don't Tell the Governor, If God was a Banker, Devil in Pinstripes, Bankrupt, The Incredible Banker*
Ravinder Singh	*I Too Had a Love Story, Can Love Happen Twice?, Like It Happened Yesterday, Your Dreams are Mine Now, This Love Feels Right, Will You Still Love Me?*
Ravishankar Etteth	*The Tiger by the River*
Reema Moudgil	*Perfect Eight*
Revathi Suresh	*Jobless, Clueless, Reckless*
Richa S. Mukherjee	*Kanpur Khoofiya Pvt. Ltd.*
Rickie Khosla	*Pretty Vile Girl*
Rikin Khamar	*The Lotus Queen*
Rimi B. Chatterjee	*Signal Red, The City of Love, Black Light*
Rimli Sengupta	*Karno's Daughter*
Rita ChaudhUry	*Chinatown Days*
Rita Gadekar	*Families at Home, Bottom of the Heap*
Ritu Lalit	*A Bowlful of Butterflies, Hilawi, Chakra: Chronicles of the Witch Way, His Father's Mistress, Wrong for the Right Reasons*
Ritwik Malik	*Because You Loved Me*

Rohinton Mistry	*Family Matters, The Scream*
Rohit Chakraborty	*The mug of melancholy*
Rohit Gore	*Focus, Sam*
Roma Bansal	*One Afternoon*
Roopa Somasundram	*Mirror Mirror on the Wall*
Roshan Ali	*Ib's Endless Search for Satisfaction*
Roswitha Joshi	*Once More, Indian Dreams, Trapped in Want and Wonder*
Ruby Gupta	*A Degree in Death, No Illusions in Xanadu, Maya*
Ruchi Kokcha	*Obsessed*
Ruchir Joshi	*The Last Jet Engine Laugh*
Ruchita Misra	*I do, do I?*
Rukmini Bhaya Nayar	*Mad Girl's Love Song*
Rupa Bajwa	*The Sari Shop, Tell Me a Story*
Rupa Gulab	*Girl Alone, Chip of the Old Blockhead, Hot Chocolate is Thicker than Blood, Daddy Come Lately, The Great Depression of the 40s*
Ruskin Bond	*Susana's Seven Husbands, A Flight of Pigeons*
S. Hussain Zaidi	*Eleventh Hour*
S.A. Chakraborty	*The City of Brass*
S.R. Saha	*Jab Se You Loved Me*
S.S. Kumar	*Frozen Waves*
Sabin Iqbal	*The Cliffhanger*
Sabyn Javeri	*Nobody killed her*

Sachin Garg	*It's My First Love Just Like My Last One, Never Let Me Go, I'm Not Twenty-Four, Come On Inner Peace...I Don't Have All Day, When Opposites Meet, We Need a Revolution,*
Saddiqa Peerbhoy	*Marry Go Round*
Sagar Sahu	*The thing between U & ME*
Sagarika Chakraborty	*A Calendar too crowded*
Sagarika Ghosh	*The Gin Drinkers, Bad Faith*
Saikat Majumdar	*The Firebird, Play House, The Scent of God, Silverfish*
Sakshama Puri	*The Wedding Photographer*
Salil Desai	*The Body in the Back Seat*
Salman Rushdie	*Fury, Shalimar the Clown, The Enchantress of Floence, Luka and the Fire of Life, Two Years Eight Months and Twenty Eight Days, The Golden House, Quichotte*
Samhita Arni	*Missing Queen, Sita's Ramayan, The Prince*
Sami Ahmad Khan	*Aliens in Delhi, Red Jihad*
Samim Ahmed	*Seven Heavens*
Samit Basu	*Turbulence, Resistance, Testing Times, A Difficult Stage, Mismatch Mayhem, Chosen Spirits, The Simoqin Prophecies, The Manticore's Secret, The Unwaba Revelations, Terror on the Titanic*
Sandeep Das	*Yours Sarcastically*
Sandeep Nayyar	*Revenge of the Chandals*
Sandip Roy	*Don't let him know*

Sandipan Deb	*The Last War*
Sangeeta Bahadur	*Jaal*
Sanjay Bahadur	*Bite of the Black Dogs, The Sound of Water*
Sanjay Bordia	*The Claim*
Sanjeev Sahota	*Ours are the Streets,*
Sanjiv Bhatla	*Mr J Has Left Us*
Sanjiv Sanyal	*Life over Two Beers*
Sarita Mandanna	*Tiger Hills, Good Hope Road*
Sarita Varma	*Girl from Fatehpur*
Sarla Barnabas	*Dream Sequence*
Sarnath Banerjee	*Corridors: A Graphic Novel, The Born Owl's Wondrous Capers, All Quiet in Vikaspuri, The Harappa Files*
Saswati Sengupta	*The Song Seekers*
Sathya Saran	*The Dark Side*
Satya Debnath	*The Crazy Harvest*
Satyajit Sarna	*The angel's Share*
Satyarth Nayak	*The Emperor's Riddles*
Saurabh Katyal	*No Flying from Fate*
Savi Sharma	*Everyone has a Story (Two parts)*
Seema Goswami	*Race Course Road: A Novel*
Shah Alam Khan	*Man with the White Beard*
Shahnaz Bashir	*The Half Mother*
Shailaja Vajpayee	*Three Parts Desire*
Shakti Salgokar	*Imperfect Mr. Right*
Shamini Flint	*Inspector Singh Investigates: A Curious Indian Cadaver*
Shamlal Puri	*Dubai Dreams*

Shamsher Chandel	*Crack of Dawn*
Shanthi Sekaran	*The Prayer Room*
Sharath Komarraju	*Murder in Amaravati, Banquet on the Dead, Winds of Hastinapur, The Puppeteers of Palam, The Rise of Hastinapur, The queens of Hastinapur, The Tree Bears Witness: A Birbal Mystery*
Sharmila Kantha	*Break in the Circle*
Sharmishtha Mohanty	*New Love*
Sharanya Mannivanan	*The Queen of Jasmine Country*
Shashi Deshpande	*The Binding Vine, The Other Man, Ships that Pass, Shadow Play, Moving On, In the Country of Deceit, Strangers to Ourselves*
Shashi Tharoor	*Riot*
Shashi Warrier	*The Girl Who Didn't Give Up, The Hangman's Journal, The Pillow Talk Movies, The Homecoming*
Shatrujeet Nath	*The Karachi Deception*
Shazaf Fatima Hiader	*A Firefly in the Dark*
Sheila Kumar	*No Strings Attached*
Shekhar Kapur	*Devi*
Shekhar Khanduja	*The End of Creator*
Sherarat E singh	*Monsieeur Singh's Loves and Losses*
Shilpi Somaya Gowder	*Secret Daughter, The Golden Son*
Shinie Antony	*When Mira went forth and multiplied*
Shiraz Mukherjee	*Tiger in You*
Shiv Aroor	*Operation Jinnah*

Shiv Kumar	*A Metro Nightmare*
Shivangi Ramsay	*Passionate Love, Mine for Tonight, Straight from a Lover's Heart, Single and Sensational, Addicted to Love*
Shiven & Mayuri	*Never Apart*
Shoba Narayan	*Return to India*
Shobha Naidu	*On the Yati's Trail*
Shobha Nihalani	*Rise of the Kalingan: Nine Book Three*
Shobhaa De	*Sethji, Second Thoughts, Sandhya's Secret, Snapshots, Sisters, Srilaaji*
Shobhan Bantwal	*The Sari Shop Widow*
Shouvik Bhattacharya	*Murder in a Minute*
Shovan Chowdhury	*The Competent Authority*
Shrabani Basu	*Victoria & Abdul*
Shravya Bhinder	*To You with Love*
Shreekumar Verma	*Maria's Room*
Shreyas Bhave	*Storm from Taxila, The Prince of Patliputra, Nemesis of Kalinga, The Prisoner of Yakutsk: The Subhash Chandra Bose Mystery*
Shrikumar Varma	*Maria's Room*
Shriya Garg	*Take one more chance*
Shruti Saxena	*Stilettos in the Boardroom*
Shubha Menon	*The Second Coming*
Shubha Sharma	*The Awasthis of Aamnagri*
Shubhakanta Behara	*The Mahanadi Dream*
Shubhangi Swarup	*Latitudes of Longing*
Shubhanku Kochar	*Everything Will be Alright*
Shujoy Dutta	*Like a pinprick to the heart*

Shweta Gnesh Kumar	*Random Rants of a Bored Housewife*
Shweta Modgill	*One Hundred Days: Her Quest, My Cure*
Sid Bahri	*The Homing Pigeons*
Siddharth Chowdhury	*The Patna Manual of Style*
Siddharth Dhanvant Shanghvi	*The Rabbit and the Squirrel*
Siddharth Obero	*The Back Benchers: The extra class*
Siddhartha Sanghavi	*The Last Song of Dusk, The Last Flamingoes of Bombay*
Siddhesh Inamdar	*The Story of Long-Distance Marriage*
Sidharth Chowdhary	*Day Scholar*
Sidharth Gigoo	*The Garden of Solitude*
Smita Jain	*Kkrishnaa's Konfessions, Piggies on the Railway*
Soma Das	*Sumthing of a Mocktale*
Somnath Batabyal	*The Price You Pay*
Sonia Falerio	*The Girl*
Sonia Singh	*Bollywood Confidential*
Sonora Jha	*Foreign: A Novel*
Soumya Bhattacharya	*Soumya Bhattacharya: You Must Like Cricket, All that You Can't Leave Behind, If I could Tell You*
Sreeju Sudhakaran	*The Great Indian Wedding Conspiracy*
Sreemoyee Piu Kundu	*You've Got the Wrong Girl*
Sri M.	*Shunya*
Srikumar Sen	*The Skinning Tree*
Srilata K.	*Table for Four*
Srinivas Rao Adige	*The Mughall High Noon: The Ascent of Aurangzeb*

Srishti Chaudhary	*Lallan Sweets*
Srividya Natarajan	*The Undoing Dance*
Stephen Alter	*Rataban Betrayal, In the Jungles of the Night, The Dalliance of Leopards*
Subhasis Das	*Mom Says No Girlfriend*
Subramanian Shankar	*Ghost in the Tamarind*
Suchita Malik	*Memsahib's Chronicles, Women Extraordinaire, Scent of the Soil, Indian Memsahib*
Sudeep Chakravarti	*Tin Fish, Once Upon a Time in Aparanta, The Avenue of Kings*
Sudeep Nagarkar	*Sorry, You're Not My Type, You're the Password to My Life, Your're Trending in My Dreams, She swiped Right into My Heart, Our Story Needs No Filter, She Friend-zoned My Love, Few Things Left Unsaid*
Sudha Murthy	*The Day I stopped Drinking, House of Cards*
Sudhir Kakar	*Mira and the Mahatma,The Seeker: A Novel, The Crimson Throne*
Sudhir Thapliyal	*Mansuri Macabre*
Sudhira Bhagat	*Acushia*
Suditi Jindal	*The Adultress, Grow Up Moon!*
Sujata Massey	*A Murder on Malabar Hill*
Sujata Parashar	*In Pursuit of Ecstasy*
Sujit Saraf	*Harilal and Sons*
Sujita Nair	*She's a Jolly Good Fellow*
Sukanya Datta	*Beyond the Blue*
Sukanya Venkatraghavan	*Dark Things*
Suman Hossain	*A Guy Thing*

Sumana Roy	*Missing*
Sumit Aggarwal	*Office Shocks*
Sumit Shahi	*Never Kiss Your Best Husband*
Sumriti Shahi	*A Lot like Love, a lil like chocolate (2011)*
Sunanda Sikdar	*A Life Long Ago, The Malhotra Bride, The Casanova's Wife, An Autograph for Anjali, Scorpio Superstar, The Marriage Predicament, Matsya, Kurma, Varaha, Narsimha, Vamana, The Runaway Bridegroom, His Drunken Wife, (and six more)*
Sundari Venkatraman	*The Malhotra Bride, The Smitten Husband, The Runaway Bridegroom, The Passionate Princess, Her Bohemian Husband, Tied in Knots, Once Bitten Twice Lucky, Matsya, Varaha, Narsimha, Parsuram, Kurma, Simha International (and 39 more)*
Sundip Gorai	*Hickory Dickory Shock! The Tale of Techies*
Sunil Gera	*Make Me Your Friend, Stars in Your Eyes*
Sunil Yapa	*Your Heart is a Muscle the Size of a Fist*
Sunjeev Sahota	*The Year of the Runaways*
Suparna Chatterjee	*The All Bengali Crime Detectives*
Supriya Dravid	*A cool, dark place*
Supriya Parulekar	*A Soulful of Lie*
Suraksha Giri	*It Happened Like This*
Suravi Ray	*Where the Sun Breaks Free*
Suravi Sharma Kumar	*Voices in the Valley, A Love Story*

Surendra Mohan Pathak	*Conman*
Susan Visvanathan	*The Visiting Moon, Phosphorus and Stone, The Seine at Noon*
Sushant Changotra	*I know you now*
Sushil Gupta	*The Fourth Monkey, First Person Singular*
Swati Chanda	*Drowning Fish*
Swati Kaushal	*Piece of Cake, A Girl Like Me, Drop Dead, Lethal Spice, A Few Good Friends*
T. Dasu	*Spy, Interrupted: The Waiting Wife*
T.S. Trimurti	*Chennaivasi*
Tabish Khair	*How to Fight Islamist Terror from the Missionary Position, Jihadi Jane, Night of Happiness, The Bus Stopped, The Thing About Thugs, Man of Glass, Filming: A Love Story*
Taj Hassan	*The Inexplicable Unhappiness of Ramu Hajjam*
Tanushree Podder	*Solo in Singapore, A closetful of Skeletons, Boots Belts Berets, Escape from Harem, On the Double, No Margin for Error, The Teenage Diary of Rani Laxmibai, Nur Jahan's Daughter*
Tanveer Singh	*It's All About Love*
Tarun Tejpal	*The Valley of Masks, Alchemy of Desire, The Story of My Assassins*
Terry O'Brien	*Vilayati Pani: A Brown Sahib Story*
Thrity Umrigar	*Everybody's Son, Bombay Time*
Timeri Murari	*Four Steps from Paradise*

Timeri N. Murari	*The Taliban Cricket Club, Small House, The Imperial Agent, The Last Victory*
Tirumurti TS	*Clive Avenue*
Tishani Doshi	*Fountainville, Small Days and Nights, The Pleasure Seekers*
Trisha Bora	*What Kitty Did*
Trisha Das	*Ms Drupadi Kuru After the Pandavas*
Tuhin A. Sinha	*Let the Reason Be Love, 22 Yards, That Thing called Love, Of Love and Politics, The Edge of Desire*
Tulika Mehrotra	*Dellhi Stopover*
Twinkle Khanna	*Mrs Funnybones*
Udayan Mukherjee	*Dark Circles*
Upendra Namburi	*A Thriller, 60 Minutes*
Upmanyu Chatterjee	*Weight Loss, The Mammaries of the Welfare State, Way to Go, The Revenge of the Non-vegetarian, The Assassination of Indira Gandhi*
Urmila Deshpande	*Kashmir Blues, A Pack of Lies*
Urmilla Deshpande & Bakul Desai	*Madhouse: True Stories of Hostel 4*
Usha Ananda Krishna	*Fallout*
Usha K.R.	*The Chosen, A Girl and a River, Monkey Man*
Usha Narayanan	*Madras Mangler, Pradyumna: Son of Krishna*
Uzma Aslam Khan	*Trespassing*
Uzma Zafri	*A Wild Rose*
V. Raghunathan	*Return to Jammu*
V. Sanjay Kumar	*Artist Undone*

V. Sudarshan	*Adrift*
V.S. Naipaul	*Half-a-Life, Magic Seeds*
Vadassery Thaiparambil Rakesh	*The Thorough Check*
Vamsee Juluri	*The Mythologist, Saraswati's Intelligence, The Firekeepers of Jwalapurum*
Vandana Kumari Jena	*The Dance of Death*
Vani	*The Recession Groom*
Varsha Dixit	*Wrong Means Right End, Right Fit Wrong Shoe, Xcess Baggage, Rightfully Wrong Wrongfully Right, A Hasty Hook-up, Ex-Factor, Danika, The Cryptic Touch, Miss Matched, Killer Moves, The Wallflowers*
Vasant Kallola	*It's Okay to Fail My Son*
Ved Mehta	*Continent of Exile, Vol. X*
Vedahsree Khambete-Sharma	*Swear You Won't Tell?*
Veena Nagpal	*The Uncommon Memories of Zeenat Qureishi*
Vijay Nair	*Let Her Rest Now*
Vikas Khanna	*The Last Color*
Vikas Rathi	*Resident Dormitus*
Vikas Swarup	*Q and A, Six Suspects, The Accidental Apparentics*
Vikram Balagopal	*Savage Blue*
Vikram Chandra	*Sacred Games,*
Vikram Khanna	*The Girl who disappeared*
Vikram Paralkar	*The Afflictions*
Vikram Paralkar	*The Wounds of the Dead*

Vikram Rana	*The Equation of My Love and Its Parameters*
Vikram Seth	*Two Lives*
Vikrant Khanna	*Secretly Yours, When Life Tricked Me; Love Kicked Me, The Girl Who Knew Too Much, Love Lasts Forever*
Vineet Bajpai	*Harappa: Curse of the Blood*
Vinod Joseph	*When the Snow Melts*
Vish Dhamija	*The Heist Artist, Nothing Lasts Forever*
Vivek Atray	*Dubey Ji Bounces Back*
Vivek jain	*The Dreamer*
Vivek Shanbhag	*Ghachar Ghochar*
Yashodhara Lal	*Just Married, Please Excuse, There is Something About You, Sorting Out Sid, How I became a Farmer's Wife*
Yasmeen Premji	*Days of Gold and Sepia*
Zarreen Khan	*Koi Good News?*

Section II: Reflections

1

Salman Rushdie's *The Golden House*: Classical Worldview for Postmodern Times

Salman Rushdie's name has been identified with magic realism for so long, but it appears that as one gets older, the traditional patterns of life or literature pull one back. In his latest novel The Golden House, Rushdie has dropped his signature magic realism and dished out traditional realism. This is not to condemn conventional notion of realism, rather to uphold it as something that has been held as integral to the art of novel, since the novel as a literary form developed in 18th-century England. The novel still has elements of postmodern style in so far as language and some of the narrative techniques like metanarrative reflexivity, ambivalence, obfuscation, multiple registers, high allusiveness, etc. are concerned. But with regard to the thematics, Rushdie takes a firm stand rather than leave it open-ended. The villain of the piece, a Mumbai mafia don with links to terrorists gets poetic justice in the end. The notion of justice has always been upheld as a humanist ideal in Greek culture—the inspiration behind Western philosophy. That, incidentally, is also the gist of Indian poetics and philosophy.

Salman Rushdie is known the world over for his fiction whose superb quality won him the 'Best of Booker' award in 2008 indicating his unchallenged sway over the Booker wining novels in the last 40 years. His appearance on the scene with his magnum opus *Midnight's Children* (1981) was a momentous event for the genre of Indian English Fiction, for, in the words of a critic, it "legitimized and privileged the till then marginalized 'other' and stood the conventional notions of the centre and margins on their respective heads. This text proclaimed the arrival of a new type of Postcolonial—not the Mimic man—not one who has accepted the 'givens' of history and politics, but one who subverted and rewrote histories, smashed the whole sorry scheme of things and moulded new realities" (Bharucha 93).

Rushdie's latest novel *The Golden House* shows him in a surprisingly new avatar. He has not only shunned some of the trappings of postmodern literature, particularly magic realism which he pioneered in Indian English Fiction and which became the hallmark of his novels,[1] but has also espoused clear moral stance. Now this is something that has been valued in Western as well as Indian poetics, but before commenting further, let us briefly go through the storyline.

Terror stalks entire world today, therefore, it is natural for an intellectual writer like Rushdie to take it up as the theme of his novel. *The Golden House* is the story of an unnamed mafia don, who grew up in Mumbai and came in contact with known goons given to extorting money from people. Later, he also stepped into the business of real estate where his highhandedness helped him mint money and grow in stature. But when his accomplices turned into terrorists to settle score with the disciplining state, he parted ways with them. The turning point was the terror attack on the Taj Hotel in Mumbai on 26/11 in which he lost his wife who had gone thereafter a fight with him.

Our don shifts to New York where he had already been investing heavily. It is here that he is acquainted with the narrator who gives him the name Nero Golden and their house the Golden House. The narrator imagines Nero asking his children, in true postmodern fashion, to choose their new identity in the adopted land and so we have the three names from the Greek classics: Petronius, Lucius Apuleius, and Dionysus, which are later abridged as Petya, Apu, and D for the sake of convenience.

Petya, the eldest, a 42-year-old, tech-savvy chap has a penchant for inventing interesting video games. Apu, the 41-year-old middle son, is a sober and romantic artist, a poet at par with Deli, as also a promiscuous metropolitan. The youngest one called only 'D' is actually born of Nero's illicit affair with a woman. He is an intellectual, idealist type and so is Riya Z, his friend. However, D is a transvestite and has feminine mannerism also. His identity grows more and more problematic with the passage of time. Hence, the use of parenthesis with pronoun 'he' (254), which changes to 'she' (266).

The family lived almost secluded life till the world around overtook them. Petya falls in love with a Somali artist Ubah, but in doing this, he unwittingly crosses his brother Apu's path who had been in love with her too. The Goldens go in their private jet to an island off Hawaii to escape the coming blizzard, where many rich people maintain habitation. At the new year party there, the 74-year-old Nero is hooked by a 27-year-old Siberian girl named Vasilisa—an interesting charter. Rene Unterlinden, the narrator, is a debutant film maker and is an important link in the story as he is at once outside and inside the narrative in the postmodern style. He is not only Nero's neighbour but also a family member in the sense that he later becomes the father of Vasilisa's baby, even though he is in love with Suchitra.

Now, the wheel of fate turns and to Nero's bad luck, Apu visits Mumbai in the company of Ubah and both are murdered by Mastan's men. Mastan was the 'unbribeable' police officer whose career plummeted due to the machinations of Nero Golden's associate Don Corleone (character based on real life don Haji Mastan). The youngest offspring D's identity ambivalence grows despite counselling. Finally, he has to go in for sex change, comes home in woman (Vasilisa's) evening dress, feels he is unwelcome and so commits suicide. Petya goes to watch Halloween parade where a fusillade of shots fired by a maverick kills seven people including Petya, and his psychotherapist Murray Lett.

The past debts have to be paid as destiny dictates. Mastan, the retired police officer, comes calling at Nero's and warns him but is himself killed within 24 hours supposedly by Nero's men. Now is the turn of final justice. A fire rages later, ostensibly from the underground gas pipes, said to be the handiwork of two Asians including a dwarf (Nero's adversary), which speedily engulfs the entire building trapping Nero, his wife and child in it. The child, Vespa, is thrown by Vasilisa through window and is caught by a labourer. So, in the end Rene, Suchitra and Vespa are alive with Vespa having been declared the inheritor of all property and Rene as the guardian by Nero on the day of Mastan's visit. Also survives the movie or the story of these life cycles.

Postmodern Traits

Rushdie is a writer of these postmodern times and his novel *The Golden House* exhibits postmodern traits in so far as style is concerned. Now postmodernism, as its high priest Jean-Francois Lyotard opined in his report *The Postmodern Condition: A Report on Knowledge*, is the negation of all grand narratives of our times like Marxism, Freudism, etc. (Bertens 142-43). On the literary front, the impact of postmodernism followed the notion of deconstruction advanced by the French philosopher Jacques Derrida in the late 1960s. Briefly, it can be said of the impact on literature that

> Postmodernism stands for freedom from tradition and authority. No centre, definite terms, boundaries or absolute truths exist. Truth is relative and subjective. The margins are as important as the centre. It stands for the contingent, the subversive and the functional. Irreverence towards authority, indeterminacy, experiments in techniques, eclecticism, pastiche, magic realism, collapse of demarcation between fact and fiction, non-recognition of boundaries, belief in relativity of critical approaches are some of the other hallmarks of Postmodern literature. What Postmodernism challenges are old style liberalism, its high moral tone with tradition and its high attendant notions of purity and authenticity considered implicit in the conventional forms of social life. (Malik and Batra 51)

Postmodernism negates the difference between the high and low art and is frequently found lacking in coherence and depth, being immersed in what Baudrillard called 'simulacra'—"where the image or the model becomes more real than the real" (Woods

26). Postmodernism got reflected as a stylistic hallmark, as Barry Lewis stipulates: "In literary terms, postmodernist fiction itself became perceptible as a kind of 'style' and its characteristic techniques and themes came to be adopted without the same sense of breaking new ground" (170). Magic realism can be considered as an important style marker of postmodernist fiction.[2]

Salman Rushdie is widely acknowledged as the pioneer of postmodern style in Indian English Literature. One can trace in him traits like "magic realism, intertextuality, meta-fictionality, extravagant farce, multi-mirrored analogy and a potent symbolic structure, the idea of reality as provisional and partial, the presence of deconstructive markers and practices etc." (Rajagopalachary 1-2). Here, in this novel, Rushdie does not use magic realism, save in the form of a two-page insert, but he does play some postmodern metafictional and reflexive tricks as in obfuscating the identity of the narrator, who, the novel states, has been "hiding behind the first-person plural, and may do so again" (22), flashes credentials like a visiting card ("I offer this brief CV now so that the reader may feel in good hands, the hands of a credible and not inexperienced storyteller": 34); asks readers for patience ("Patience: I will not reveal all my secrets at once": 39); knows his mental faculty will be suspected ("I say this while I am still in full possession of all my mental faculties": 130); questions self about the logic of the story ("Plausible. And yet one is not wholly convinced": 138), etc. This is to assure the reader in the postmodern spirit that the worlds outside the text and inside are not different.

The narrator, being placed outside the Golden family, can feign ignorance about intimate matters but later he is sucked into the vortex; thus he is outside as also inside the narrative. Rushdie also displays circularity and ambiguity in narration while referring to the city of Bombay, from where the protagonist Nero Golden had migrated. The name of the city and country India are kept in abeyance until page 19 as "the city that could not be named in the country that could not be identified" (16). After page 19, this self-imposed gag is lifted, but again, for reasons known to him only, Rushdie goes in for anonymity of city and country on page 114.

Rushdie has created postmodern situation in which people of different nationalities come together in New York which they call home—imaginary homelands—as Rushdie postulates in his book by the same name. There is the Indian mafia don as the protagonist, along with his sons, his new Russian wife Vaselisa, the Bulgarian narrator, the retired Burmese diplomat, the Australian doctor, the Somali girlfriend of Apu, etc.

Postmodernity converges with contemporaneity, with the now and the near, with our ephemeral and immediate experience as it mocks the veracity and claims of permanence of hallowed texts, of revered icons and the biblical promises. In this context, the narrative itself becomes suspect and turns into metanarrative. The metanarrative underlines the postmodern present in the lives of the characters too. The characters in *The Golden House* lead their lives within the binaries and they are conscious of these. "Even as my personal happiness increased, so did my unspoken self-criticism," remarks Rene (260). Commenting on the poststructuralist instability of semantics, the narrator says to Apu: "...the word spiritual, which was now applied to everything from religion to exercise regimes and fruit juice, needed to be given a rest, for perhaps a hundred years or so" (226).

The Golden House is a postmodern text in the sense that the use of allusions from literatures of the world as also reference to artistic works of all-time standing, placed alongside quotes from contemporary popular verbal and visual media make this work a pleasure to read and cherish. So, we often see the scattered allusions to Shakespeare, Aeschylus, Sophocles, Roman myth sitting comfortably with the recent news of escape from the Minnesota jail of two murderers! (261). As in Rushdie's other novels, Hindi film music (*Tuhi Meri Shab Hai...*) is heard in a Manhattan street (128). Rushdie completes the background of the song and tells us that it is from a 2006 Kangana Ranaut-starrer *Gangster* (102-03). An overload of references, however, hinders the flow of narrative at times:

> As I stared at Vasilisa Golden silhouetted against a window beyond which lay the winter waters of the Hudson she looked to me like one of the goddesses of the screen [...] like Jeff Daniels in *The Purple Rose of Cairo*. I thought of Ornella Mutti bewitching Swan in Schlondorff's film of Proust; of Faye Dunaway as Bonnie Parker with her sensually twisting mouth captivating Warren Beatty's Clyde Barrow; of Monica Vitti in Antonioni shrinking erotically against a corner and murmuring *No lo so*; of Emmanuelle Beart clothed in nothing but beauty in *La belle noiseuse*. I thought of the Godardettes Seberg in *Breathless* and Karina in *Peirrot le fou* and Bardot in *Le mepris*, and then I tried to rebuke myself, reminding myself of the powerful feminist critiques of new wave cinema, Laura Mulvey's 'male gaze' theory.... (177)

Mixed language use is the condition of the postmodern fiction as there is blurring of boundaries between serious and popular fiction. *The Golden House* uses a mix of literary and colloquial forms. It is not bombastic as it was in *Midnight's Children* or *The Satanic Verses*. Ironic understatements, which subvert meaning in post-structural sense, abound like while talking of the family life of the Sicilian aristocrat Vito, Rushdie notes: "... disillusioned by Palermo, by the Mafia and by his father too, grew up to make his home in New York and became determined to lead the opposite life to his father's, utterly faithful to his wife Blanca, but refusing to spend a single evening stuck alone with her and the children at home" (34). But Rushdie can bring up emotions through conventional rhetoric where needed, as for example, while talking of the violence in America:

> I walked the streets in a blind rage and all at once it was as if all the anger gathering in the air poured into me too, I could feel it, the anger of the unjustly dead, the young men shot for walking in a stairwell while black, the young child shot for playing with a plastic gun in a playground while black, all the daily black death of America, screaming out that they deserved to live, and I could feel, too, the fury of white America at having to put up with a black man.... (146)

Issue of Identity

An important theme touched upon in the novel is identity. The question of identity has become extremely vexed as postmodernism marks the fluidity of identity whereas post-coloniality underlines its importance in our times. "God is dead and identity fills the vacuum," comments Riya in the novel (72). Indeed, for the migrant in any country, it becomes a matter of life and death. We find the contemporary world riven by identities based on class, caste, sex, colour, race, religion and, most of all, politics. It can be seen as a disruptive construct that is outcome of political tensions in oppressive societies where the majority tries to impose its norms on the minorities. It becomes "decisive and a strategic, deliberate mode of separation and the practices and methods of keeping cultures and social groups separated" (Marfield 44). Quoting Nasser Hussain, Marfield explains, "As is the practice in modern cosmopolitan society, the tendency of the dominant culture is to romanticize the link between culture and identities. Thus, ideological and social constructed forms such as African-American, Asian-American and so on become a necessary discursive practice in expressing and accentuating differences" (55). However, the hyphens in these constructs as in the theoretical emblem 'postcolonial' point to postmodern ambivalence only.

We love to flaunt our identities inspired by narcissism of the tallest order. Rushdie refers to the Museum of Identity,[3] which further underlines the importance of identity as the

> mighty new force in the world, already as powerful as any theology or ideology, cultural identity and religious identity and nation and tribe and sect and family, it was a rapidly growing, multidisciplinary field, and at the heart of the Identity Museum was the question of the identity of the self, staring with the biological self and moving far beyond that. Gender identity, splitting as never before in human history, spawning whole new vocabularies that tried to grasp the new mutabilities. (72)

It is these 'mutabilities' that are in focus at the end of arguments. Postcolonial theory shows identity is relative in the context of the colonizer and the colonized or the dominant and the dominated. The issue is discussed in the novel in some depth with references to the mythical notions of *ardh-narishwar* or grammatical particles denoting sex. The conversation between D, Riya, and Ivy Mantel hinges on the issue of D's sexual identity:

> 'Or maybe transfeminine, because you're born male, identify with many aspects of femaleness but you don't feel you actually are a woman.'
>
> 'The word woman is being detached from biology. Also the word *man*.'
>
> 'Or if you don't identify with woman-ness or man-ness maybe you're non-binary.' (111-12)

They discuss the grammatical pronouns used in different languages for denoting sex. Finally, Riya sets his doubts to rest with the words: "You can choose who you want to be, sexual identity is not a given. It's a choice" (112). Elsewhere, D and the professional psychologist debate what is woman, mind-body problem, choice and freedom, etc. (250). Nero, like anyone from the older generation, is unable to comprehend the idea of mixed sexual identity like women without women's parts, man with surgically constructed organs (307).

Classical Worldview

The discussion on identity is, however, to be qualified in that Rushdie's characters hardly change; their inner identity remains stable. They are flat in Forster's terminology and so the fluidity of character remains confined to discussion only. The characters, in fact, come out larger than life. Despite the fact that the protagonist is a former don, Rushdie, through his skilful narration, is able to win over reader's empathy for him. One tends to agree with the critic who avers:

> For all its literary bravado, the brilliance of its practised riffs, this latest Rushdie novel is not about attack or even showing off. It is a work of mourning: Greek tragedy, Greek threnody. Speaking of which, Greek myth and Roman history laminate this novel all over with their dark gold: Jason and his Argonauts chasing the Golden Fleece, Apuleius' story of metamorphosis in *The Golden Ass*, Roman Emperors, Furies,

> Muses, Hubris, Nemesis, the gods Dionysius and Pan, you will recognise each of them in these bloodied pages. (Nair)

Indeed, the novel upholds the classical viewpoint. The foremost concern of classics from Aristotelian days to Renaissance period and onward to the eighteenth-century practitioners of neo-classicism had been the human being and how he could and should be made perfect. 'Know thyself' was the motif of ancient Greek humanism which inspires all Western thought. While values like morality, justice and courage were high in hierarchy, hubris was placed at the lowest level. In Homer, we find "moral reflections on the behaviour of men, the foolishness of mortals, the misery and transitoriness of life, and the wickedness of injustice" (Thilly 9). It is the same with Hesiod, who in his *Works and Days* attacks the foibles of his time and presents moral maxims, as also with others like Aesop (of *Aesop's Fables*) and the gnomic poets. Horace believed literature to be a vehicle of instruction as well as delight, and this is what best fits Rushdie's novel under discussion here.

The moral slant in literature was viewed favourably and indeed practised by the neo-classicists of the 18th-century England like Alexander Pope and Dr Samuel Johnson, etc., for whom ancient Greek and Latin masterpieces were classics or ideals for them to follow. Poetry was designed "to yield both instruction and pleasure to the people who read it. Not art for art's sake, but art for humanity's sake was a central ideal of neoclassic humanism" (Abrams 184). The moral approach continued to hold sway until the 19th-century realist movement caught on in literature sending ideals based on antiquity out of use. However, morality cannot be totally banished from the world, so we have literary figures and critics like Mathew Arnold, T.S. Eliot, Paul Elmer More, and lately Yvor Winters, Edmund Fuller, etc. Irving Babbit, a known humanist and Eliot's teacher wrote in his essay "Genius and Taste": "Truly great literature conforms to standards, to the ethical norm that sets bounds to the eagerness of the creator to express himself" (138).

It is not only the Western classics that espouse morality as something important, but the Indian classical works too stress moral principle not only in literature but in all knowledge-imparting texts.[4] In fact, *dharma* itself is defined in moral terms—as that which ought to be practised (*ya dharyate sa dharma*). Thus, the moral end is not religion-specific in the sense that it cannot be identified with any organized religion.[5] This dharmic (based on *dharma*) view should inform literature, according to the Indian poetics.

Moral and Philosophical Issues

Rushdie's classical proclivity is further substantiated by his focus on the moral and philosophical questions which have always stared mankind in the eye. This novel debates lofty questions and mysteries of life and world—self, society, literature, etc.—from different perspectives, all of which raises its stature above the run-of-the-mill novels. Almost every character, including Nero, grows philosophical. Apu is already devoted to mysticism. Rene and Suchitra discuss the goings-on in the Golden House and elsewhere in the world in philosophical vein. At one place, Suchitra remarks to Rene: "Be profound. Own your tragedy. Find your freedom. Resolve your ambiguity" (285).

In Chapter Two, the protagonist asks the key moral question: "What is a good life?" This is something that would be miles away from a postmodern mind. "The question (overt or implied) now asked by the professionalist student, the State, or institutions of higher education is no longer 'Is it true?' but 'What use is it?'", notes Lyotard (51). This is the world of utilitarians now, but Rushdie's answer underlines his worldview: "In these our cowardly times, we deny the grandeur of the Universal, and assert and glorify our local Bigotries.... In these our degenerate times, men bent on nothing but vainglory and personal gain—hollow, bombastic men for whom nothing is off-limits if it advances their petty cause—will claim to be great leaders and benefactors, acting in the common good..." (7). The novel, therefore, is a critique of postmodern thinking.

The conflict between good and evil does not require the mediation of religion, as the narrator observes: "I had been brought up by those dear departed Belgians [his parents] to believe that 'right' and 'wrong' were ideas that came naturally to the human animal, that these concepts were born in us, made. We believed that there was a 'moral instinct': hard-wired into the DNA in the way that, according to Steven Pinker, the 'language instinct' was. This was our family answer to the religious allegation that persons without religion could not be moral beings, that only the moral structure of a religious system validated by some sort of Supreme Arbiter could give human beings a firm grip on good and evil" (147). The narrator seems to be airing Rushdie's views, who, while answering an interviewer, said:

> ...there's a lesson there that you can't avoid learning about the power of religions and fanaticism to unleash this kind of horror. I think it's quite clear that in my life, or anybody in my generation, anybody growing up in independent India in the last half century, knows that. They know about the capacity that lurks inside that religious belief when pushed to the extreme to unleash extreme violence. (Deena 21)

Rushdie perceives the postmodern world from a classical moralist's position. It becomes evident even in his views on contemporary politics. Rushdie comes down heavily on the Trumpian kind of politics that controls the world today. Rushdie's assessment is that "The world outside the haunted house had begun to feel like a lie. Outside the house it was the Joker's world, the world of what reality had begun to mean in America, which was to say, a kind of radical untruth: phoniness, garishness, bigotry, vulgarity, violence, paranoia, and looking down upon it all from his dark tower, a creature with white skin and green hair and bright, bright red lips" (278). This postmodern world is not to Rushdie's liking, for he believes in classical values of truth and morality.

Conclusion

Summing up, it can be said that the novel *The Golden House* has the format of a postmodern thriller that is full of chases and murders, but the message enshrined is the classical one that has been valued in all literatures, whether Western or Eastern until postmodernism raised its head: It is that human action or character becomes one's destiny. Fate justly punishes you for evil deeds. This is also the gist of the *Karma* theory upheld in Indian philosophy and justice is the value upheld in ancient Greek literature. Surprisingly, this is clear to Nero—a proud man—who confesses to Riya towards the end of the novel: "You accuse me and I am guilty of it and fate has punished me by taking my children. One child dead at the hands of my enemies, one by his own hand, one at the hand of a madman, but all three are my punishment and my burden to bear forever, yes, and their mothers too" (336). Nero Golden is, thus, wiser but it is too late and he also meets his doom for having set the wheel of justice in motion the moment he chose the evil course in life. Rushdie's worldview castigates the protagonist's hubris. Rene comments, "After Hubris comes Nemesis: *Adrasteia*, the inescapable" (261). This justifies the punishment which makes the message classical and universal.

NOTES

1. Talking of magic realism, one notes its prevalence in most of Salman Rushdie's novels. The use of magic realism informs the storyline of his first novel *Grimus*, which pictures a magical Calf Island where immortals live who can also undertake celestial travel. The story is basically about Flapping Eagle, an Indian who drinks a magic potion and lives for more than 700 years. In *Midnight's Children*, the protagonist and all those born on the midnight hour of Aug. 15, 1947 possess telepathic powers. In *The Ground Beneath Her Feet*, the protagonist gains extra vision as a result of an accident. In *Satanic Verses*, in the first chapter, Gibreel and Saladin Chamcha are shown falling from the aeroplane, with the latter transforming into a goat-like creature. In *Luka and Fire of Life* also, we find the entire scenario is marked by things linked to magic, as for example, flying carpet, the city of Dreams, the land of Lost Childhood, River of the Magic World, etc. In *The Enchantress of Florence*, the human turns into a witch. Rushdie, however, did not use this technique in *Fury*, his seventh novel published in 2001. Fantastic happenings are the staple of Rushdie's fiction which take place "without the narrator registering surprise or commenting on their strangeness" (Faris 281), thus fulfilling the condition of a magical realist text.

2. Barry Lewis, in his essay in the anthology *Routledge Companion to Postmodernism*, identifies these markers of postmodernist fiction as temporal disorder, i.e. blending of history with fantasy; pastiche; fragmentation or the breaking up of plot, character, setting and theme, which were earlier considered the cornerstones of fiction; looseness in chaptalization; obsession with dread of existence and of losing freedom; and the permeation of text and the world, with author or real historical personages entering fiction.
3. The replacement of traditional museums by identity museums has been trending lately. Rice Hall of George Washington University explains: "...the notion of the traditional museum as we've come to know it—a cold, looming temple of glass-cased collections from an antiquated, imperial past—has given way to a proliferation of museums designed to celebrate the shared experiences of a particular ethnic, racial, or religious group. But [...] 'identity museums', whether they focus on Asian Americans, Jewish Americans or other groups, are creating a distorted cultural narrative that is far from black and white marble" (Hall).
4. Knowledge in Indian tradition is suffused with socially relevant and useful values. Regarding the purpose of literature, "Most Indian theorists are agreed on literature's purpose being the promotion of commonly accepted ends of life. Bharata [the first great theoretician in Indian drama] at the very beginning in no uncertain terms asserts that literature is a discourse of knowledge—*pancam veda*—a knowledge text. The art experience therefore is perceived as a transforming experience as the *ananda* (joy) experienced is illuminating, enlightening, liberating—the experiencer acquires new, affirmative cognition and thereby escapes from his narrow self and his inherent worldly tendencies and becomes nobler than he actually may be" (Kapoor 163-64).
5. Professor Makarand Paranjape avers that the concept of *dharma* is different from religion: "Modern secular religions like Humanism or Marxism have a *dharmic* element in them. Dharma is common to Hinduism, Buddhism, Jainism, Sikhism, the indigenous religions and to Zoroastrianism, Islam and Christianity, faiths which have their origins outside our land but which have many local adherents now. That is why, the faith of this country is known as *sanatana* dharma, the eternal dharma, and is not to be identified with any one form of

what has now come to be known as Hinduism" (85). Taking up the works of two authors—Raja Rao and Salman Rushdie, Paranjape comments that "a Raja Rao or a Salman Rushdie despite their totally dissimilar values and philosophies, may be seen as similar in that they both wish to act upon society, to alter it in ways they consider good and beneficial. Both are, in that sense, practitioners and teachers of dharma, though one is traditional, the other modern; one Vedantic, the other Leftist; one religious, the other secular; one majoritiarian, the other minoritarian, and so on" (96).

WORKS CITED

Abrams, M.H. *A Handbook of Literary Terms*. New Delhi: Cengage Learning, 2009.

Babbit, Irving. "Genius and Taste." *The Nation*. 7 February, 1918. <http://www.unz.com/print/Nation-1918feb07-00138/>

Bharucha, Nilufer. *World Literature: Contemporary Postcolonial and Post-Imperial Literatures*. New Delhi: Prestige, 2007.

Deena, Seodial Frank. *Salman Rushdie's Global Philosophy: Critical Essays*. Delhi/Sydney: Prestige Books International, 2018.

Faris, W.B. "Sheherazade's children: Magical realism and postmodern fiction." *Magical Realism: Theory, History, Community*. Eds. L.P. Zamora and W.B. Faris. Durham: Duke University Press, 1995, pp. 163-90.

Forna, Aminatta. "The Golden House by Salman Rushdie review—A parable of modern America." *The Guardian*. 16 September 2017. <https://www.theguardian.com/books/2017/sep/16/the-golden-house-salman-rushdie-review>.

Hall, Rice. "Role of the Identity Museum." *GW Today*. 14 November 2012. <https://gwtoday.gwu.edu/examining-role-identity-museum>.

Kapoor, Kapil. *Comparative Literary Theory: An Overview*. New Delhi: DK Printworld, 2014.

Lewis, Barry. "Postmodernism and Fiction." *The Routledge Companion to Postmodernism*. London/New York: Routledge, 2001, Edition 2011, pp. 169-81.

Lyotard, Jean-Francois. *The Postmodern Condition: A Report on Knowledge*. Trans. Geoff Bennington and Brian Massumi. Manchester: Manchester University Press, 1984.

Marfield, Randy. "Cosmopolitan Culture and Corrosion: Salman Rushdie's Dialogue on Identity." *Salman Rushdie's Global Philosophy: Critical Essays*. Ed. Frank Seodial Deena. Delhi/ Sydney: Prestige Books International, 2014, pp. 43-57.

Nair, Rukmini Bhaya. "The Golden House: Salman Rushdie's bark is still strong but the bite less sharp." *The Hindu*. 16 September 2017. <http://www.thehindu.com/books/rushdies-bark-is-still-strong-but-the-bite-less-sharp/article19690000.ece>.

Paranjape, Makarand. *Towards a Poetics of the Indian English Novel*. Shimla: Indian Institute of Advanced Studies, 2000.

Rajagopalachary, M. "Re-presentation of History in the Recent Indian Fiction in English: An Overview." *Kakatiya Journal of English Studies*, Vol. 29, 2010, pp. 1-7.

Rushdie, Salman, *The Golden House*. Gurgaon, India: Penguin, 2017.

Thilly, Frank. *A History of Philosophy*. New Delhi: SBW, 2005.

Woods, Tim. *Beginning Postmodernism*. New Delhi: Viva, 2010, Reprint 2013.

2

Rohinton Mistry's *Family Matters*: A Postcolonial Humanist Text

Rohinton Mistry is widely acknowledged for his postcolonial approach to the marginalized. In his novels, he has not only highlighted the marginal position of the poor and the destitute in the Parsi community but also in the wider Indian society. In *Family Matters*, we find he locates the marginalized within the family set up also. The aged people are objects of neglect, more so in poor families where financing the upkeep of old people seems burdensome. As is his wont, Mistry shows the impact of dirty politics on ordinary, politically unattached lives. Politics is also responsible for the fall of the city of Bombay from a cosmopolitan to a ghettoized one. As an intellectual, Mistry cannot escape casting a glance at the declining numbers of the Parsi community. He also comes up with his views on how the community can forge links with other communities. For his focus on the Parsi identity, political suppression, and the weak and the destitute in society, Mistry comes out as a great postcolonial humanist.

Rohinton Mistry, an Indian Parsi writer who migrated from Bombay (now Mumbai) to Canada in 1975, is a product of post-colonial times. Beginning with his *Tales from Ferozsha Baag*, a collection of short stories published in 1987, Mistry has written till date three major novels, viz. *Such a Long Journey* (1991), *A Fine Balance* (1997), and *Family Matters* (2002) and a novella *The Scream* (2008)—a limited edition (only 150 copies) published as a fundraiser for a Canadian charity. In all these fictional works, the community of Indian Parsis (also written as Parsees) is mainly in focus. And yet it would be injustice to the writer in case he were only considered to be representative of his community, for his concerns transcend to acquire a humanistic outlook. This is postcolonialism at its best and most relevant in the contemporary world.

Re-defining Postcolonialism

Postcolonialism, which started with the theorization of the struggles of the colonized people for freedom, has indeed come a long way. India was among those which fought this battle against the erstwhile British rulers. Mahatma Gandhi, not only led the struggle in the first-ever successful non-violent experiment, but also formulated ideas for a postcolonial society in India. His innate spirituality enabled him to see all as equal and, therefore, the idea of subjugation whether by an alien power or by our own people of fellow subalterns was an anathema to him. He was equally emphatic about the native culture which was reflected in his espousal of village industry and the concept of Ram Rajya. It is a pity that he did not live long enough and those who claimed to be his heirs so smoothly sidestepped his philosophy and indulged in the same kind of politics which the British practised so that the plight of the subalterns in our society continues to be miserable.

Sometime later in Africa, Ame Cesaire and Leopold Senghor talked of the Black identity that had been suppressed by the colonizers. Franz Fannon theorized that constant negative portrayal of the native by the colonizer led the former to believe in the very lies that the latter propagated about them. The native even tries to mimic unsuccessfully Western cultural practices and don 'white mask' but all the same, it points to the cultural domination. The Arab scholar, Edward Said, analyzed the skewed Orientalist approach of the colonizers. His distinction of self vs. other became seminal to postcolonial thought.

In the 1990's, the Indian academic Homi Bhabha, modified the concept of mimicry to incorporate hybridity in it. The hybridized native is situated between his adopted Englishness and original Indianness—a state of in-betweenness and the same holds true for the colonizer, the later part evoking disbelief in many quarters. It was left to Gayatri Chakravarti Spivak to raise the fundamental problem of inadequacy of representation of the subaltern because he was not heard, nor did he have the clout or power gained through English language. All representation of the Third World, at present, is a Western discourse (Malik 143-47).

Clearly, the chief concern of postcolonial studies is the status of the 'other' as colonized or the oppressed, regardless of gender, class, race, creed, etc. This stress on the value of justice is a humanistic concern which further leads to the issue of identity—of the subjugated and the subaltern which is sought to be effaced or mutilated by the colonizer or an authoritarian set-up. Born of the struggle for independence, Postcolonial theory has a definitive political edge and it favours opposition to any regime that aims to suppress people a la colonizer.

Along the line somewhere, the colonial narrative had an interface with the postmodern globalized world wherein movement across political boundaries and geographical continents is on the increase. The spaces wherein the immigrant comes into contact with the people in the host country and subsequently his culture interfaces with the native culture there is ever on the increase, calling for dealings on equal terms even if the past relationship had been along colonizer/colonized axis or the racial lines of white/black or brown. This, then was and is the current scenario facing postcolonial studies.

Further on, taking up the case of the subaltern and the weak within any free society, postcolonialists feel that they are pitted against an increasingly commercialized world with no scope for taking into account the adverse effect that the globalization brings to bear on them. It is in the fitness of things that from this point of departure, the postcolonial theory must evolve to become a more inclusivist and broader humanist approach in the global village if it has to stay relevant in postmodern times. In fact, even Frenz Fanon, who was a champion of violent overthrow of the colonizer, recognized the importance of building solidarity of colonized people on the basis of a shared history of suffering, regardless of their racial identities. This, according to a scholar, is "a form of humanism that Fanon seeks," and in this "Fanon's humanism anticipates the work of several postcolonial theorists, notably that of Leela Gandhi (2006) and Ashis Nandy (1987 and 1998)" (Nayar 29). So far as the current scenario is concerned, "recent trends in postcolonial theory have come to embrace the language of cosmopolitanism and humanism as viable alternatives for a postcolonial future—the UN Universal Declaration of Human Rights 1948 provides an alternative to postcolonial theory's revisionist humanism—the re-cognition of difference," says Pavan Malreddy (1557).

However, humanism is not the sole preserve of the updated postcolonial theory. It has always been valued in Parsi and Indian cultures which show a lot of similarity in many areas. These are among the oldest civilizations in the world. Parsis—the people of ancient Iran—belonged to the Indo-European branch of the Aryans and their history goes as far back as 2000 B.C., when Prophet Zarathushtra is believed to have been born. In his novel *Family Matters*, Mistry makes Nariman Vakeel tell his grandson about the glory of the ancient Iran. The migration of the Parsis from Persia (now Iran) to India started after the invasion of ancient Persia by the Arab Muslims. It continued from 785 to 1021 A.D. and they settled on the Gujarat coast under an agreement with the local ruler at the root of which lay the sentiment of humanism only. The Parsis have faithfully kept their word to live in harmony with other communities, and their reputation as peaceful, industrious people contributing to the uplift of their adopted land is well established.

The Storyline

With these musings on the postcolonial theory as the setting, let us go over the story of the novel briefly. It revolves around a lower middle class Parsi family of Bombay (now Mumbai). The head of the family, Nariman Vakeel, is a retired professor of English literature. In his late seventies, he suffers from Parkinson's disease about which his step-daughter Coomy is more concerned than his step-son Jal. He lives with them in a building named Chateau Felicity. Both siblings, though well past their marriageable age, are still unmarried. They are the children of Palonji Contractor, the former husband of his wife Yasmeen, both of whom are deceased now. Nariman and Yasmeen's daughter Roxana is married to Yazed and has two young sons—Murad and Jehangir. This family lives in Pleasant Villa which was gifted to them by the professor.

The story opens with the concern shown about the professor who has had a fall while crossing the road and broken his ankle. He is taken to hospital and his leg is put in cast. After a two-day stay there, he is brought back home in an ambulance. Later, the doctor attending on him says the ankle would take some more weeks to get set. This news dampens Coomy's spirits as she is already fed up with looking after the old man, particularly at moments of nature's call. So, a week after the fall, the professor is shifted to his daughter Roxana's small flat and assured that it was for a few days only. Surprisingly, she had not been informed about the accident earlier.

As the days drag on, Coomy's fertile brain hatches an ingenious plan to avoid receiving back the professor. Jal deliberately hammers the roof of Nariman's room so that the plaster falls down. Thereafter, both of them visit Roxana and deliver the disturbing news of a leaking roof making it impossible to host Nariman. As expected, Yezad and Roxana are a worried lot now. They want some financial support from Coomy which the latter refuses straightaway leading to exchange of some unsavoury words between them. To save her face however, Coomy engages an amateur handyman Edul residing in the same building to repair the 'leaking roof'. The novice that he is, an iron beam while being hoisted up, falls down on Edul and Coomy, killing the two then and there.

Meanwhile, Yezad, under financial burden due to the upkeep of his father-in-law, tries gambling for some time. In a politically vitiated climate, Yezad reports to his boss the fictitious demand from Shiva Sena activists for money in lieu of permission to keep 'Bombay' instead of 'Mumbai' on the signboard of the sports emporium where he works. The owner of the emporium, Mr. Kapoor is in deep love with every old thing about Bombay.

He won't hear of such a thing and instead would part with money. On the appointed day, however, real Shiv Sena men descend demanding change of name but before they speak, Mr. Kapoor castigates them for their supposed demand and throws the money which action offends them so much that they murder Kapoor. Yezad is shaken by this sudden turn of events and considers himself responsible for Kapoor's murder. The all-round downslide makes Yezad turn to prayers to find solace.

Coomy's death brings about the badly needed turnaround in the lives of these people. As per Jal's plan, Yezad's flat is sold for forty lac rupees. Some of the amount is spent on the its renovation and the rest is kept in bank deposits, the interest from which is sufficient to see all of them through life. All of them now shift to this spacious accommodation. After a year, Nariman passes away due to Parkinson's disease. The Epilogue, entirely Jehangir's point of view, shows Yezad passing his time in reading religious scriptures and praying. He is now a self-righteous Zoroastrian Parsi who frowns upon any sign of modernity. However, in Jehangir's eyes he is a bigot only. The narrative throws up a number of issues like the terror unleashed by the political outfit in the city, the gambling operations, economic hardships of the characters and impact on children, and finally the issue of guilt and redemption. As a postcolonial writer, Mistry's concern about the Parsi community and race are highlighted.

Parsi Identity

The postcolonial issue of identity is an important one that finds focus in this novel. Mistry is aware of the dwindling number of Parsis the world over. The total population of the Parsis in India has gone down from one lac in 1961 to 75000 in 1987 census (Haldar 102) and is estimated to be around 60000 at present. The Government of India has declared the community as endangered and announced several incentives to check the extinction of this wonderful community (Murphy). In *Family Matters*, Dr. Fitter and Mr. Masalawala have a lively discussion on the issue of depleting numbers.

> "The experts in demographics are confident that fifty years hence, there will be no Parsis left."
>
> "Extinct, like dinosaurs," said Dr. Fitter. "They'll have to study our bones, that's all."
>
> Jal smiled. He liked the doctor despite the gruff personality and bluntness. His humour epitomized the Parsi spirit, he felt, the ability to laugh in the face of darkness.
>
> "You will be named Jalosauras," said Dr. Fitter. "I will be Shapurjisauras. If they find my father's bones, we will have a Pestonjisauras with a pugree on his head. And our inspector here, who loves his Scotch, will be the powerful Whiskysauras, a magnum of Blue Label tucked under his arm. In the meantime, eat, drink, and be merry." (345)

As to why the community is facing this predicament, a look at their history will help. The Parsi community, we find that the period before the independence of the country was crucial to the development of the community and its outlook. It is common knowledge that the Parsis cooperated with the British and came to be seen as their cohorts. "The Parsees dressed like the Europeans, smoked, drank, played cricket and pursued English education but the inner Parsee life remained unchanged" (Kumar qtd. in Batra 15). With the British they launched on business voyages like the opium trade to which renowned author Amtav Ghosh's *Ibis Trilogy* (2019) is devoted. This cooperation with the British, in turn, led to a certain high-brow attitude among them which alienated them from the bulk of the Indian populace. After the country gained independence, the Parsis, who were quite well-off economically, withdrew themselves into a cocoon, so to say, and devoted themselves mainly to economic activity. Those who found it difficult to adjust to the new reality crossed the shores of the country to settle abroad or nursed dreams of migrating to western countries. Parsi intellectual Nilufer Bharucha aptly remarks: "In decolonized India, the exalted position enjoyed by the Parsis during the Raj has been eroded and increasing dominance by the majority Hindu community has marginalized them. Parsis today are trying to reorient themselves to this new much reduced role" (42).

Yezad, the central character in this novel too nursed such a dream but he could not go to Canada and this botched plan left a scar on his psyche. Beset with economic hardships here, many Parsi young men and women keep on postponing marriage—till the time they get good employment or by the time they get accommodation in a costly city like Mumbai where a large number of Parsis live. Their number has also been dwindling over the past few decades due to the rat-race for success which marks the educated and prosperous members of the community. They feel threatened as a small island in the vast oceanic waters of a populous country.

Another significant factor relevant in this context is the obsession with purity in the Parsi community. Until 2017, they forbade strictly the entry of any non-Parsi into its fold through marriage. On the other hand, any Parsi girl marrying a non-Parsi was banished from the community. This led to fall in numbers of this community. Only in response to vehement protests by the young Parsis was this injunction removed. The treatment meted out by Nariman to his lady-love Lucy or later by Nariman's children to him have similar pattern. The plot is mum about Nariman's decision to marry Yasmin even when he loved Lucy. The only plausible reason is that he buckled down under parents' pressure who went by the societal code. At the cross-road in his life, Nariman repressed his desires which stage a comeback in his dreams.

The identity of Parsis, therefore, becomes an urgent focus of attention. There is a lot of space given to the identity markers like their lifestyle, history, myths, way of worship and the current problem of dwindling population. The westernized lifestyle of the Parsis is also reflected in his works by Mistry. Whether it is the surfeit of English rhymes and song-lines in *Such a Long Journey*, the birthday celebrations in *pucca* English style in *Family Matters*; the handling of love-sick Lucy by a married Professor or the way of addressing his father-in-law as 'chief' by Yezad in *Family Matters*, English culture seems to have permeated the Parsi lifestyle to a great extent.

While these conditions have left an imprint on the social psyche of this race, the Parsis do try their best to impart knowledge of their religion and value system to the young. These efforts do not necessarily succeed at all times. Yezad used to tell his sons the story of his father's valour in displaying loyalty to the bank in which he worked during fierce riots in the city. For this, he was rewarded with a clock that hung in their house and which Yezad zealously guarded as a valuable symbol of honesty and bravery of his late father. Whereas the mythical story of Faridoon and Zuhaak as told by Nariman to the grandchildren symbolises the eternal nature of the struggle between good and evil, the heroic deed of Yezad's father is brought in to convince the sons of the modern relevance and desire to live by that ideal. The children, however, were hooked to Enid Blyton books to adopt their role models and reference points from—something over which Yezad frets and frowns again, fearing children would develop an unhealthy mindset. Roxana, on the other hand, feels proud of her son feeding his grandfather (108).

Politics and Humanism

Postcolonialism is intimately tied to politics as it came into existence due to the political struggle of the colonized against the colonizers. As such, in Mistry's fiction, the political angle does creep in. In fact, it forms the main plank in the novel *Such a Long Journey* in which an armyman and a bank clerk—both Parsis—suffer due to the machinations of the Prime Minister Indira Gandhi. Thus, the public-private boundaries get blurred in his fiction. Similarly, in his novel *A Fine Balance*, characters—both poor Parsis and Hindus suffer during the infamous phase of Emergency promulgated in 1975 by the same Prime Minister. In this novel, Mistry remorselessly peels the veneer off the face of the political class. Similarly, in *Family Matters*, he comes down heavily on the Shiv Sena, a political party in India, for its parochial outlook. This party launched a campaign to change the name of the city from Bombay to Mumbai as the latter is the original name of the city—a postcolonial move indeed but then it comes into conflict with the spirit of cosmopolitanism. Mistry underlines this conflict beautifully in the novel.

In *Family Matters*, Husain is Yezad's colleague working in the same emporium. He lost members of his family in the post-Babri riots that rocked Bombay for a long time. Mr. Kapoor, himself a victim of the 1947 riots that accompanied the vivisection of India, tries not to remind Husain of the riots. Husain hardly retains the bitterness of the past, which could have been a normal phenomenon in any ordinary mortal. Another humane character is Vilas, who works in the adjoining book shop and as a side-job, writes letters for the illiterate migrant labourers who come to Bombay from far-off places to earn a livelihood. Thus, the total influence of the individuals working with Yezad should be positive.

As a postcolonial humanist text, the novel oozes with a humanistic spirit. It goes to the credit of Rohinton Mistry that the ambit of his sympathy is wide enough to include those who have not attracted much the attention of ordinary writers. In his novel *Family Matters*, therefore, Mistry takes up the status of the aged besides focusing on the subaltern within the Parsi community and the marginalized in other communities. In his novel *A Fine Balance*, a major portion has been devoted to the rural poor of India who belong to the Hindu community.

Yezad is the one who has to support his family with a limited income to which the care of his father-in-law has been added. Yezad's wife keeps monthly income apportioned in different envelopes so that she does not exceed the monthly budget allocation for different expenditures. His son considers it his duty to support his father and starts accepting petty bribe from classmates in return for okaying their homework as monitor of the class. His other son Murad walks home from school to save the bus money. If a made-up leaking roof was a problem in Jal's house, it is the real prospect of rain upsetting arrangement of an extra bed in the balcony so that Nariman can be accommodated safely in the bedroom. The way Murad tries to create a make-shift room in the balcony is indeed heart-wrenching:

> "Daddy and I will dress the balcony in a raincoat and gumboots and cap."
>
> Rummaging among the shelves outside the kitchen, they found two small plastic sheets, enough to cover the spaces in the wrought-iron railings but nothing large enough to make a roof.

> "Ask Villie," suggested Yezad to Roxana. "She might lend us a tarpaulin or something." (109)

This picture of a lower middle class Parsi family is hard to believe since they are mostly known for their fortunes and a few of them actually occupy Fortune and Forbes lists of wealthy persons in the world—Tata, Wadia, Godrej, Poonawala, etc. But Mistry is truly a postcolonial humanist. Therefore, his attention turns towards the lower rung of Parsi community. But then, essentializing and homogenizing has always been suspect in the eyes of the postcolonial writers and thinkers. The Western colonialists resorted to stereotyping to easily comprehend the native people. So, Mistry's Parsi characters Jal, Coomy, Yezad—all occupy liminal space which is more realistic portrayal.

Of all the characters in *Family Matters*, Yezad's professional life has been depicted in detail. He is fortunate to have got a humane employer in Mr. Kapoor whom he also respects for his intellectual leanings, something rare for a businessman. Kapoor is inseparably and emotionally linked to Bombay and the name of his shop, viz. Bombay Sports Goods Emporium does not seem to have been selected casually. He cherishes the memory of old Bombay through paintings and pictures preserved over a long period by him and laments the depredation brought about by the changing times. Being aware of similarity of Yezad's interests, Mr. Kapoor presents him some valuable pictures from his personal collection and Yezad is appreciative of the spirit of sacrifice behind this gesture.

Not just pictures, Mr. Kapoor also loves the people of Bombay for their cosmopolitan spirit. A Hindu himself, he has least qualms in celebrating Christmas or other festivals belonging to different communities. This approach is diametrically opposite to Yezad's when, egged on by his orthodox Parsi circle, he arranges for the immersion of non-Zarthustri images in sea waters. Kapoor also tries his hand at being one of the myriad Bombayites, commuting daily by local trains. A novice in this art, he suffers but does not complain. It is a philosophical decision, as he explains to Yezad, "I want to embrace everything my city has to offer. I want to mingle with her people, be part of that crush of bodies in the streets and trains and buses. Become one with the organic whole that is Bombay. That's where my redemption lies" (346). What is a philosophical decision for Kapoor is fantastic rhetoric for Yezad. The motivation for this experiment came from a common platform scene in which the daily passengers helped a latecomer chasing the train to board it. But when Kapoor tries to savour the same spirit, the daily commuters just laugh at him and do not extend the helping hand. The reason, as he analyses it, is the fine clothes and shoes that he puts on. So, he would now get ill-fitting cheap clothes from the pavement vendors (348). His search for the human values of fellowship and comraderie comes to an end when Yezad treacherously hatches a heinous plot to extract money from him taking advantage of the fear psychosis created by the Shiv Sena. But Kapoor never compromises on values dear to him. He has the guts to throw money in the face of the 'extortionists' rather than talk peace with the people who want to change the cosmopolitan character of his dear Bombay city. He becomes a martyr to a cause.

As in the other novels of Mistry, people belonging to the lower middle class have a formidable existence. Their life is beset with a thousand and one problems: their clocks stop, the taps run dry at six in the morning, their grocers cheat them regularly and getting adequate accommodation is well-nigh impossible. In this crowded city, even *kholis* in a modest *chawl* are rented out in shifts of 8 to 12 hours (138). The train travel for the daily commuters involves no less than Tarzan's antics (137). In an interview, he said, "Strange as it may seem, the individuals who make up the Parsi community are human beings, of flesh and blood, heirs to all joys and sorrows of mortals, capable of behaving as nobly and as despicably as any other, as they go about the business of living life that is inevitably filled with laughter and tears and meanness and kindness. And that is why their stories are universal" (Arzan). For Mistry, the commonality of lived experience is important even as the induction of an uncommon event upsetting fine arrangements is the necessity of a piece of fiction.

Salvation through Prayer

Mistry's humanism comes in conflict with faith. The particular situation in the novel has been twisted and turned to expose various dimensions of the conflict. Mistry's skepticism with regard to faith shines through this web. He is firmly on the side of humanism. What we see towards the close of the novel is a Yezad who is full of remorse for having forsaken the lofty human values and fallen prey to greed. The spiritual values provide sustenance to man in troubled times, but selfishness presents a stumbling block here. This is seen in Coomy's character, who, faced with the unwelcome prospect of hosting her ailing father, invents the excuse of a leaking roof: "An act of God is no one's fault". Jal is prevailed upon to cooperate but is reportedly "uncomfortable with casting God in a supportive role in their deceitful drama" (184). In a masterstroke of poetic justice, she pays with her life for having driven "Pappa" out of her home. God does play a sporty role, however, as the 'Bombay Sporting Gods Emporium' signboard would indicate after the 'o' in 'Goods' has been blown away by storm (370). And then, Yezad's proposed plan is disposed of queerly by God as a real Shiv Sena man turns up in place of the fictitious one leading to the murder of an innocent Kapoor.

Yezad is flabbergasted and his guilt cries for similar reward but then it seems God's justice is tempered with mercy; mercy because Yezad has repented. During the period of financial crunch caused by the additional burden of hospital bills of his father-in-law, Yezad starts visiting the fire temple. The latter phase involving Mr. Kapoor's murder, for which he thinks himself responsible, makes this practice of visiting the *agiary* and praying there a compulsion for him. His wife Roxana feels pleased with his new-found "faith in prayer that had descended like a blessing upon him and their house" (445). To Roxana "belief is not essential. The prayer sound itself will bring him peace and tranquillity" (445).

Is Yezad's surrender total? It would require deep probing, for we are entering the domain of the subconscious and the mystical. It is hardly possible for one to know one's own self fully. When it is the question of one's relationship with the Absolute, the problem becomes doubly confounded, for the Absolute hardly speaks the way He used to, in Biblical times. Even then, Job had such a difficulty resolving his doubts. It requires perhaps the sagacity of the sages of *Bihadaranyak Upanishad* to interpret the thunderous sounds to which T.S. Eliot refers in *The Waste Land*. When questioned by Jehangir about the prospect of getting a new job, an unemployed Yezad's reply is, "God is great. If He wants me to, I'm sure I will" (433).

Yezad has his moments of revelation. The initial phase involving his visits to the fire temple seems to be having a salutary effect on him. The one, who hated attending to ailing Nariman for the foul smells, is now seen serving tea to him and giving him a shave. Analysing the self, he feels that the young would do well to remember death. "Carrying your death with you everyday would make it hard to waste time on unkindness and anger and bitterness, on anything petty." Also, he has the feeling that if you knew a person long enough, he could elicit every kind of emotion from you, every possible reaction, envy, admiration, pity, irritation, fury, fondness, jealousy, love, disgust. But in the end, all human beings became candidates for compassion" (358).

Yezad's metaphysical discoveries, however, seem to distance him from the humanist ideal. He hardly fits in with the simple image of a loving father. Jahangir recalls the name-game that his innocent mind had invented as a child. The youngster's later point of view is authenticated through first person account in the 'Epilogue' section of the novel. Having found out the histories/ meanings of the names of other members of the family, Jehangir thought that together they made a perfect family: "They were blessed, they possessed the whole world, they had their own guardian angel, and Mummy's dawn light shone upon all of them. Yet Mummy and Daddy were fighting and unhappy..." (289). At that time, Yezad laughed and joked, whistled and played with the children. All that is passé. Now, "when he is home, he's either praying or reading, and says the music disturbs him" (465). Murad thinks his father has "gone over the edge... deep into the abyss of religion" (493). "You're becoming more and more fanatical," he is forced to say to his father (486). Jehangir goes to the extent of observing that his real father "is gone, replaced by this non-stop-praying stranger" (500).

Even though he has not been able to act honestly in life, Yezad would very much like his sons to tread the righteous path. For this, he invokes the help of God: "O Dada Ormuzd, bless my sons, keep them healthy and honest, look after all our family according to Your will, help me do what is Your will..." (437). But his younger child Jehangir is a typical new generation brat who cannot accept things as they come to him. The child's internal conflict is manifest in his longing, which seems to be the writer's as well, "If only Dada Ormuzd could help me understand! Why must prayer and religion lead to so many fights between father and son? Is that His will?" (466). Which, in effect, is the question that humanists ask of spiritualists.

The theme of the novel *Family Matters* reminds one of Eliot's play *The Family Reunion*. Both have some similarity as far as the title and the theme go. Harry, the central character in Eliot's play is haunted by his guilty conscience (which even takes the shape of the classical Eumanides) for his desire to kill his wife, who falls overboard a ship and gets drowned in sea waters. He ends up atoning not for his sin but for that of his father who had likewise desired to kill Harry's mother as he was infatuated by Amy's sister Agatha who restrained him in the name of the then-unborn child, viz. Harry. The *Family Matters* does not share Eliot's approach in looking at the events *a la* original sin committed by Adam for which posterity was held accountable. However, the culpability here appears more concrete even when the essential concern remains the same, i.e. the equalization of desire and deed at the site of sin.

Jehangir's is a choric comment on the futility of factitious and facile faith. He yearns for a genuinely humane order that touches the innermost depths of the self and is not confined to spaces marked by his father in the drawing room. Towards the end of the novel, he is told that post-death, all the requirements of food and clothing, etc. of his grandfather would be met by Dada Ormuzd. As the first person account of Jehangir shows, he is immensely amused at the idea of this "clothing and catering service run by God". Nor does he understand the rationale of constant muttering the name of God while at the same time disregarding His creations; not attending to the cries of Nariman is a case in point.

WORKS CITED

Batra, Jagdish. *Rohinton Mistry: Identity, Values and Other Sociological Concerns*. New Delhi: Prestige Books, 2008.

Bharucha, Nilufer. *Rohinton Mistry: Ethnic Enclosures and Transcultural Spaces*. New Delhi: Rawat Publications, 2003.

Eliot, T.S. *The Waste Land*. *The Complete Poems and Plays of T.S. Eliot*. London: Faber & Faber, 2004.

——. *The Family Reunion*. *The Complete Poems and Plays of T.S. Eliot*. London: Faber & Faber, 2004.

Ghosh, Amitav. *Ibis Trilogy*. New Delhi: Penguin, 2019.

Haldar, Santwana ed. *Rohinton Mistry's Such a Long Journey: A Critical Study*. New Delhi: Asia Book Club, 2006.

Malik, R.S. and Jagdish Batra. *A New Approach to Literary Theory and Criticism*. New Delhi: Atlantic Publishers and Distributors (P) Ltd., 2014.

Malreddy, Pavan Kumar. "(An)other Way of Being Human: 'indigenous' alternative(s) to postcolonial humanism," *Third World Quarterly*, 32:9, 2011, pp. 1557-72.

Mistry, Rohinton. *Tales from Firozsha Baag*. London: Faber and Faber Ltd. 1987.

——. *Such a Long Journey*. London: Faber and Faber Limited, 1991

——. *A Fine Balance*. New York: Vintage Books, 1997.

——. *Family Matters*. London: Faber and Faber Limited, 2002.

Murphy, Rosalie. "India: Government Joins Efforts to Grow Parsi Population," *Pulitzer Centre*, 22 April 2015. <https://pulitzercenter.org/stories/india-government-joins-effort-grow-parsi-population>

Nayar, Pramod K. "Franz Fanon: Towards a Postcolonial Humanism," *IUP Journal of Commonwealth Literature*, 2011.

Omar, Sidi M. "Humanism Reconsidered: Postcolonial Humanistic Proposals." *Recerca Revista de pensament i anàlisi*, April 2012, pp. 143-61. <https://www.researchgate.net/publication/304524949>

Arzan. "Rohinton Mistry: In Conversation." *Parsi Khabar*. 5 January 2015. <https://parsikhabar.net/individuals/rohinton-mistry-in-conversation/9320/>

3

Shashi Tharoor's *Riot*: Fine Specimen of History-Fiction Interface

There are no two opinions about Shashi Tharoor being a versatile personality: he is an acclaimed writer, a suave diplomat, a conscientious politician, an extraordinary orator, a committed human rights activist and so on but primarily he is a writer. Starting his career in 1978 with the UNO, he rose to be its Under-Secretary-General. In the aftermath of the end of cold war, Dr. Tharoor held many key posts. He was the official candidate of India for succession to UN Secretary-General Kofi Annan in 2006, and came a close second to the present Secy.-General Ban Ki-moon. Our focus here is his contribution to the world of letters. He is an award-winning writer of a dozen books of fiction and non-fiction. His fictional work, bearing a rather unusual title *The Great Indian Novel* (1989) is considered a classic and has run into 28 editions so far.

Tharoor's novel *Riot* is not merely a stylized work; it is also a thought-provoking work of fiction. Published in 2001, well after the notorious riots that followed the December 6, 1992 demolition of the Babri mosque, the novel places the plot in February-October 1989 time frame. It deals with the build-up of tension between Hindus and Muslims in an obscure town, culminating into a major conflict claiming some human lives. This account of recent history is amalgamated with a romantic relationship between the collector of Zalilgarh, the zero point, and a young American girl who was associated with an NGO working for the welfare of women. The story gives ample opportunity to the writer to bring up the cultural differences between India and America. Apart from these, Tharoor focusses on the process of history writing and hints at its inadequacies and limitations. In these postmodern times, history is believed to be subjective and contingent rather than objective and eternal. Hence, the ambiguity and lack of finality to the issues touched in the novel.

The story begins with a twenty-four year old American girl Priscilla Hart coming to Zalilgarh, a fictitious place in India, to work on a women's health project. It is clear that she possesses the idealism of youth which brings her so far away from home. A torrid love affair develops between Priscilla and V. Lakshman, the collector of the district. As the latter is a married man with a daughter, this extra-marital affair brings in its wake a lot of tension which forces him to call it quits finally, but then it is immediately followed by Priscilla's death. While they are together, they discuss love, religion, customs, etc. from their cultural positions. Months before Priscilla's death, tension had been brewing in Zalilgarh as firebrand Hindus linked to R.S.S. had been mobilizing people for building a Ram temple at Ayodhya. A procession was taken out by the Hindus which was attacked by some Muslim hotheads leading to violence in which some people lost their lives. The timing of Priscilla's death coincides with the communal clashes but it remains unclear till the end as to who killed Priscilla.

Priscilla's parents, who are divorced, travel to India to find out the cause of her death. An American journalist accompanies them. As their investigation progresses, the details of Priscilla's stay in India emerge slowly. Through various documents like the transcripts of meetings, diary entries, newspaper reports, etc., we are told about the developments. The novel also includes discussions on the communal build-up on the issue of the Ram Mandir at Ayodhya. All the stakeholders, namely Hindu and Muslim leaders, administrative officials, etc. make their viewpoints clear.

Stylistic Aspects

The first thing that impresses the reader upon opening the book is its narrative style. As mentioned earlier, Tharoor has used a mélange of formats like transcripts of interviews and conversations, newspaper reports, diary and journal entries, etc. to convey the story. This style makes it more convincing for the readers who, unconsciously though, look for the primary source of information. Secondly, the jumbling up of different textual forms in the novel lends a metaphorical touch to the scrapbook which the protagonist of the novel Priscilla Hart used to maintain and which was reported missing but actually handed over as a souvenir by the Superintendent of Police Gurinder Singh to his friend Lakshman, the district collector, who was deeply in love with Priscilla.

The narration is not linear and there is frequent back and forth movement through time. The narrative is even broken in parts as in the case of the interview which Randy Diggs had with the S.P.; it spans the pages 126-34, 148-54 and 172-79. The piecemeal disclosure of information has been done at strategic spots in the text. The language used is quite simple which, but for the loaded theme and long discursive passages, could have placed the novel in the category of popular fiction.

The reader gets different viewpoints of a single event/ issue. This technique was effectively used in *Rashomon*, an award winning film made in 1950 by a Japanese director Akira Kurosawa. It was a crime thriller in which different characters—a bandit-rapist, the woman, her husband, a priest and a woodcutter—all had different stories to tell of a single incident (Rashomon 1950). This distrust of a definite truth comes to the fore when Lakshman tells Priscilla:

> "The Truth! The singular thing about truth, my dear, is that you can only speak of it in the plural. Doesn't your understanding of the truth depend on how you approach it? On how much you know?"
>
> She bites her lip. "Either something is true, or it's not," she says a last.
>
> "Not so my darling," I declare. "Truth is elusive, subtle, many-sided. You know...". (137)

As such, the text can be said to have the Rashomon Effect. Oscar Wilde seems to be Tharoor's favourite litterateur as he has been quoted umpteen times in the novel. Truth has been defined by Wilde as 'one's last mood' (204).

Another stylistic device is soliloquy—a part of the stagecraft, which has been used by Tharoor in the form of letters written by Priscilla to her friend Cindy Valeriani in which she writes unhesitatingly about each and every development, but no letter from Cindy appears in the novel, nor is there any hint of a response from her in the letters written by Priscilla. On the whole, the fragmentary style of narrative fits in well with the fragmentary nature of reality recognized in postmodernism.

New Historicist Approach

It is not merely the style that reflects postmodernist leanings; Tharoor's views on history, as deduced from the overall philosophy of this novel, also show a postmodernist bias. The novel provides his views on a number of issues concerning our society and politics. He is for an inclusivist approach so that opposition, of any type, can be accommodated. That is the basis of longevity of Indian culture and religion as also of the success of democracy in our country. He, therefore, is not afraid of dissent. On several occasions, Tharoor has been known to celebrate the diversities and contradictions found in India. Raising a toast to the resilience of Indian democracy, Lakshman remarks, "We have given passports to a dream, a dream of an extraordinary, polyglot, polychrome, polyconfessional country" (45). This approach has brought into mainstream those who had radical differences. A clear example is the Indianization of communism as manifest in the participation by the various Communist parties, particularly the CPM, in general elections to which they were fundamentally opposed. Lakshman also lauds the "world's first and farthest-reaching affirmative action program" (44) to counter the ill-effects of age-old discrimination against the untouchables. "So Hinduism is the best antidote to Marxism" (43), he concludes.

On the issue of communal tension, Tharoor deems it best to present the different viewpoints and then, like a true artist, leave it to the reader to judge for himself. With regard to the Babri mosque which became a bone of contention between the Hindus and the Muslims, Tharoor starts with the views of the majority Hindu community expressed by Ram Charan Gupta as he is interviewed by the journalist Randy Diggs (52-62, 120-24). Gupta, a member of the RSS, is a hardliner who criticizes the appeasement of Muslims, like the provision of Muslim Personal Law at the cost of common civil code, ban on owning of land by any non-Kashmiri in Kashmir, etc. He dreams of building a Ram temple at Ayodhya and thereafter take up the disputed sites at Mathura and Kashi. Ram Charan quotes historical evidence also:

> There is plenty of historical evidence for our claims. Joseph Tiffenthaler, an Austrian Jesuit priest who stayed in Awadh between 1776 and 1781, wrote about how the famous temple marking the birth of Ram had been destroyed 250 years earlier and a mosque built with its stones. A British court even pronounced judgement in 1886, and I quote: "It is most unfortunate that a masjid should have been built on land specially held sacred by the Hindus.... But as the event occurred 356 years ago it is too late now to remedy the grievance. All that can be done is to maintain the status quo.... Any innovation could cause more harm and derangement of order than benefit. (120-21)

Lakshman, the district collector is proud to be a Hindu but the Hinduism that he practises is not the narrow-minded, sectarian, ritualistic type; it is eclectic and liberal. It is symbolized by the Vedic *sloka* his father had taught him which means "Let noble thoughts come to us from all directions of the universe" (146). Therefore, while members of other communities feel proud in being what they are, "the Hindus say they are proud to be... secular" (146).

The opposite viewpoint of Muslims is articulated by Prof. Mohammad Sarwar, a Muslim historian, who is in Zalilgarh to do research on one Ghazi Miyan, worshipped as a warrior saint by both Muslims and Hindus of the area. He draws his inspiration not from Jinnah but Maulana Abul Kalam Azad, who felt that by demanding a separate country, the Muslims separatists were only disowning the large country that India was. "India is not complete without us, that we are no less Indian than the most chauvinist Hindu" (110). He looks at the demand for Pakistan raised in pre-partition days in a different light. Rather than settling for what he calls 'second-class citizenship, a result of our association with the original sin of Partition', he would want his fellow Muslims to assert before Hindu bigots: "I am as entitled to it [India] as you are" (110). He rues the day when Jinnah and his followers acted, "in the name of all Indian Muslims, to surrender a portion of our entitlement by saying that the homeland of an Indian Muslim is really a foreign country called Pakistan" (110).

The history of two-nation theory lies at the root of the Hindu-Muslim conflict, "But who owns history? This is, in many ways, what this whole Ram Janmabhoomi agitation is about—about the reclaiming of history by those who feel that they were, at one point, written out of the script. But can they write a new history without doing violence to the inheritors of the old?" asks Sarwar (110). He feels that the Hindus "want revenge against history, but they do not realize that history is its own revenge" (147). This indeed is the crux of the matter but only if ordinary people—the ones who shout slogans for one party or the other, could transcend the time slot they occupy and have a bird's eye-view of a broader slice of time!

Sarwar is peeved over the 'demonization of collectivity' (113)—over his co-religionists wanting him to change his liberal ways. He castigates the Rajeev Gandhi Government for kowtowing to the conservative Muslim lobby in the infamous Shah Bano case. He is determined to 'resist this minority complex that the Hindu chauvinists want to impose' upon him (114). Minorityism is only a mindset and not a demographic reality for him. This is the picture of an ideal Indian Muslim but then Sarwar is not a stereotypical Muslim; he is also a learned historian.

A historian has a different kind of straitjacketing; it is the discipline—the epistemological format of his subject that he is called upon to abide by. As a historian, Sarwar expresses inability to admit the existence of Ram. If true, then pin-pointing the exact place of lord Ram's birth is well-neigh impossible. According to him, Ram temples did not exist before tenth century, even though the text might have been there as an epic and not as a sanctified scripture. "The Rama cult, and its offshoot the Bhakti movement, rose during the period of the Muslim conquest of North India and the establishment of the Delhi sultanate, when Hinduism was on the defensive" (182).

The administration looks at it from the standpoint of law and order which aspect is discussed by the superintendent of police when he is interviewed by the journalist (126). Gurinder finds fault with both sides. The tension had been building up as the Ram-Shila pujan (worship of bricks to be used in building the Ram temple) was in progress. On the eve of the fateful day, some Muslim bikers stabbed a Hindu youth. Next day, as the Hindu procession started, some elements in it incited the Muslims with their provocative sloganeering. The police had made elaborate bandobust to thwart any trouble, but both the sides seemed to have made preparations for a violent confrontation. At one point in the narrow street, the procession was attacked with a crude bomb which badly injured a Hindu youth. The collector quickly took away the injured in his car to the hospital, but the news of attack spread like wild fire and led to clashes in which some people lost life. Priscilla also died around the same time.

Since the developments concerning the demolition of Babri mosque and the movement for building Ram temple belong to recent past and are fresh in public memory, there is hardly any need of evidence for it. Coming to the ground reality at the local level, Tharoor, as per his own admission, drew upon the ground-level experience of Harsh Mander, a former civil servant who published *Unheard Voices: Stories of Forgotten People* giving the account of communal riots that took place in Khargone in Madhya Pradesh where he was posted at the time of communal flare-up. Many of the details of communal clashes, the Ram-Shila Pujan programme, the procession taken out on Sept. 30, 1989, hurling of the bomb from the double story house, handling of situation by the DM and the SP, rationing 10 kilograms of wheat to all families in the dalit basti, the prejudiced judicial officer, the local MLA, etc. have clear affinity with the details given in Mander's book (190-200). As such, these lend a touch of authenticity to the narrative by bringing in history-fiction interface.

Tharoor takes potshots on different political parties for their opportunism. He finds the communist parties double-faced. Sarwar was a student leader in his college days and had met Rudyard Hart who was employed with the coca cola company. The convoluted views of the young communists can be gauged from the way a female student guzzled coca cola—an American product—proclaiming that it was her "way of exploiting the exploiter!" (87). The same girl grew to be a teacher in an American university.

On the opposite side, there is also the naïve viewpoint of an American—Rudyard Hart, Priscilla's father, who enlightens Mohammad Sarwar on the Indian problem "You have too much history. Far more than you can use peacefully. So you end up wielding history like battle axe, against each other. Whereas we at Coke don't care about history. We'll sell you our drinks whatever your history is. We don't worry too much about the past" (205). America is known for its lack of history—that probably is taken to be a blessing by Hart.

But where the West tried to comprehend India, it came up with a skewed approach—Orientalism, as Edward Said named it. The Orientalist approach of the West is also castigated in the novel. Ram Charan is at pains to point out that the West cannot comprehend the contentions and complexities of India—"a country whose population is more than fifty per cent illiterate but which has produced the world's largest pool of trained scientists and engineers" (231). Ram Charan tells Randy Diggs:

> Even before you arrive in Delhi, you foreign presswallahs already have your biases, stereotypes, predilections about India, and they never change with experience. Some of your clichés are romantic ones: John Masters, Ganga Din, the Bengal Lancers, Kipling's innocent Western jungle boy surrounded by the dark animals of the Hindu kingdom—you know them all. But their stories are not my stories, Mr. Diggs.

> You are writing Western stories for a Western audience and telling them you are writing about India. (229)

Apart from the Babri mosque imbroglio, this novel also mentions the feelings of the Sikh community in the wake of the Operation Bluestar to flush out the Khalistan militants from the precincts of the Golden Temple (194). While it created the likes of Simranjeet Singh Mann who spearheaded radical politics, people like Gurinder Singh, the Superintendent of Police at Zalilgarh, were persuaded by a victim's family in his own community to continue to be in service. Without passing any judgement, Tharoor, like an artist, only presents the two options. The hint cannot be missed that politics in India has created hurdles in the path of national integration.

Politicians and Bureacrats

That the politicians in India queer the pitch is no news. To present these politicians in true light, the artist in Tharoor changes tack. As he did it in his acclaimed novel *The Great Indian Novel*, Tharoor tries his hand at light verse here also. His poem 'Advice to the World's Politicians: How to Sleep at Night' written in blank verse fits in the context. It lambasts the politicians who, unmindful of the sorry state of affairs around them, have a sound sleep:

> No, do not think
> of the solitary tear, the broken limb
> the rubble-strewn home, the choking scream;
> never think
> of piled-up bodies, blazing flames,
> shattered lives, or sundered souls.
>
> Do not think of the triumph of the torturer
> the wails of the hungry,
> the screams of the mutilated,
> or the indifferent smirk
> of the sleek. (92)

Tharoor does not spare the middle class and takes them to task for their complacency and lack of concern for others. In the poem "I am an Indian" (95), he details the routine of a well-to-do Indian:

> I am an Indian, with a roof above my head;
> When I've had enough of the working day, I fall upon my bed;
> My walls are hard, my carpets soft, my sofa cushions red.
> What kind of an Indian? You said.

The artist in Tharoor is at his best when he describes the affair between Lakshman and Priscilla. They had chosen a deserted old building at one end of the town. It was called 'kotli'. Priscilla would reach there on Saturdays on her bicycle which she would discard in the shrubbery. After a while, the collector would drive up to that place, leave the car in the care of the driver at some distance and go meet the girl in a room. They had sex regularly and neither of them was a novice in the art. As the details that came to light after Priscilla's death indicate, the driver had sensed it. Who killed her remained a mystery. The finger of suspicion could be raised at many people. Priscilla had been active in creating awareness among women regarding family planning. A pregnant Muslim woman, frail in health and already a mother of seven children, had been advised by her to go in for abortion without bringing it to the knowledge of her husband who would have objected to it. He did come to know and vowed to wreak vengeance on the helpless foreigner.

Geetha, the collector's wife had been informed by Gurinder about the affair between Lakshman and Priscilla. She even approached a godman to do some puja, "use tantra, do the tandava, use anyone and anything" (227). The collector himself could be a suspect since he had first promised to marry Priscilla but then went back on his promise. The reason, at first, was Priscilla's previous affairs in America and later the concern for his daughter Rekha who loved him very much. Finally, the communal clashes could claim the life of any one who happened to be at 'the wrong place at wrong time'. It was explained to Priscilla's parents that she might have been seen in that 'out-of-the-way place' by the Muslim fanatics who used that place to make bombs and fearing that she might alert the administration may have eliminated her. Priscilla's scrapbook which her mother tried frantically to find had already been given by the S.P. to the Collector, his old friend—as a keepsake! How interested parties can 'play' with the evidence is amply brought out by the way the mystery behind Priscilla's murder is kept intact. While the district collector Lakshman excuses himself on the pretext of shortage of time, the police chief Gurinder Singh beats about the bush and would not like to come to the point while talking to Priscilla's parents.

Tharoor, in the true vein of an accomplished artist, presents the different aspects of a conflict. He seems to stand aloof while the characters make known their varying perceptions. If one wishes to get hold of Tharoor's views, one must turn to the second section (pp. 55-109) of his non-fictional work *The Elephant, the Tiger and the Cellphone*. He also makes a reference to this novel *Riot* in his article "The Politics of Identity" in this book. His approach to the communal problem is shaped by his liberal views and his appreciation of the differences and complexities found in India. In *Riot*, Lakshman and Sarwar come closest to Tharoor in regard to the latter's philosophy.

Towards the end of the novel, while talking to journalist Randy Diggs about Priscilla's murder, Lakshman asserts that the administration also wants to know the truth. At the same time, he remarks, "Whose truth? There's not always an easy answer" (236). The mystery behind the murder is juxtaposed with the mystery surrounding the authenticity of the Ram Janmabhoomi. The suggestion is clear: if one cannot come to a definite conclusion with regard to an event that took place a few days ago, how could we be sure about what happened centuries ago. Considerations such as these have cast a spell of doubt in our times on the entire process of history writing. Leaving aside the accepted historical evidence, therefore, the advocates of new historicism give equal credence to non-historical records also.

The debate on the historicity of the Ram Janmabhoomi still continues and may never come to an end. On the one hand are the discredited historians with their doubtful paraphernalia. On the other are the keepers and practisers of faith for whom tradition is more important than any factual information. True, the Babri mosque was built in 1528 and since then, there have been many political moves, both by the British rulers of yore and by the indigenous governments in the state to serve their ends. The religious leaders did their bit to confound the issue.[1] However, the story of Ram has come down to us through the collective memory of people of India spread all over the length and breadth of the country. There are a number of places and temples linked to the characters and events of Ramayana both in India and Sri Lanka. Tempers normally run high when there is a confrontation between followers of two different faith systems. Markandey Katju, former Chief Justice of the Supreme Court of India and present Press Council of India chairman has rued the naïve mindset of the majority of people which helped continual communal clashes in the country. Creating conflict was very easy here. "All somebody had to do was make a mischievous gesture of disrespect to a place of worship and people start fighting one another" ("Reunification").

However, Tharoor being a postmodern writer, must treat history and fiction as not very distinct categories. The postmodernists do not find much of difference between the way of writing of history and literature. In fact, historians have long been using the narrative mode of history-writing. The facts are located and then these are joined with the help of a narrative justifying mostly the cause-effect approach. If the narrative is not amenable to this approach, they would try some other approach like part-whole, topological or contextual. Also the historians are selective in the choice of evidence and are guided by their ideology. Salman Rushdie, who has used history in the manner of a postmodernist narrative in his *Midnight's Children*, underlines the role of historian rather than of history in carrying the people along, through the power of narration, Saleem Sinai aptly remarks: "What actually happened is less important than what the author can manage to persuade his audience to believe" (263).

Through their historical narrative, the historians have been romanticizing, interrogating and problematizing history. Hayden White rightly emphasizes that "the techniques and strategies that they [historians and novelists] use in the composition of their discourse can be shown to be substantially the same, however different they may appear on a purely surface or dictional level of their texts" (121). Apart from the contingent knowledge of the topic at hand, what are common to a historian and a writer as they render reality in their individual ways are their prejudices, misconceptions, imagination and command of a very inconstant medium, i.e. language. As such, we believe now that historical records are not absolutely true but relational and open to multiple interpretations. On the other hand, the novelists have taken themes liberally from history and depended on history for structuring their works. For example, Walter Scott introduced into historical setting imaginary characters, situations, etc. to make the plot viable and interesting.

Linda Hutcheon, a leading theoretician of our times, has fine-tuned these considerations into the concept of historiographic metafiction. Alluding to the line of demarcation drawn earlier between literature and history, she comments:

> However, it is this very separation of the literary and the historical that is now being challenged in postmodern theory and art, and recent critical readings of both history and fiction have focused more on what the two modes of writing share than on how they differ. They have both been seen to derive their force more from verisimilitude than from any objective truth; they are both identified as linguistic constructs, highly conventionalized in their narrative forms, and not at all transparent either in terms of language or structure; and they appear to be equally intertextual, deploying the texts of the past within their own complex textuality. But these are also the implied teachings of historiographic metafiction. (Huthceon 105)

The novel *Riot* resonates with Hutcheon's formulation. Tharoor has also commented obliquely on the writing of history in this novel. In his view, all viewpoints are to be taken into consideration just as all formats—journals, diaries, newspapers, letters, etc. have been brought in to construct the plot. The novel is indeed an artist's rendering of reality in the manner of historiographical metafiction.

NOTE

1. In a book *Ayodhya: The Dark Night* (HarperCollins) launched recently, co-authors Krishna Jha and Dhirendra K. Jha have come out with the story of how "on the night of Dec. 22-23, 1949, an idol of Ram Lalla 'mysteriously' appeared inside Ayodhya's Babri Masjid, setting in motion a chain of events that was to change the course of Indian politics in later decades." The plan at that time was to "pitchfork Hindu Mahasabha as a major political player in post-independent India." (Bhattacharya)

WORKS CITED

Bhattacharya, Amit. 'A midnight raid that changed course of history.' *The Times of India*. 6 Dec., 2012. New Delhi Capital ed.: 10. Print.

Hutcheon, Linda: *A Poetics of Postmodernism: History, Theory, Fiction*. New York: Routledge, 1988. Print.

Tharoor, Shashi. *Riot*. New Delhi: Penguin, 2001, Reprint 2003. Print.

——. *The Great Indian Novel*. New York: Penguin, 1989. Print.

——. *The Elephant, the Tiger and the Cellphone: Reflections on India in the Twenty-first Century*. New Delhi: Viking Penguin India, 2007. Print.

Mander, Harsh. *Unheard Voices: Stories of Forgotten People*. New Delhi: Penguin, 2001. Print.

'Rashomon 1950'. Web. 10 Jan. 2013. <http://www.imdb.com/genre/Drama>

'Reunification of India, Pakistan only solution to Kashmir: Katju.' *The Hindu*, 9 Dec. 2012. NOIDA/Delhi ed.: 9. Print.

Rushdie, Salman. *Midnight's Children*. New Delhi: Vintage, 2011. Print.

White, Hayden. *Tropics of Discourse: Essays in Cultural Criticism*. London: The John Hopkins Univ. Press, 1982. Print.

4

Arundhati Roy's *The Ministry of Utmost Happiness*: A Politico-Literary Response to Terrorism

The long-awaited second novel from Arundhati Roy has finally appeared after a span of 20 years, under the title *The Ministry of Utmost Happiness*. What we saw after the appearance of her first novel was the evolution of the Booker prize winning novelist into an activist. That was probably responsible for her diversion into non-fiction and publication of books opposing armament, industrialization, globalization, etc. She has openly opposed the nuclear explosion carried out by India in 1998, the American policy in Afghanistan and Israel's policies in West Asia, but her two books, viz. *Kashmir: The Case for Freedom* (2011) and *The Hanging of Afzal Guru and the Strange Case of Attack on the Indian Parliament* (2013) brought to the fore her political views on the sensitive issue of Kashmir.

The present book, viz. *The Ministry of Utmost Happiness*, a political novel by all accounts, as it refers to political personages, but more than that has the political issues at its core which trigger most action. As compared to her last and only other novel *The God of Small Things* (1992), the literary attributes, by no means inconsequential, take secondary place in relation to the writer's political philosophy articulated in this novel. There are several strategies adopted to advance the agenda; these are: being selective in the choice of material, investing negatives with emotional capital through deft use of language, and creating an insider-character to support the opponent's viewpoint. All these make the novel a dystopic one which refuses to note any positivity around or any ray of light at the end of the tunnel.

Storyline

There are tell-tale indicators of dystopia like the graphic of a grave with a flower on it on the cover of the book. The title *The Ministry of Utmost Happiness* sitting oddly with the cover picture sarcastically suggesting grave as the purveyor of highest form of happiness. Inside, we find that the book is dedicated to "The Unconsoled". Besides, the action in the story actually begins and ends in a graveyard.

The novel begins with the birth of Aftab, supposedly a boy but whose male organs are not sufficiently developed. As he grows, he exhibits girlish tendencies and is naturally attracted towards *Khwabgah*, the name given to the house of *hijras* (neuters) in old Delhi. There are other *hijras* there living under the tutelage of Kulsoom Bi and Aftab enters it as Anjum. There are arrivals and departures of transgenders of different types. The author takes pains to describe the lifestyle and functioning of the *hijra* community.

Unfortunately, Anjum has to go to Ahmedabad at the time when communal riots take place there following the Godhra train passengers' massacre. Anjum gets stuck in Gujarat for some time and when she returns, she joins protestors in Delhi. Anjum is so upset with what she saw in Gujarat that she shuns the Khwabgah and shifts to a graveyard and makes it her abode. Slowly, some other characters like Saddam Hussain, a Hindu-turned-Muslim, who started as a security guard but tried hand at many professions unsuccessfully, also join her. A blind Imam (Muslim priest) is a regular visitor here. In this way comes up the Jannat Guest House & Funeral Services. To keep the place going, Anjum steals electricity from the mortuary (68) and the security guard Saddam runs fake drug business (78).

The location of the narrative now shifts to Jantar Mantar in New Delhi where protesters of all shapes and denominations gather. The motley crowd includes the victims of the infamous Bhopal Gas Tragedy as also the activists of Delhi Kabaadi Wallahs Association, Sewage Workers' Union, Manipuri

Nationalists, Mothers of the Disappeared in Kashmir, and so on. But more than that is the presence of the Gandhian (Anna Hazare) and Aggarwal (Kejriwal) that links the description to real time happenings. There is also a protestor by the name Azad Bhartiya, and then an abandoned baby adopted finally by Anjum and given the name Miss Jebeen the Second by the author.

Chapter 7 titled "The Landlord" (incidentally, the last chapter too has the same title) is the monologue of Biplab Dasgupta, a senior army officer posted in Afghanistan, who has come to visit his house in Delhi, part of which is let out. He is an important character who enlightens the readers about the 'inside' news concerning the functioning of the government and the army. There are two tenants in his house and one of them, S. Tilottama is his friend of college days. Nicknamed Tilo, she is described as an unconventional girl who dressed immodestly and smoked cigarettes. Naga (Nagraj Hariharan), son of the foreign secretary, is his classmate too. Thirty years later, they come into contact with one another in different roles. The two men love her but Tilo takes Musa Yeswi, another college friend, as her husband, after his first wife and daughter Miss Jebeen the first, had died in police firing in Kashmir. The marriage takes place in Delhi. After marriage, Musa joins the ranks of militants, even though he keeps visiting Tilo periodically in Delhi. Tilo also goes hunting for Musa in Kashmir once, giving the writer opportunity to describe the activities of the terrorists and the army. In Kashmir, she makes love to Musa in the houseboat, is impregnated, but goes in for abortion when she returns to Delhi.

Towards the end of the novel, Musa dies, and within weeks, Tilo marries Naga, who was known as a revolutionary student leader but is now an investigative journalist, "cultivated" by the army. Roy details the ways in which the terrorists camouflage their moves, how the stone-pelters communicate and how even women sympathizers lead them to safe hideouts. How Musa organizes Tilo's stay in his kin Gulrez's houseboat, lets her cool heals for two days (or does he keep a watch from somewhere to see if security forces have got wind of it) and after his rendezvous with her, escapes camouflaged under a woven grass mat and pots of vegetables (374)!

Narrative Style

The novel is fragmented and unwieldy and is short on cohesiveness and conciseness. It is not one novel, rather it is a mix of two novels; one dealing with the *hijra* community and the depressed class, and the second with the issue of terrorism in Kashmir. Even the third short narrative focussing on a woman Naxalite is sought to be linked loosely towards the end. Instances like the entry of Azad Bhartiya in the early part of the novel is tenuously related to the main storyline. His presence in the end to locate the Naxalite mother of Miss Jebeen, the Second is equally an add-on, not integral to the structure of the story. The long letters written by Bhartiya or Revathy are meant to fill pages just like the notes left behind by Tilo that cover pages 245-61 and the repetitive memoranda or reports of police stations. Also unnecessary details of the illness of Tilo's mother could have been avoided without doing any harm to the narrative. There is just too much to be roped in: "...her myriad minor characters and political discussions [...] cause the narrative threads to slip from her hands, leading to a bewildering lack of momentum and focus" (Rooney). That leads to lack of artistic control, as another critic comments: "... unlike *Americannah* or *Twelve Killings, The Ministry of Utmost Happiness* lacks the creativity and subtlety needed to turn issues and themes into an engaging literary masterpiece" (Lahiri).

As if this were not enough, there is an exasperating mix of registers also—Urdu poetry, mundane reportage, personal notings, etc., which test the reader's patience—"frustratingly rambling", as a critic comments, "shockingly uneven in its register. Soaring to flights of irony and poetry one moment, plunging into anodyne reportage the next, it appears to be composed by several minds and hands, unable to decide its tone and texture" (Ghoshal).

Selective

However, we are more concerned about Roy's worldview, which, to say the least, is dystopic. Even though history of post-independence India consists of numerous events and developments, Roy is selective and chooses the ones that show the ugly and the rotten side of the body politic. When she takes up the issue of militancy in Kashmir, she describes the negative developments in great detail in this unwieldy narrative. So far as positive features are concerned, she mentions in passing only, so that the overall impact is one of despondency and frustration.

Her selection includes the state of emergency imposed in India, the insurgency that rocked Punjab, the 1984 anti-Sikh riots, the Union Carbide Gas Tragedy, Gujarat riots of 2002, anti-Dalit events, 9/11, Maoist insurgency, displacement of people due to the building of dams and other issues which were espoused by her as an activist. Chapter 3 captioned "The Nativity" refers to the birth of a new India in ironic undertone. The drive to make the unnamed city beautiful meant removing the villages and unauthorized colonies—Roy's pet topic since the Narmada Bachao Andolan days. "Thousands of beggars were rounded up and held in stockades before being shipped out of the city in batches. Their contractors had to pay good money to ship them back in" (99). It looks like a take on Rohinton Mistry's *A Fine Balance* that deals with the emergency regime in India and its impact on the slum dwellers. Roy's novel mentions that 3000 people died on the streets last year! The people evacuated are settled on the city's outskirts "in the bright swamp rightly compacted with refuse and colourful plastic bags, where [...] the air was chemical and the water poisonous. Clouds of mosquitoes rose from thick green ponds" (100). So much for the new India!

In this upended cruel and dystopic world, Saddam, formerly Dayachand, kills his father to save his own life when a marauding crowd accosts them on suspicion of having slaughtered a cow. The location is a local police station where his father has been put behind bars because he has not been able to bribe police officer as much as demanded by him. At another place, reference to such incidents comes up again and Roy's research finds another unheard of consequence: "They accuse you of eating beef and then take over your house and your land and send you to a refugee camp. It's all about property, not cows" (402).

Relationships, in a dystopic world, just do not work out the way they should. Tilo's two marriages do not last long, the first because Musa was killed, and the second for reason best known to the couple. Tilo goes in for abortion because "She worried that the little human she produced would have to negotiate the same ocean full of strange and dangerous fish that she had had to in her relationship with her mother. She did not believe that she would be a better parent than Maryam Ipe" (391). People are strange in the world if you live a life on your own terms and fail to establish a working relationship with the world. Besides, how do we assume that the other person—in this case the aborted baby—would too have the same inclinations and fate as the mother's?

Roy's major focus is the situation in Kashmir. She has had to admit that insurgency has played havoc with the tourism business in Kashmir. She knows that the meaning of Azadi for the terrorists is Islamization "*Azadi ka matlab kya* [What's the meaning of freedom?]: *la ilaha illallah*" (374). They enforce their 'protocol' about women's dress even on Tilo! This is "stupidification, idiotification...First Azadi, Then Annihiliation. That's the pattern" says Musa (371). The question that Roy fails to answer is why does Musa stick to terrorism? And why is he projected as an idealist hero in the novel?

Even in situations, where the hand of the terrorists is clearly seen, Roy tries to look the other way. In Kashmir, the terrorists use every trick to befool people and to incite them against the army and the government. The novel notes an incident in which an empty duffel bag was touted as the body of a killed Kashmiri and buried in the presence of thousands of people. Later the place was fenced and a board proclaiming it as Mazar-e-Shohadda was posted there. Years later, when a young stone-pelter (protestor) asked the mastermind of the event, he was told, "This is the trouble with you youngsters, you have absolutely no idea how wars are fought" (311). However, influenced as Roy is by the terrorist camp, the novel states that some people ascribed this rumour to the Rumours Wing of the army!

If Roy were to be believed, then the Indian army is doing nothing, save some stupid things and we are all living at the mercy of the terrorists only. Thus, Roy explains that a fidayeen plan to attack an army camp was aborted only by the terrorists! (276). Similarly, a tailor wanted to have his photograph carrying gun. He was taken away by terrorists to their hideout and his wish was fulfilled. Back home, he was taken prisoner by the BSF as they came to know of his visit to the terrorists' enclave. Roy wonders childishly if it was worth it? There are several such stories which Roy has picked up from the people sympathetic to terrorists. These find the pride of place in her novel on some twenty pages under the section titled "The Reader's Digest Book of English Grammar and Comprehension for Very Young Children by S. Tilottama" covering pages 271 to 284. Wonder if Roy got permission to use the title of the well-known journal! Though the length of the stories is described as 'two *beedis* and four cigarettes', yet the addition of words "full of marijuana" here would have explained things better!

Emotional Investment

Another strategy to achieve the goal of backing terrorists' viewpoint is to invest an unfortunate incident with a lot of emotional capital. So, Miss Jebeen's the First's funeral comes in handy for emotional overcharge. The emotionally charged letter written by the mother of Miss Jebeen, the Second or the numerous Urdu couplets with English translation, even though superfluous, are meant to play on sentiments of readers. Roy makes use of rhetoric to raise tempers as while describing the envisaged return of peace after many years, she says in a satiric vein:

> ...when the militancy was declared contained by the government, and tourist traffic restored to the valley, "after the major militant groups had turned (or been turned) on each other [...] after spies and informers had [...] been killed by their handlers, after renegades absorbed into regular day jobs by the thousands of NGOs [...] after senior bank managers had appropriated the unclaimed money that remained in dead militants' bank accounts, after the torture centres were

> converted into plush homes for politicians, after the martyrs' graveyards grew a little derelict and the number of martyrs had reduced to a trickle (and the number of suicides rose dramatically)...." (320)

There is an element of puzzlement, or even bewilderment when Roy tries to comprehend the mind of the common people. Ordinary people crave for peace and security so that they can earn their livelihood and bring up their families. So, when the government offers them hope to start own business and offers cheap loans from banks, they can hardly withhold the temptation to secure monetary benefits where they can. But it is not to the taste of the newly-turned militant Musa: "We were fighting and dying in our thousands for Azadi, and at the same time we were trying to secure cheap loans from the very government we were fighting. We're a valley of idiots and schizophrenics, and we are fighting for the freedom to be idiotic and—"(359), says Musa. The comment made by a young critic seems pertinent that the writer probably did not want to write the book: "*The Ministry of Utmost Happiness* looks like a tome, feels like an epitaph, and seems to be born out of a pregnancy that author-activist didn't quite want. It feels like a creature expelled from the body, covered in uterine slime and blood, premature—simply because despite the obscenely long gestation period, it doesn't seem like a finished thought" (Sen).

Use of language is a recognized tool to invest or divest a description of its meaning. Roy describes the whole phenomenon of terrorism as "call for martyrdom that came from across LOC" and that people favoured it *after due consideration*. Check the use of rhetoric:

> They followed the new Pied Pipers [Pakistani handlers of militants] up into the high meadows and alpine glades where training camps had been set up. Only after they had been given guns of their own, [...] after they had weighed the odds and decided it was a viable option, only then did they allow the rage and shame of the subjugation they had endured for decades, for centuries, to course through their bodies and turn the blood in their veins into smoke. (313)

Roy is clear that these people included "blackmarketeers, bigots, thugs and confidence tricksters", who lapped up the free bounties of grenades "being distributed so generously like parcels of choice mutton at Eid" and "grafted the language of God and Freedom, Allah and Azadi, on to their murders and new scams. They made off with money, property and women./ Of course Women./ Women of course./ In this way the insurrection began" (314). Surprisingly, this kind of insurgency fuelled by foreign power and fanned by shady people becomes dear to the writer.

Roy's bitterness is scattered all over the novel. Her new terminology includes the phrase 'surplus people/mothers/ children' for the poor, who get crushed under rich men's cars while asleep on pavement. Did no poor inept or drunken driver ever ride roughshod on road? The graveyard incident in which a goat is slaughtered is painted with an eerie relish that adds to the macabre atmosphere of the graveyard. (70). Historian Ramchandra Guha faulted Roy long back, when she espoused the cause of environment, for her exaggeration and simplification of things: "Ms. Roy's tendency to exaggerate and simplify, her Manichaean view of the world, and her shrill hectoring tone, have given a bad name to environmental analysis" (Guha).

Roy's use of words fails to hide her prejudices. The "bewakoof" (idiotic) kitten thrown overboard into water "didn't know how to live in a *mintree* occupation" (377), but it's the armyman Amrik Singh who is shown "bewakoof" as he kills Gul thinking him to be Commander Gulrez. Well, if you call military presence 'mintree occupation', slam army repeatedly in the novel and mock audaciously their motto pinned on the wall (384), your narrative cannot be called objective. For Roy, the situation in Kashmir is reminiscent of a civil war; the use of terminology indicates it: "Bandipura is 'liberated', they [the army] say" mocks the terrorist in his diary (281).

Roy comes out as a politician disparaging the politicians not belonging to her party. Starting with scandalous reference to Maneka Gandhi's Bombay Dyeing advertisement (34) in which she featured wearing a towel only, she names Indira Gandhi and Sanjay Gandhi without any camouflage, but she disparages PM Vajpayee as the lisping poet PM and Manmohan Singh as a "Trapped Rabbit" (104). Prime Minister Narendra Modi is, for her, "Gujarat ka Lalla" (104). She cannot withhold the temptation to refer to the suit that he wore on one occasion: "LallaLallaLalla woven into the pinstriped suit gifted to him" (91). All through, the use of rhetoric is made to create prejudice, as in the following description: "...army camps and torture centres that had mushroomed across the Valley. When the fighting began and the Occupation tightened its grip..." (311). Roy is known for her command of English language and the knack for coining memorable phrases. Despite this, she uses freely four-letter words and inane and unquotable phrases with English translation. She even banks upon expletives to lead a chapter to climax. (124). Her politically provocative use of language is seen at worst in her own version of English Alphabet. (208).

Confessional

The third strategy adopted by Roy is to put her words into the mouth of an armyman to show it all coming from the horse's mouth. The penultimate Chapter 11, also titled "The Landlord" is the monologue by the key army officer Biplab Dasgupta, who admits that the ordinary people have now started attacking the army, purportedly in retaliation for army's excesses on people. "And to think that all my life I have been a part of it. It's all I can do to stop myself [...] to ridicule—the sacked, drunk, conscientious objector" (430). He is shown meeting Musa, the prime terrorist portrayed in the novel, who grins and says, "We may turn out to be wrong, but we have already won" (431).

The officer also mocks Hindu nationalism (165); cultivates a firebrand student leader Naga now a journalist who happily capitalizes on the information given by the officer, exposing "crimes of the Indian State" (166); lays bare the greed of the armymen, who compete for rewards by falsely exaggerating their actions, etc. (176). Elsewhere, Roy puts the blame on the army for wanting to maintain the status quo so that they can sell to the militants the arms for money (228)!

One may hit upon occasional reports of corruption in the army, but by and large, Indian army has had far better reputation which is mischievously sought to be sullied by Ms. Roy. Who can forget the missions like Sadbhavna in which the armymen provided education to children and saved the local people during floods that wreaked havoc in the valley? Roy refers to this particular episode in one sentence and in her own partisan manner: "The army performed stunning helicopter rescues for TV crews" (264), but what stands out is the confession of the narrator Biplab:

> The inbuilt idiocy, this idea of jihad, has seeped into Kashmir from Pakistan and Afghanistan. Now, twenty-five years down the line, I think, to our advantage, we have eight or nine versions of the 'True' Islam battling it out in Kashmir. Each has its own stable of Mullahs and Maulanas. Some of the most radical among them—those who preach against the idea of nationalism and in favour of the great Islamic Ummah—are actually on our payroll. (170)

Perhaps Ms. Roy would believe even the Daesh or ISIS to be brainchild of Indian army too!

History-Fiction Interface

The present novel deserves comment both with regard to its theme as also the narrative style. Taking up style here, one must note Roy has used the fictional form to comment on recent history which is intertwined with politics. History and fiction share a mutual and important relationship since from the very beginning. Many writers have done it before, and of all the literary masters, Shakespeare is one brilliant example, whose numerous historical plays use history "not merely as a source of material for writing plays, but also for providing insight into the history and politics of his times" (Dhar 10). He is the best when it comes to commenting in a pure literary and indirect manner on current political situation. But of course, a novelist of Roy's ilk hardly calls for that comparison. Another stalwart John Dryden used his poetic art in *Absalom and Achitophel* with the overt aim to advance the prospects of the king Charles II who was embroiled in a feud with the parliament over the question of his successor. Dryden's verse poem was thoroughly political, yet it was a brilliant witty artistic piece that is enjoyed till this day. In Indian English Fiction category, we come across some brilliant examples of the use of recent history in novels. Salman Rushdie uses it in an artistic garb of magic realism in his novels like *Midnight's Children* which brought him the Best of Booker. Shashi Tharoor has made a balanced appraisal of all sides to the Babri dispute in his novel *Riot*.

Fictionalizing recent history in our times when the reading public is more aware of politics, demands a detached stance if it has to appeal to the reader who would rather approach a political commentator for political views than a literary writer. *The Ministry of Utmost Happiness*, however, comes out as a political novel rather than a pure artistic attempt. It can be seen that the strategy of emotional investment in sordid events, is offset by the other strategies of selective culling of matter, use of language in a provocative and even profane manner and the insider's confession to buttress own prejudiced stance. Therefore, the scenes which should have aroused empathy in the reader appear artificial and fail to achieve this artistic end.

When it comes to using historical material for fiction, one has to choose from among several versions or create one's own version to fill the gaps convincingly and carrying the potential to advance the writer's point of view. One such concrete way is to use actual newspaper clippings or copies of official record to buttress one's point. In *Lajja*, Taslima Nasreen makes more than adequate use of actual newspaper reports. In *The Hungry Tide*, Amitav Ghosh has given the real life characters in his note at the end of the novel. These lend credence to the fictional episodes and characters. In *Such a Long Journey*, author Rohinton Mistry creates a replica of the real-life Nagarwala which almost conforms to reality. Not in Roy's case. In contrast, Roy's acknowledgements do not show any such link, either to a character or even to a single memorandum or diary entry of which there is a surfeit in the novel.

Counterpoint

Lest the fictional accounts are lapped up by the gullible without adequate proof, it is imperative that these are pitted against realistic accounts too. So, let us turn to a real-life character who has been in the midst of it all, and though Indian army is known for its secular credentials, we have incidentally a Muslim gentleman, Syed Ata Hasnain, who was corps commander in J&K. Having retired quite some time back and therefore, without any liability to conform to the governmental view, he wrote recently in a national daily, ruing the fact that the terrorists had organized their side of what he calls a 'hybrid conflict' involving not only armed conflict but also other domains, viz.:

> ...promotion of radical ideology, creation of intense alienation, keeping the organs of government on tenterhooks and incapable of governing, intimidation of government agencies, media and private citizens, gun running and narcotics to sustain finances, and lastly and perhaps most importantly maintaining financial conduits for the unimpeded flow of money into the conflict system." The financial conduit also includes the Pakistani embassy in New Delhi where the visiting separatist leaders are provided cash in gift packets! ("There")

Hasnain warns that this is a complex proxy war waged by Pakistan and in this the separatists have been "projecting their cause through literature, social media, media patronage, mosque power, direct engagement and creation of structures which can be activated in minutes to respond to diverse situations" ("There"). Roy's account in the novel supports the last item in this list actuated through the womenfolk who guide the terrorists through the alleys of Srinagar and other cities, with stone-pelters appearing at short notice. But what Roy fails to perceive is the invisible propaganda unleashed by these people with the covert backing of Pakistan, through Indian literature and media. Roy is unconsciously influenced by the discourse created by them. The present government has done well at least to crack down on the money being pumped into the coffers of terrorist organizations by the powers inimical to India, through innocuous channels like the border trade. Effective action on this front has revealed the fault lines in the structures espousing the cause of "azadi". It has also revealed the myopic vision of some of the national political parties.

Core Issues

The core issues that demand examination and re-defining are the following: (i) the politics of the subcontinent, (ii) the threat to democracy from terrorism, (iii) the equation between religion and terrorism, and (iv) the terrorists' claim to human rights. In an article published long back in *The Guardian*, Roy had said, "I spoke about justice for the people of Kashmir who live under one of the most brutal military occupations in the world" (Chamberlain). She needs to acquaint herself with the inside situation in countries like North Korea, China, and Pakistan itself to understand the meaning of the term. Putting a question mark on legitimacy is untenable in a democratic set-up despite its various flaws (and which system is bereft of it?).

Roy is justified in expressing her sympathy for the people of Kashmir who have been suffering for long. But Roy uses her heart not the brains to analyse the vexed problem. Her novel fails to go deeper into the history to trace the chain leading to present problems. Pakistan, in fact, never reconciled to the merger of Kashmir with India back in 1947 when immediately after the Partition, it sent its army dressed as Mujahideen fighters to annex the state coaxing the ruler of the state to accede to India. Starting with the West Pakistan's atrocities in East Pakistan leading to the birth of Bangladesh, Pakistan reactive policy of 'a thousand cuts' through indoctrinated jihadi terrorists, ethnic cleansing of Kashmir by driving out the Hindu Pandit community, the unleashing of terrorist attacks all over India including Kashmir—a policy still followed by the Pakistan army and the ISI. Roy fails to fathom the issue as also how the peace initiatives undertaken by successive governments to bring Pakistan to see reason paid back with attacks on Kargil heights or army bases at Pathankot, Uri and so on.

To her, if the people of Kashmir are terrorized into demanding Azadi, they should be granted it, but supposing this were to materialize, what would be the future scenario? It would not stop at that. Rather it would mean relapsing into the two-nation theory on the basis of religion. In that case, all Muslim-dominated areas must secede from India. How is that going to bring peace? Roy evinces the tendency to flow along with her rhetoric and forget her own protestations of secularism or she wilfully abstains from deriving lesson for future from history through a dispassionate and unbiased study. According to Wilkinson, "If unchecked, terrorism can easily escalate to a civil war situation, which the terrorist may seek to exploit in order to establish a terrorist-style dictatorship" (*ibid.*). And we have seen this happen in the emergence of the Daesh or ISIS! So, there could be no hope at the end of the tunnel if India were to catapult to the terrorists' wishes.

The problem of terrorism which is talked about in the novel deserves more insight than is available with the writer. The largest body of terrorists threatening the world today is doing so in the name of religion. On the face of it, no religion claims to support terrorism but we know that fundamentalists tend to be exclusivist with regard to other religions and some of them even support militancy to advance their agenda. Without discussing it further for want of scope here, I shall like to quote Dalai Lama, the Buddhist spiritual leader, who said recently: "People cease to be Muslim, Christian or any group the moment they become terrorists" ("Ultras embrace"). Non-violence and universal love are the founding principles of all great religions.

The bogey of violation of human rights is often raised by the terrorists when they are at the receiving end in a judicial forum. The chief plank of the writer's protest is the issue of human rights on which she takes an idealist stand. The issue of reconciling the ends of human rights with control of violent extremism is indeed challenging. The moot question is whether one, who openly flouts the human rights of peaceful innocent people by killing them like mosquitoes is entitled to appeal for safeguarding his human rights. Democratic societies, as Wilkinson says, are "clearly vulnerable to terrorist attacks because of the openness of their societies and the ease of movement across and within frontiers. It is always easy for extremists to exploit democratic freedoms with the aim of destroying democracy" (196). In the case of subversion supported by an outside state, and for the mistake of treating a state's terrorist as freedom fighter, the states "must adopt the clear principle that 'one democracy's terrorist is another democracy's terrorist" (Wilkinson 207).

WORKS CITED

Chamberlain, Gethin. "Arundhati Roy faces arrest over Kashmir remark". *The Guardian*. India. 26 October 2010. Accessed 17 Sept., 2017. <https://www.theguardian.com/world/2010/oct/26/arundhati-roy-kashmir-india>

Dhar, T.N. *History-Fiction Interface in Indian English Novel*. New Delhi: Prestige, 1999.

Ghoshal, Somak. Book Review: The Ministry Of Utmost Happiness By Arundhati Roy. *HuffPost*. 2 June 2017. Accessed 2 Sept., 2017. <http://www.huffingtonpost.in/2017/06/01/book-review-the-ministry-of-utmost-happiness-by-arundhati-roy_a_22121017/>

Guha, Ramachandra. "Perils of extremism". *The Hindu*, 17 December 2000. Accessed 12 August 2017. <http://www.thehindu.com/2000/12/17/stories/1317061b.htm>

Hasnain, Syed Ata. "There is no military solution in J&K, separatist finances should have been targeted much earlier". *The Times of India*. 5 August 2017, p. 14.

Lahiri, Oeendrala. "The Ministry of Utmost Happiness' Is Timely, but Not Deserving of the Booker". *The Wire*. 1 Sept., 2017. Accessed 22 Oct., 2017. <https://thewire.in/172939/ministry-utmost-happiness-arundhati-roy/>

Rooney, Kathleen. "The Ministry of Utmost Happiness: Arundhati Roy's long-awaited new novel is grand and perplexing". *Chicago Tribune*. 19 June 2017. Accessed 15 Sept., 2017. <http://www.chicagotribune.com/lifestyles/books/sc-ministry-of-utmost-happiness-arundhati-roy-books-0621-20170622-story.html>

Roy, Arundhati. *The Ministry of Utmost Happiness*. New Delhi: Penguin Random House, 2017.

——. "The Monster in the Mirror". *The Guardian*. London. 13 December 2008. Accessed 12 August 2017. <https://www.theguardian.com/world/2008/dec/12/mumbai-arundhati-roy>

Sen, Jhinuk. "The Ministry of Utmost Happiness review: A one-dimensional story told in sterling prose." *Catch News*. 20 June

2017. Accessed 12 Aug., 17. <http://www.catchnews.com/culture-news/the-ministry-of-utmost-happiness-review-a-one-dimensional-story-told-in-sterling-prose-66494.html>

"Ultras embrace terror, lose religious identity". *Times of India*, 19 Oct., 2017, p. 13.

Wilkinson, Paul. *Terrorism versus Democracy: The liberal state response*. New York: Routledge, 2001. Third Ed. 2011.

5

Rajat Mitra's *The Infidel Next Door*: Centering the Marginalized in Own Land

"When a man fights for truth, he is the loneliest" (173), says Nitai, a character in this novel and this sums up the idealistic message which the author Rajat Mitra wants to give. A page turner coming from a psychologist may not be something new, but this debut novel from Rajat Matra touches upon the issue of exodus of the Hindu minority in Kashmir—a theme that does not have many takers among novelists these days.

This is perhaps the only book from the genre of Indian English Fiction that has a very balanced perspective on the issue and does not seem swayed by the prevalent intellectual discourse. The writer has worked at the ground level for many years with criminal justice systems on cases of human rights violations. He has studied the emotional life of both—the victims and perpetrators of ethnic violence. Despite the author being from a domain different from literature, this novel has all the adornments of a literary piece. The way he has crafted characters and arranged the action shows him as a true artist. His prose style is simply endearing.

Of late, interest in Kashmir has risen and quite a few writers like Urmila Deshpande, Abhay Narayan Sapru, Anita Krishnan, Feroz Rather, Humra Quraishi, Nitasha Kaul, Ravi Dhar, and Shahnaz Bashir have published novels based on life in Kashmir. Not long ago, Arundhati Roy's *The Ministry of Utmost*

Happiness appeared, which, contrary to the title, presented a cynical view of things. Mitra's novel, however, ends on an optimistic note, with engaging perspectives on historiography, politics, and religion.

Aditya Narayan, born under auspicious stars to a family of Kashmiri Pandits who lost their forefather at the hands of the fanatic king Aurangzeb's men as they were piqued at the refusal of the tenth Sikh Guru Teg Bahadur to convert to Islam. Aurangzeb's forces let loose a reign of terror in Kashmir because Kashmir was supposed to be the stronghold of Hindu culture and the Pandit community had approached the Sikh Guru for help. Aditya's guru, referred to as Gurudev in the novel, demands as *gurudakshina* from him to rebuild the Adi Sankar temple near Srinagar, because "If this temple survives, Hinduism will survive in Kashmir" (59). Gurudev believes that when your *dharma* is under attack, it is the priest's role to "move away from doing prayers and remove *adharma* from society" (61). Aditya, along with his parents, goes to Srinagar and starts the construction of the temple which is presently in ruins. Close to its boundary, is a mosque. In re-building the temple, he faces stiff opposition from the hotheads among the Muslim community.

The Imam of the mosque is a liberal Muslim and has adopted the orphan girl Zeba and brought her up along with his son Anwar who becomes a stone-pelter under the influence of Haji chacha, the villain of the piece, but due to love for his sister, he saves the life of Aditya whom he had, at first, tried to kill. His friend Javed loves Zeba but she develops a soft corner for Aditya drawing hostility from the Muslim community. However, Aditya, through his Gandhian ideals and gentle behaviour wins the heart of Zeba and is able to generate soft feelings in Anwar too. Javed, Anwar's friend is also soft towards Aditya.

Zeba, however, is married to Haji chacha's son Salim who is a terrorist. There are many twists and turns in the story that involves repeated attacks on Aditya and other Hindus. The time period is the 1990s, when the exodus of Kashmiri Hindus started. Finally, Aditya renounces the world. The story ends with Aditya's permission to Anwar to write on the ruins that the destroyed temple is a symbol of intolerance and his wait for friend Aditya represents hope.

Aditya Narayan comes out as an ideal person, too good to be true. He is deeply spiritual person and has no interest besides performing the rituals at the temple and keeping it in order. The intent of the novelist seems to be to have such a character to serve as a means to build bridges between the two communities. The novel reflects Mitra's knowledge of the philosophies of Hinduism and Islam as also his insight into corruption and political bungling that has brought the valley to this pass.

Kashmir Situation

As a newcomer to Kashmir, Aditya is pricked at the discrimination that the Kashmiri Pandits face in Kashmir: "Javed, I see pandits stop to give way to Muslims on the streets. I just wonder. Pandits and Muslims have common ancestors. A few hundred years ago, all were Hindus. So that makes us brothers. Then why the conflict?" (96). The novelist details the misconceptions which the Muslims have about Hindu religion and way of worship. What comes out is that the education of the Muslim children in madrasas is partly responsible for a narrow vision of religion. For the teachers there, what matters is the difference between a believer and a non-believer called *kafirs*. They believe that the holy Quran "directs every true Muslim to deal in specific ways with kafirs" (41).

The public discourse outside school is controlled by fanatics like Haji chacha for whom azadi (freedom) means "when our land will be free of infidels" (53). He is seen spewing venom everywhere. The terrorists receive plenty of money from foreign countries. There are slogans written on the walls of houses of Hindus asking them to leave or face the consequences. The terrorists have double standards. They disallow shopkeepers to keep fancy clothes and cosmetics for women but as a shopkeeper says they themselves are the biggest customers because they purchase such stuff for their wives and mistresses (259).

The pandits come to the temple one last time before leaving Kashmir to save their lives and honour of their daughters. All this reminds one of the infamous Mughal Kings Aurangzeb, during whose reign such oppression took place. The head of a Pandit family asks Aditya to hide his wife's jewellery in the temple as the militants are reportedly looting the people leaving Kashmir. The situation is akin to the one that prevailed during Partition in 1947. It is unimaginable as to how in free India, such discrimination and terror prevail in a corner of the country.

The army is often at the receiving end in Kashmir even when it is taking on the terrorists. However, the novel presents a positive picture of the Indian army. When a Captain treats the teenage boy like his son after the latter is caught throwing stones at him (64). Towards the end of the story, we find the same army man, now a brigadier, meeting Anwar and appreciating his work.

The invisible hand of the mischief makers supported by Pakistan is hinted at in the narrative at several places. Chicanery and deceit come in handy for the terrorists and their sympathizers. Some such persons, in the guise of army men, are seen beating Kashmiris on flimsy excuses and even abducting them. Anwar is surprised that in each case, Haji chacha would reach the home of the victim sooner than the incident took place (176). Clearly, he is the mastermind fomenting trouble.

The role of police under the command of politicians is suspect. When Aditya stages a protest *dharna* in front of the police station for not registering a rape case, the policemen try to dissuade him but he is steadfast. When Javed and his other Muslim friends join Aditya, the political class is flabbergasted. Under orders from their political masters, the policemen stage an attack on Aditya and burn the tent. The Chief of Police's orders are clear: "Any act of solidarity by a Muslim toward a Hindu is not to be given publicity. Our instructions are that no pandits stay back in the valley, and they don't get a chance to be united, least of all with Muslims showing support for them" (228).

The peculiar situation in Kashmir makes some irritating practices a part of life there, like too many roadblocks where people would queue up for frisking and answer awkward questions about their movement. A little fumbling could be taken as a hint of something fishy and the fellow will be sent to the interrogation centre. Once a person comes out with signs of harassment, he becomes an easy prey for the militants to bolster their number. People like Haji chacha even stage-manage highhandedness of police or fake army men to create militants in this manner. He has also objection to Anwar's sympathy for a Hindu boy being beaten by Muslims on suspicion of his being a police informer. When Aditya says that he could be innocent, Haji chacha observes: "How does it matter if one is innocent or not?" Anwar's query: "Chacha, in a revolution are we boys only numbers?" (241) shows he has identified himself with the Hindu victim.

There is the height of corruption in the police force. Even when you go to the police to find the whereabouts of your missing kin, you are asked to pay, and there are fixed rates! (330). Everything is rotten in a state like this, and people lay blame at their adversary's door just to implicate him and get him removed from scene, just like it happened in Javed's case who was betrayed by a friend.

Hinduism

The novelist does not go into details of Hindu rituals, even though those forming daily routine of the priests are noted in a referential manner. Aditya is an ideal Hindu priest, working steadfastly for his spiritual progress and the re-construction and upkeep of the Adi Shankar temple. For this purpose, he drives away the emotions that are evoked by Zeba's interest in him. This is a trying period for him as he admits to Nitai, "I am a priest, Nitai. I can only say that the awakening of love has been far more tormenting for me than it has been in the discovery of God" (224).

Aditya is a personification of the Gandhian principles of dedication to non-violence and truth which requires courage of a rare degree and he refers to Guru Tegh Bahadur as endowed with that courage. The army general talking to Aditya is impressed and admits he is now in a position to tell his children why Hinduism could not be destroyed in Kashmir (176). When he is released after brief imprisonment following the fictitious case of trying to disrupt peace in Battmazar, he prays not just for those who died in that massacre but also for the perpetrators of the genocide (187). His views on religion per se reflect his liberal approach. When Zeba asks Aditya if his religion makes a separation between believers and nonbelievers, Aditya replies in the negative.

To be fair to the writer, the writer does not shield Hinduism on the issue of intra-faith discrimination. He brings in the two siblings belonging to *doom* caste who are treated as untouchables by Aditya's father. It is the self-same Nitai, the untouchable, who saves the newly built temple from burning down after the fanatics among Muslims set it on fire. He also saves Aditya when he is attacked on the street by Muslims boys. Aditya's father Krishan Narayan is unable to reconcile to all this. Aditya tries to reason with him:

> "It needs purification for prayers to start again."
>
> "I won't sit in this prayer, Baba."
>
> Krishan Narayan tried to argue with him. "The lower castes do such jobs. Don't get too emotional."
>
> "Baba, it is we Brahmans who distorted the shastras to create untouchability, not the shastras". (149)

Aditya starts teaching Nitai Vedas and in this, his mother stands by him. When his father objects, Aditya states clearly, "Baba, the scriptures also say a Brahman is the one who searches for knowledge. That makes Nitai a Brahman too" (166). All this is too much for the orthodox Krishna Narayan, and so, after the death of his wife, he decides to leave for vanaprastha. Before proceeding, he bares his mind saying the temple belongs to his son and wife, was never his. Clearly, the older generation has difficulty in shunning the age-old practices even when these go against the core principles of Hinduism. Mitra rises above the divisions of casteism when we see his characters—a Brahmin and an untouchable finding common cause in fighting for truth. Says Nitai: "Dada, I thought there was no one more lonely than an untouchable. But now I realize, when a man fights for truth, he is the loneliest" (173).

Aditya is a liberal idealist who practises what he preaches and is very much qualified to tell Zeba that Hinduism treats all religions as so many rivers "which in the end lead to God like the rivers merge into the sea" (113). Her father, the Imam, was of the opinion that "praying to deities led to pride, vanity and ego making one forget submission to Allah" (122). Aditya's mother Gayatri tells her about the Vedantic view of creation that locates God in all animate beings and even in inanimate objects. When Zeba sees her bathing and dressing the idol of the Lord, she discovers a different relationship between man and God (120).

Islam

If Aditya is icon of liberal Hinduism, Anwar becomes a liberal Muslim following interface with Aditya, even though in the past he had been the pioneer of stone-pelters in the Kashmir of 1990s and meant to drive away Aditya and destroy his temple. The author's focus is on invoking the inner self because it is the only instrument to fight obscurantism and orthodoxy. Aditya tried to kill Aditya by throwing him into the frozen river but having done so, when he came home, he could not have sound sleep. He was confronted in that state by his sister Zeba after which he spilled the beans that he was coaxed to do this by his beloved Misba, a fanatic Muslim. Along with her, Anwar went out and saved Aditya from sure death. Thereafter, he was a changed man. He knew he would be mocked by the hard-core Muslims in the midst of whom he was hailed as an expert stone thrower, but his concern was more to avoid any aspersion on Zeba on this count.

As a practising psychologist having worked with cases of trauma and violence, Mitra comes across many psychological conditions affecting young people. As such, he is able to depict convincingly the change in Anwar who admits: "On the one hand, I feel I have let everyone down, on the other hand, I feel a lightness in my heart" (198). To this, Javed, his friend and the other pacifist who is converted through Anwar's example, explains: "You hear the voice of God in your ears, when you save your enemy from dying" (198).

Prof. Baig, the Vice Chancellor of Jammu University is a brave and upright Kashmiri intellectual who places the composite culture of Kashmir above religion. The Vice Chancellor tells Aditya about the island in the Dal Lake called Battmazar (graveyard of the non-believers) which means the graveyard of the non-believers (Hindus). The darkest period of Kashmir history was during the Pathan reign (1752-1819) when untold oppression of Hindus took place. The Hindu families were taken to the island, given the choice between converting to Islam or mercilessly buried alive with head visible above ground, and left to die in that state. Surely, not many people have heard about it. The Vice Chancellor is a true historian who even after being questioned by the police, stands by his version and publishes full article on Battmazar. The meeting with the Vice Chancellor is an eye-opener for Aditya too who asks his mother: "Ma, when we pray to God, we call him by different names. Does it make a difference to God?" (83).

Mitra quotes Will Durant to note that the Islamic conquest of India was the bloodiest one in the history of mankind (79). The kind of Islam that the terrorists seek to impose in Kashmir is highly prejudicial, communal and a threat to the dignity and safety of women. The common slogan doing the rounds is "Will make Kashmir into Pakistan with pandit women without their men" (235). Anwar is shocked. "When did having Hindu women as your property become the idea of azaadi? This is not what I believed to be azaadi," he asks (243).

The author takes on the utopian dream of a pan-Islamic world haunting many Muslims. Anwar, a conscientious youth, is restless because some basic questions haunt him all the while, to satisfy which he visits a seminary. There a moulvi rightly observes: "These students only talk of how to make the world an Islamic place. They don't understand that for one thousand years our ancestors tried to do that" (275). This is as unrealistic as the dream of kings of past like Alexander, Genghis Khan, Napoleon or Hitler, to rule the world.

Women's Predicament

The novelist deserves kudos for journeying into the psyche of the women characters to lay bare the impact of terrorism in Kashmir. In fact, this is what places fiction, a genre of literature, above history, for while history gives bare facts and leaves the emotional part untouched, the novelist is able to bring out the true picture of the inner self of individuals. He may be accused of not going by the scientific method, by reason or logic in describing things and depending on emotions, but the fact is that imagination has a big role here. While fictionalizing history, a novelist analyzes the past with emotions and tries to delve deep into the inner feelings of people belonging to past. Noted litterateur Khushwant Singh rightly asserts: "It is a simple formula: Use our heart not your head, your emotion not reason" (Singh 2).

The novel depicts faithfully the state of the Kashmiri Muslim women. The chief female character, Aditya's love, Zeba suffers from double whammy, having been adopted by the Imam from an orphanage. Even though the Imam is not a fanatic, yet he fails to assert himself under pressure from Haji chacha and others. Zeba watches Aditya and the construction of the temple. Aditya's radiance and pure lifestyle attracts her and she starts loving him silently. However, when the militants threaten Aditya and his mother also tells Zeba that love demands sacrifice, she marries Salim who had been chosen by her family. It is not a happy married life that she has because Salim is a confirmed militant who takes her as wife after he had murdered his first wife. Zeba feels that he comes only for sex to her but she remains loyal to him.

After coming back from police station where the cop leered at her and asked provocative questions, she mused that to both, the cop and Salim, she was "just a sexual vessel with no individuality" (258), which speaks volumes about the status of women in Kashmiri society. Salim is found to be a promiscuous person but then "Women were supposed to accept infidelity and other transgressions by their men and maintain a culture of silence" (258). Compare this to the nasty talk of her relationship with Aditya which is supposed to be the cause enough by the terrorists to coax Salim into murdering her in cold blood.

Slowly, Pakistan-sponsored militancy took hold of the liberal society of Kashmir. The militants banned cinema and girls going out without *burqa*. Zeba feels that *burqa* erased her identity. She would never like it for her daughters. The lumpen elements in society are hardly deterred by this cover. As she walks down in *burqa*, she hears a comment from two boys living in the neighbourhood that her buttocks were nice (258). Without *burqa*, when the same boys saw her, they would address her as 'chachi' (aunt), so *burqa* wearing, instead of providing safety, had further made her insecure.

The terrorists would even disfigure the face of the girl who flouted their orders, by throwing acid on her face. One such victim is given a bed in the hospital ward where Aditya is admitted in critical condition. The militants come searching for him but the girl outsmarts them by shifting him to the adjoining room and then when militants see her face, they choose to leave hospital. There is black humour in her comment that having seen her disfigured face, they won't return (292). This is really a pathetic situation created in the novel.

Historiography

Past can take different shapes for different reasons according to the needs and requirements of a novelist. But historian cannot mould the past according to his needs. "History can be romanticized, sensationalized, interrogated and problematized. The novelist may critique it satirize it, play with it, even trivialize it. All these different purposes can not only have far-reaching implications for his fiction, but also determine his arrangement of events and characters, his choice of modes of presentation and narrative strategies" (Dhar 27).

The novelist bases his novel on the history of Kashmir, rather he supplements it also. As to the relevance of a literary author in the field of history, Collingwood, a well-known scholar of history can be quoted here. While talking of the work of the historian and the litterateur, he notes:

> Each of them makes it his business to construct a picture which is partly a narrative of events, partly a description of situations, exhibition of motives, and analysis of characters. Each aims at making his picture a coherent whole, where every character and every situation is bound up with the rest. The novel and the history must both of them make sense; nothing is admissible in either except what is necessary, and the judge of this necessity is in both cases the imagination. (2)

While dealing with history, a novelist is faced with several problems and in order to appreciate the novelist's work, we must understand what exactly is the art of fictionalizing history. According to the *Encyclopedia Britannica*, fictionalizing history is "a work of fiction that attempts to convey the past age with realistic detail and fidelity to historical fact" (64). But historical facts have been proved to be unworthy of the credit that we have given them all along, for the New Historicists tell us that history is handmaiden to authority. It is the king who gets written in history what he desires. Therefore, Aditya points out to the judge, "To write about Battmazar in olden times meant sure beheading. [...] My ancestor was beheaded for refusing to convert and none of my ancestors after him had the courage to return" (186). It is not the history that told the present generation of pandits about the genocide committed by the Pathan era rulers, rather it is the memory of the ghastly tragedy that percolated down the generations of Kashmiri pandits, and which demands to be given its due. J.P. Sartre, the well-known French philosopher, rightly observes:

> Since the past is no more, since it has melted away into nothingness, if the memory continues to exist, it must be by virtue of a present modification of our being everything in present: the body, the present perception, and the past as present impression in the body all is, actuality, for the impression does not have a virtual existence qua memory, it is altogether an actual impression. (Sartre 160)

This novel, therefore, rightly raises the question of history and the way to learn it, which, as Prof. Baig, the Vice Chancellor of Jammu University states, "Through stories. Kashmiris preserved the stories of atrocities on them by word of mouth" (80). Baig insists on re-building the temple, which, coming from a historian, means memory is being recognized as a reliable history.

Undoubtedly, the memory continues to haunt people. When Aditya asks Prof. Baig if the history of a people is different from the memory they carry of past, he replies, "History, Aditya, dies a thousand deaths, but no memory. Memory holds us together and gives us hope when wars, massacres tear our continuity apart. [...] It is our memory that heals us, not history, from injustices of the past. History puts a blind on us, making us believe that we are prisoners. History is like an empress, angry with a whip in hand, who demands obedience to the written word. Memory is the mother who holds us in embrace, protecting us when our soul needs answers" (87). So, unless the memory dissolves with the passage of time or through mollification in right manner, the bitterness remains.

It is also true that memory can be a double-edged sword. It can be understood with reference to the monument raised to India's Partition at Amritsar. One view is that it will bring back memories of mayhem and probably re-kindle the spark of revenge. On the other hand, it is believed that the present generation, which is uninvolved and is gifted with present-day intellectual capital, will take it in the right spirit and vow to eliminate hatred for future.

But professor infuses hope in Aditya when he says, "They [Kashmiri Pandits] carry their homeland in their hearts this time. Whenever societies have done that even if it takes twenty, fifty, hundred, even a thousand years, they have returned to their land. It will happen to your people too one day" (251). In a hard-hitting article, Prof. Baig asks the Kashmiri Muslims that if they perpetrate collective violence upon pandits, what right do they have to claim victimhood? (253). Prof. Baig, it must be said, is endowed with what is called 'historical consciousness', i.e. the faculty to take a broad view of history and its place in moulding people's lives. Historical consciousness," states Rao, "may be described as one's awareness of not the confluence of the moment, the milieu and the individual but also the sensibility that enable one to abstract meaning out of the Maya of human existence" (Rao 118).

Solutions

The author presents psychological solution to the problem of terrorism in Kashmir, when the army officer orders release of Salim, a confirmed terrorist so that people "talk of him as a traitor who betrayed his comrades in exchange for freedom" (344). Kashmir, he says, is full of criminals with halos of martyrs and creating martyrs will help terrorists' cause only. It is the creating of martyrs that keeps the movement in Kashmir alive" (344). The writer has done well to append a glossary of meanings of Hindi and Urdu words besides explaining such terms in footnotes too.

The other solution that the novel suggests is the Gandhian one because "unarmed courage in the face of certain death leads us to a feeling of connection to life and brings a change in our heart" (311). Mitra has crafted the character of Aditya Narayan, who, through his peaceful satyagraha—the insistence on carrying on his mission—is also able to influence Muslims like Zeba, Anwar, and Javed. Javed loses his life as a result of highhandedness of security men.

Anwar's courage is appreciated even by the army men, but more than that he is a conscientious young man, who is keen to know answer to three questions, viz. (i) Can a call for violence toward infidels and their women from mosques be justified?, (ii) If I wanted to kill an infidel first and then end up saving his life, do I veer away from the path of being a Muslim?, and (iii) While Haji chacha wants him to act according to the verses on infidels in the holy book, his father says he should be compassionate towards everyone as Islam is a religion of compassion (273). Clearly, he is a true humanist rather than a narrow-minded Muslim.

Non-violent approach, in our times, is under cloud just as Mahatma Gandhi's status as the person responsible for India's freedom is being questioned with the argument that the British had no capacity left after the end of the Second World War to hold on to the India. In addition, the radical opposition coming from Subhash Chandra Bose's Indian National Army, the Naval Revolt, the several tribal revolts, etc. had further incapacitated the British. Non-violent opposition, as Anwar's example shows, works with conscientious adversaries, and to think the British had that mindset would be a misnomer.

Style

The 366-page novel is divided into 100 short chapters, but it goes to the credit of the author—he should know it being an experienced psychologist—that he keeps the interest of the reader alive creating suspense wherever the story seems to sag, like on page 56, the narrative ends with "What do they mean by my background? And what do they mean by seeds that give birth?" muses the young girl Zeba. Thus, the fact that Zeba is an orphan is leaked at the right moment through a letter written by her mother 13 years ago. The writer has done well to append a glossary of meanings of Hindi and Urdu words besides explaining them in footnotes too.

Any novel endears itself to the readers and leaves a lasting impression when it is able to arouse, through effective narration, the emotion of pathos. There are several instances in the novel where the reader feels moved. One such is when Zeba talks on phone from a store to a doctor of the mental asylum where her mother was kept. The revelation about her mother's death is too much to bear for Zeba and when she tries paying for the phone bill, the shopkeeper does not accept it and having overheard the conversation, wishes her peace of mind. This is *kashmiriyat*, or rather *insaniyat* indeed (142).

Conclusion

The discourse in Kashmir is vitiated due to the machinations of a fanatic fringe among Muslim population egged on by Pakistan and further compounded by corruption. It's not that all Muslims think alike, there are people like the Imam who preach the essence of religion, and there are people like Krishan Narayan who are unable to free themselves from the conservative mindset with regard to untouchability. But Aditya Narayan, the protagonist, is a true Gandhian figure who, despite performing the daily rituals as a *pujari* of the Hindu temple, believes in the cardinal virtues of religion.

There is no denying the fact that the current intellectual discourse in India is pro-Left, and a skewed one with a distorted view of religion. For those who think nothing of conversion which lies at the root of the exodus of Kashmiri pandits, the novelist observes through a pandit character, "The conversion is the scar that doesn't let you heal. When after centuries of following a faith, you give it up on being forced, your soul never accepts it. It remains a trauma and lies embedded deep inside. It is passed on to the future generations making them violent" (267).

The present-day intellectual discourse identifies secularism with looking askance at anything related to Hinduism, so much so that admitting that one is Hindu by religion seems like one is admitting backwardness. On the other hand, talking of the interests of the minority community is the only thing legitimized by this discourse. It is, therefore, admirable on the part of Rajat Mitra to put things in proper perspective by putting the Hindu and the Muslim points of view side by side in a judicious manner.

WORKS CITED

Collingwood, R.G. *The Idea of History*. London: Oxford, 1961.

Dhar, T.N. *History-Fiction Interface in Indian English Novel*. New Delhi: Prestige, 1999.

Mitra, Rajat. *The Infidel Next Door*. North Charleston, USA: Create Space Publishing, 2017.

Rao, A.V. Krishna. *Nayantara Sahgal: A Study of her Fiction and Non-Fiction*. Madras: M. Seshachalon & Co., 1976.

Roy, Arundhati. *The Ministry of Utmost Happiness*. New Delhi: Penguin, 2017.

Sartre, Jean-Paul. *What is Literature?* Trans. Bernard Frechtman. London: Routledge, 2001.

Singh, Khushwant. *Delhi: A Novel*. New Delhi: Penguin, 1990.

6

Kiran Desai's *The Inheritance of Loss*: Home as the Structural Principle

Home is not, it is said, constituted by the four walls; it is a symbol of security and comfort—an abode of solace in times of crisis and a multiplier of joy in times of happy living. Home has a unique appeal for its inmates not only because physical conditions mould mental state but also because home points to the presence of family in it. Thus, the emergence of the institution of family added to the importance of home which lies at the intersection of nature and culture. Only a person who does not have home or is far removed from it knows its value. There is no dearth of folk-songs in all cultures that sing of the travails of the *pardesi* or the one who has to stay away from home. How one feels at home in home is described by Robert Frost thus in his dramatic poem "The Death of the Hired Man":

> "Home is the place where, when you have to go there
> They have to take you in."
> "I should have called it
> Something you somehow haven't to deserve."

Home is, thus, a natural choice for leading most part of our life; it is a place of rest and if possible, of work too. Also, the limits of home expand or contract in different contexts. It could be any territory from the small, walled in space in which one spends most of one's lifetime to the entire country one calls one's 'home country'. This later concept is evoked when one is out of one's own country. Home then, in all its manifestations and interpretations, constitutes the governing principle of the narrative of the Man Booker Prize winning novel *The Inheritance of Loss* by Kiran Desai, acclaimed daughter of the well-known Indian novelist Anita Desai. The title of the novel with its negativistic overtone, however, refers only to the sense of loss felt by Biju mainly, and by Sai partially towards the end of the novel. The narrative hinges predominantly on the search for home, so much so that it can be called the structural principle of the novel. This is the Tomashevskiian bound motif that is essential to the causal-chronological sequence of the novel. The *Routledge Encyclopedia of Narrative Theory* subsumes it under the category of Narrative Thematics about which it states:

> Narrative Thematics is a plot-oriented approach with roots in formalism and structuralism. Formalst analysis reduced narratives to their smallest, indispensable thematic elements, motifs, in order to analyse narrative structure. Tomashevskii distinguished bound motifs, which are logically essential to narrative action and its causal-chronological coherence, from free motifs, which remain logically inessential to it. (Pyrhonen 598)

This essay focusses on the concept of home as used in the novel on literal as well as metaphorical planes. An attempt has been made to underline the convergence of concerns regarding the place of origin, security, and employment with the structural pattern of the novel and how these fashion the causal and chronological aspects of the novel.

When we talk about home, habitat forms an integral part of the idea of home. A pleasant environment can make or mar our joyful experience of life. Sensory experience affects the emotional and intellectual life of the people, except of those who have attained perfect dissociation of sensibilities or detached themselves totally from the world. That is why we are concerned about environment. Desai's focus on the geographical nature, apart from being an aesthetic embellishment, also forms an allied motif of home. To link the script of the narrative with the underlying concept of home calls for technical ingenuity and a commitment to ecological welfare, both of which Kiran Desai displays in ample measure.

The poem by the Argentinian poet Jorge Luis Borges that serves as the epigraph in *The Inheritance of Loss* states nostalgically: "My homeland is the rhythm of a guitar, a few portraits, an old sword, the willow grove's visible prayer as evening falls." He also laments the loss of countryside to the greedy metropolis and of his own inability to 'arrive'. This quite befittingly hints at the theme of the novel. As the narrative begins, we find Sai, the 16-year-old luckless daughter of a couple that perished on a Vienna road, approaching a decrepit colonial building called Cho Oyu, in search of a new home. The house is in Kalimpong, a picturesque hill station in the Darjeeling district of West Bengal. The retired judge Jemubhai Popatlal Patel, who presides over this estate happens to be her maternal grandfather but he is a singular personality in that he jealously guards his privacy. Even though Sai has the judge's blood running in her veins, and has been orphaned through a cruel trick of fate, Jemubhai only grudgingly consents to allow her to stay here.

It appears the judge's formative years were responsible for this lack of warmth. He left his home at the age of 22. From his ancestral village Piphit in Gujarat, he travelled to Bombay to catch a ship for Liverpool, England, for studies. His search for lodgings took him to some "twenty-two homes before he arrived at the doorstep of Mrs. Rice on Thornton Road. She didn't want him either, but she needed the money and her house was so situated—on the other side of the train station from the university—she was concerned she wouldn't be able to find a lodger at all" (45-46). All the same, he suffered from an overdose of anglophilia which effaced his tender feelings, if any, for home and the people in it. His reaction to the flattering description of his homeland in the library book in England is indicative of this acquired mindset:

> He read a book entitled Expedition to Goozerat: "The Malabar coast undulates in the shape of a wave up the western flank of India, and then, in a graceful motion, gestures toward the Arabian sea. This is Goozerat. At the river deltas and along the malarial coasts lie towns configured for trade...."
>
> What on earth was all of this? It had nothing to do with what he remembered of his home, of the Patels and their life

> in the Patel warren, and yet, when he unfolded the map, he found Piphit. There it was—a mosquito speck by the side of a sulky river. (117)

Later, he joined the judicial service in India, then under British rule. As a result, he had been thoroughly anglicized in etiquette and manners and considered himself a notch above others—his close family members included. He is not able to appreciate the value of home for an orphaned granddaughter. This attitude is seminal to the development of the plot as the seeds of conflict are sown here.

Adopting Home

Sai's adoption of home, as such, remains incomplete just like her affair with the 20-year-old science teacher Gyan, which, if successful, could have made the search of home more meaningful and complete. At Cho Oyu, she has the company of a cook who tells her stories of spirits and of his son Biju, who is trying to find home in America. His status is that of an illegal immigrant and like thousands of others, he is trying hard to get the green card.

If the consciousness of home lies at the deeper level in the novel, that of the habitat is felt at the surface level, at the level of allied motif. The idyllic description of the hill station shows Desai's ecological consciousness, which she has inherited from her mother. If Nanda Kaul merges with the atmosphere in *Fire on the Mountain*, in *The Inheritance of Loss*, it is the house that merges with the landscape: "When she looked back, the house was gone; when she climbed the steps back to the veranda, the garden vanished. [...] The gray had permeated inside, as well, settling on the silverware, nosing the corners, turning the mirror in the passageway to cloud" (2). Exotic details of nature—of flora and fauna and lush vegetation—at the foot of the Kanchenjunga presents a veritable feast for the nature lover. Even the solitude of the inhabitants of Cho Oyu has been described in terms of the giant squid spotted there on rare occasions: "No human had ever seen an adult giant squid alive, and though they had eyes as big as apples to scope the dark of the ocean, theirs was a solitude so profound they might never encounter another of their tribe. The melancholy of this situation washed over Sai" (2). The house is a crumbling structure in which a "thousand deceased spiders lay scattered" (12) on the attic floor. A saucer of milk and a pile of sweets is placed by the cook to pacify a pair of black cobras living in a hole. The archetypal cook, as his namelessness suggests, lives in harmony with nature believing that "The natural world exists in its own right and other beings have a will, a way of their own and their own stories" (Drengson 20).

Sai's parents had also gone to Russia to earn livelihood and to realize a niche, as the environmentalists would say, but unfortunately they met with a fatal accident. That is why Sai, who had been studying in a convent, had to come to her only surviving relative—Jemubhai. In a sense, none of the human beings living at Cho Oyu are the original inhabitants of this place. The building was built by a Scotsman who left India in 1957. The neighbours "the landmarks of her new home" (48) include among others Lola and Noni, two Anglicized sisters, Uncle Potty, an anglophile from Lucknow and Father Booty, a Swiss national who came here 45 years ago and never thought of going back, satisfied as he was with the pastoral setting into which he established a dairy. Kalimpong is fundamental niche or the original home for none of them; each one was trying to realize the niche. This, in all, builds the exposition part of the novel, though the information is non-linear in the true postmodern style.

Sai gets emotionally involved with Gyan, her teacher of Nepalese origin, who lives in the poverty-stricken Bong Busti. Home is also a metonymy for class and Gyan was ashamed of letting her see his home even when she wanted to (167). Transcending the economic and cultural barriers, however, nature brings them together. Against the scenic backdrop of the Delo lake or by the shores of the Teesta river, they tell each other tales of themselves and their families. While nature brings them together thus, the cultural politics creates a gulf between the two lovers. The growing discontent among the Indian Nepalese takes the form of Gorkhaland agitation. Gyan joins this movement and is brainwashed so that he distances himself from Sai and even uses harsh words for her. There is a nasty quarrel between the two. Gyan places his geo-ethnic identity above everything else. He berates his beloved and mocks at the 'fake English accent' and 'powdered faces' of 'that fussy pair' at Cho Oyu. He now looks down upon them as encroachers on his homeland.

This mood does not last permanently. When Sai drifts away, he tries to make amends but whether the two are able to unite or not remains an open-ended issue in the novel. Gyan reminisces and feels "the trouble was that he'd tried to be part of the larger questions, tried to become part of politics and history. Happiness had a smaller location, though this wasn't something to flaunt, of course" (272). Home is also a metaphor for a secure haven. Gyan has realized the difficulties on this path and ended abruptly his honeymoon with the GNLF. His offer to locate the missing Mutt confirms that he is much mellowed now.

The placid life in this beautiful place, disturbed by the unrest among native Nepali community, has its roots in the forcible boundary adjustments done by the erstwhile British rulers and thereafter by our own government on the basis of linguistic organization of states. The GNLF activists, who rob the judge of his old arms, consider the region their original home and therefore want it declared Gorkhaland. When the land belonging to the Bengali sisters is encroached upon by the Gorkha activists, they assert: "This is our land!" But the Gorkhas would have none of it (240). While the legitimacy of the hill retreats of people like Justice Jemubhai, Father Booty, Noni and Lola is questioned by the GNLF cadres, their own credentials as inheritors of land might not go beyond a particular point in past, caught up as they are in the "mythic battles of past vs. present, justice vs. injustice" (295). Even if a group has been here for several generations, the fact remains that it is true so far as the recorded history goes. One cannot make history a ground for claiming a piece of land in these postmodern times when any identity, leave aside the one based on settlement, is fluid and changeable.

The crisis in the lives of these people living in India comes with the questioning of their right to home. Father Booty's home is found "as illegal as he was" (228) by the police since he had forgotten to get his papers renewed. Sisters Lola and Noni too would lose home which Lola's late husband Jaideep had bought—it became clear after Lola had had a talk with the Pradhan of the GNLF cadres whose indecent utterances pained her long after she left the place (252).

Homeless in US

Trying to realize his own niche is Biju in far-off America, moving from one ill-paid job to the other and also, while working in stuffy kitchens, coming in contact with people from other third world countries—from Pakistan to Zanjibar. He learns that Indians have spread far and wide. They are trying to search for home or realize niches in Guyana, Kenya, Chile, South Africa, Fiji, New Zealand, Canada, etc. For Biju, it was the new home: "When he returned *home* at the basement of a building at the bottom of Harlem, he fell straight into sleep" (58). He also learns that Indians are discriminated against in many countries from Uganda to Guadeloupe (77). Even in the lottery system that was adopted for granting visas, Indians were not allowed to apply. Thus, racial prejudices present hurdles in securing home in the world even in postmodern times.

In America, the conditions of work for illegal immigrants are not sound. They live in constant fear of being spotted by the police and are exploited by cheats on the pretext of helping them to get green card. In the severe New York winter, Biju has to put a padding of newspaper under his shirt to keep himself warm. He weeps over his predicament (51). From Baby Bistro to Brigette's, Biju woks in many restaurants before he is finally rendered jobless. In the process, he learns a lot of strategies for survival even as his search for home in the land of plenty remains elusive. The craze for green card drove him mad at times: "He walked to the far end where the homeless man often slept in a dense chamber of green that seemed to grow not so much from soil as from a fertile city crud. A homeless chicken also lived in the park. Every now and then Biju saw it scratching in a homey manner in the dirt and felt a pang for village life" (88). Desai also depicts a homeless American whose images pop up on various pages in the novel. His debut picture in the novel follows:

> Biju had been nervous there from his very first day. "Howdy," a man on the steps of his new abode had said, holding out his hand and nodding, "my name's Joey, and I just had me some WHEES-KAY!" Power and hiss. This was the local homeless man at the edge of his hunting and gathering territory, which he sometimes marked by peeing a bright arc right across the road. He wintered here on a subway grate in a giant plastic-bag igloo that sagged, then blew taut with stale air each time a train passed. Biju had taken the sticky hand offered, the man had held tight, and Biju had broken free and run, a cackle of laughter following him. (59)

The talk about home will not be complete if its macro form—the home-country—is not discussed. International politics enters this discourse about home through the backdoor. Kiran Desai makes her characters talk about colonialism which was, simply put, all about divesting the native people of their home. The owners of the Brigette's restaurant are shown reading the *New York Times* report which mentioned how the third world people, the "former slaves and natives" of the myriad newly decolonized nations, came to America "screaming colonialism, screaming slavery, screaming mining companies screaming banana companies oil companies screaming CIA spy among the missionaries" (134). That in effect means the colonized are aware of the machinations of the powerful in the world to capture their home country's politics and economy through economic imperialism. People like Achootan want green card as a matter of right with the logic which he had developed in England: "Your father came to *my* country and took *my* bread and now I have come to *your* country to get *my* bread back" (135). This is raw logic but surely it has a lot of sense in it.

In this away-from-home, globalized scenario of New York, the identity gets transmuted, transferred and translated in so many ways. Desai describes in numerous snapshots the multiple dimensions of the "lack of clarity of vision" (155) in this regard. The scene in the café is indicative of this obfuscation:

> Confusion was rampant among the "haalf 'n' haf" crowd, the Indian students coming in with American friends, one accent one side of the mouth, another the other side; muddling it up, wobbling then, downgrading sometimes all the way to Hindi to show one another: Who? No, no, it was not they pretending to be other than who and what they were. They weren't the ones turning their back on the greatest culture the world has ever seen.... (155)

Desai examines the construct of home inside out. What about the exploitation of Indians by Indians in America? Do the exploiters forget their common home (shared niche), after they have, what they imagine, 'realized niche in the States? When Biju slipped on some rotten spinach in the kitchen of Gandhi Café, the owner Harish-Harry refused to call in a doctor, because according to him, it was Biju's responsibility to keep the floor clean. Again, when the compensation for lost baggage is being doled out only to the NRIs and not to Indians, the former could afford to maintain a cool posture, looking thoroughly civilized while the latter having lost greenbacks are screaming (298). So, being civilized, which is a cultural phenomenon as against natural, is tied to simple selfishness.

Driven by want and harassment and self-pity, nostalgia for home overtakes Biju so strongly that in his imagination, he can smell the humid air of Kalimpong and hear the sound of silver grass. Finally, he decides to return to India. As ill luck would have it, he is robbed of everything by the Gorkhland militants before he lands at Cho Oyu and meets his father. What comes as a climax without any denouement or resolution is not only this material loss but also the loss of hope of home in the US but regaining of home back in India. But for him, the loss is still worth inheriting, because he has finally reached back home. Sai too is inheritor of loss of any patron—her parents dead, her grandfather loving dog Mutt more than her and Gyan yet to come back to her, but she gains insight into the myriad ways in which life moves and realizes "Never again could she think there was but one narrative and that this narrative belonged only to herself, that she might create her own tiny happiness and live safely within it" (330). In this respect, the title of the novel *The Inheritance of Loss* tells half the story.

The novel does discuss subtly several issues. It underlines the fact that while the concept of home is in consonance with nature and every creature craves for one, human culture politicizes it. We can lay claim to a place as our original, ancestral, ethnic, or racial home at the cost of historical knowledge only. Man tends to interpret motives of purity of race or claim to a piece of land to suit his present existential needs only. The nature-man relationship has ever been problematized as Desai's remark towards the close of the novel suggests it without assigning any value to it but, all the same, giving it a biocentric focus: "All night it would rain. It would continue, off and on, on and off, with savagery [...] the town would slide down the hill. Slowly, painstakingly, like ants, men would make their paths and civilization and their wars once again, only to have it wash away again" (323). Surely, the quest for home as a manifestation of the existential aspirations of man would not be thwarted merely because of this tussle between nature and culture. Leonard Lutwack's observation about the earth could fittingly sum up this submission: "It is a hostile, alien place; and yet also man's true home" (qtd. Howarth 86).

WORKS CITED

Desai, Anita. *Fire on the Mountain*. London: William Heinemann, 1977.

Desai, Kiran. *The Inheritance of Loss*. New Delhi: Penguin, 2006.

Drengson, Alan. 'Novels, Philosophical Studies and Ecocriticism.' *Indian Journal of Ecocriticism*. Osle India, Aug. 2009.

Frost, Robert. "The Death of the Hired Man". *Poetry Foundation*. https://www.poetryfoundation.org/poems/44261/the-death-of-the-hired-man

Howarth, William. 'Some Principles of Ecocriticism'. *The Ecocriticism Reader*. Ed. Cheryll Glotfelty & Harold Fromm. Athens: The University of Georgia, 1996.

Pyrhonen, Heta. "Thematic Approaches to Narrative." *Routledge Encyclopedia of Narrative Theory*, eds. David Herman, Manfred Jahn & Marie-Laure Ryan. London: Routledge, 2005, 2008.

7

Chetan Bhagat's *The 3 Mistakes of My Life*: A Study in Strategies of Popular Fiction

'The biggest-selling English-language novelist in India's history', proclaims the blurb on the jacket of the book *The 3 Mistakes of My Life*, quoting the *New York Times*. There is no doubt about it and what is more, Bhagat is also credited with having thrown open the floodgates of popular fiction in India so that on an average, around a hundred novels belonging to this category now appear in a year in India. Nevertheless, it also is a fact that Bhagat remains a writer of light fiction and employs the strategies that focus not on conveying great ideas to readers but on raising the saleability quotient of his novels in the market. The purpose of this paper is to study these strategies and to speculate on the future of.

A popular novel—the category to which Bhagat's work belongs—is defined by J.A. Cuddon as one that has a wide readership belonging to middle or "low-brow" category. Such a novel "may not possess much literary merit". According to him, "Many a best-seller, historical novel, novel of sensation, thriller and novel of adventure has been so described. Some of the well-known British popular novelists have been: Warwick Deeping, Howard Spring, R.F. Delderfield [...]. Such a list might be greatly extended" (685). One might add here that everyone has, at one point of time or another, read such popular writers like Barbara Cartland, Agatha Christie, Erle Stanley Gardner, Sir Arthur Conan Doyle, Dan Brown, J.K. Rowling et al., and might remember characters like Sherlock Holmes, Perry Mason, Harry Potter for the whole of one's life.

The commonest observation about popular fiction is that it is formulaic and stereotypical, and it uses artifacts that have often been used. It may also be called formulaic in the sense that the prospective reader approaches it with a certain measure of foreknowledge of what exactly he is to find in it. In this, it can be contrasted with serious or literary fiction which does not conform to this pattern. There is an element of mystique built around a canonical work and a reader may prefer to go by a reviewer's recommendation in choosing a work, for it cannot be predicted like popular fiction.

Although most popular varieties of popular fiction are based on detective, romantic, scientific, and adventurous themes, there can be other variants also like autobiographical, historical, social, etc. Popular fiction deals with almost any theme which has hogged the attention of society. In the Indian context, one can expect to find day-to-day problems facing society on the whole like caste and gender divisions, crime and corruption etc. in these novels. Similarly, political events also provide rich fodder for the popular fiction mill. In a nutshell, distinction between popular and literary fiction in respect of theme may not be tenable.

What better defines this difference is the treatment. In case of serious fiction, one or several or all of the following features may be found: minute observations regarding physical and mental situations and actions, deeper insight into problems, wider coverage of humanity, beauty and richness of language and imagery, and other stylistic flourishes and deviations. In case of popular fiction, the treatment is simpler and it is nearer to normal life of people most of whom do not always speak grammatically correct and literary kind of language like the characters in most serious literature are represented doing. While the literary novelist may occasionally use swear words to faithfully denote the linguistic register of his fictional characters, the popular novelist would use cuss words mainly to add spice to his prose just as he puts in a surfeit of sex scenes to tempt ordinary readers most of whom look for cheap thrill.

Serious fiction would cater to a reader who is grounded somewhat in the nuances of literature, but popular fiction would appeal to a reader with an average level of education and comprehension. With the passage of time, a popular fiction writer develops his fan club which he seeks to satisfy. On the other hand, the writer of serious literature is motivated by certain artistic/aesthetic vision. There are several theories about trivial literature; some of them accuse it of promoting status quo-ism with regard to distribution of power, while some others believe popular literature to be the site for negotiation and contestation in a society always on the move.

Elizabeth Lowell,[1] a prolific American popular fiction writer, with more than fifty works belonging to different categories of popular fiction to her credit, contends that accessibility is the "hallmark of popular fiction". Regarding the creative effort put in a popular novel, she avers,

> In popular fiction, the only critics who really matter are the readers who pay money to buy books of their own choice. Reviews are irrelevant to sales. Readers of popular fiction judge an author by his or her ability to make the common language uncommonly meaningful, and to make an often-told tale freshly exciting. The amount of effort a reader puts into this fiction is minimal. That, after all, is the whole point: to entertain readers rather than to exercise them.

Lowell castigates literary fiction for its pessimistic outlook, based mainly on Marx, Freud and Sartre. On the other hand, the philosophy of most popular fiction is optimistic; that is why it beats literary fiction at the sales counter.

> The underlying philosophy of much popular fiction is more optimistic: the human condition might indeed be deplorable, but individuals can make a positive difference in their own and others' lives. The Muses of popular fiction are Zoroaster and Jung, the philosophy *more classical than modern*. Popular fiction is a continuation of and an embroidery upon ancient myths and archetypes; popular fiction is good against evil, Prometheus against the uncaring gods, Persephone emerging from hell with the seeds of spring in her hands, Adam discovering Eve. In a word, popular fiction is heroic and

> transcendent at a time when heroism and transcendence are out of intellectual favor. (italics mine)

As Lowell admits, the philosophy of popular novel may be inspired by classical principles—something upheld in the canonical literature also which gives primacy to high artistic and intellectual qualities and humanistic concerns, and which has the power to enlighten as well as delight the reader. But these are the views of a creative writer, who may be accused of glorifying her trade. In order to have a balanced picture, we shall also take up the views of a known culture critic in the next section of this article.

Moreover, the entire concept of canon is dubbed elitist by the postmodern critics. It is suspected to be the handiwork of privileged class in society which sought to reign in the minorities and the counter movements to strengthen the framework laid down by it. The major objection of the postmodern critics is to the overarching Eurocentrism in canon formation which has been broadened to fit in the binary mainstream/marginal in different literatures of the world. There is no doubt that Eurocentrism is an irrational notion begotten by the former colonial powers, for no single race or nation can arrogate to itself the wisdom of mankind for all time. But putting it at par with the 'mainstream' category world-wide is not simply broadening its ambit but resorting to a mischievous and reductionist syllogism.

II

In our times, when cultural study of literary works reduces much of the sheen surrounding them, it is natural to suspect some materialist strategies deliberately adopted to make a novel a sales wonder. Even as the popular writers have their fan clubs, the publishers too, carry on large-scale surveys to find out what actually can sell in the market. Hefty advances are given to promising or proven writers, hype created, books launched with much fanfare and even awards manipulated to prop a work or an author. This is very much like the making and launching of commercial feature films. In fact, Bhagat's novels have a structure that shows their affinity with popular Hindi films—the most visible form of popular culture in our times. His novels have simple stories which do not require any mental exercise to reveal layers of meanings as found in canonical works. Like a Hindi *masala* film, Bhagat's novels too bring together disparate elements like fancy, facts, idealism, suspense, crispy dialogues, humour, sex, etc. that appeal to the youth; after all, the novels target the youth as their readers.

The first and foremost aspect of a work of the popular category is its relevance to the life of its consumers. Since Bhagat's novels predominantly have young readers, he is expected to take up issues concerning youth. *Five Point Someone* had the sub-title 'What not to do at IIT'. Since the writer himself is an IIT-ian, some of the young readers are suspected of having approached the novel with the hope to get some tips with regard to entry into the haloed precincts of an Indian Institute of Technology. Relating of the story partly in autobiographical manner persuades the reader to believe the account as true. Some young readers expectedly looked forward to knowing about the inside story of a reputed academic institution which they probably wanted to enter and could not, so that the novel promised to satisfy their curiosity in this regard. Either way, it ensured a large reader base to the writer.

Bhagat's second novel *One Night @ the Call Centre* came along at a time when the BPO business had touched heights and the call centres in Bangalore and Gurgaon symbolized the metamorphosis of Indian business from traditional to modern lines. The generally overnight work-schedule dictated by the imperative of catering to the U.S.A.-based clientele, the put-on western accent of the long-distance young callers from India, attractive pay packages and a new work-place culture introduced by the M.N.C.'s combined to entice the youth who found fresh opportunities knocking at their door. The novel was bound to sell like anything.

Bhagat's third novel *The 3 Mistakes of My Life* cashes in on the cricket-fixation of the nation and cuts across all age barriers. Besides, the writer has tried to dabble in a political theme also by linking the story to the post-Godhra riots in Gujarat. This inclusion shows Bhagat no longer wishes to keep his readership base limited to the youth even though the key characters are young people. The story of his fourth novel *2 States: The Story of My Marriage* begins at the Indian Institute of Management, Ahmedabad, where Krish, a Punjabi boy from Delhi and Ananya, a Tamil girl from Chennai are fellow students and then it is the usual boy-meets-girl kind of story. The story is related in the autodiegetic mode, deservedly so because it is broadly based on the author's own love life. Bhagat and his wife Anusha, who are from Delhi and Tamil Nadu respectively. The cultural differences and the ensuing conflict reminds one of the Hindi movie *Ik Duje Ke Liye*. In fact, Bhagat's penchant for including a numeral in the title of each one of his novels also puts one in mind of some superstitious film producers who select the titles of their movies on some such considerations (Nasir Hussain, for example, selected titles of films beginning with the Hindi alphabet *a*). The latest novel is *Revolution 2020: Love, Corruption, Ambition*. There is surely no revolution in the book, save a journal by that name; it is all about the three things mentioned in the sub-title. A youth taking to corrupt ways of the world to succeed in politicized milieu of India is not a new thing but then the novel ends on an idealistic note with Gopal sacrificing his love for the betterment of his sweetheart! It appears like a take on the old Hindi movie *Sangam* in which a character with the name Gopal did the same thing!

Taking up Bhagat's novel *The 3 Mistakes of My Life* as a case study, we find that the story encompasses events in the lives of three close friends—Ish (Ishan), Omi, and Govind (the narrator), all of whom come together to start a retail cricket goods shop. Ish, who has been a district-level cricketer, takes under his wings a young boy named Ali who is gifted by nature in that he can see in slow motion a ball that has been delivered by a fast bowler. This special gift reminds one of Salman Rushdie's magic realism that finds expression in the magical power granted to the children born on the midnight of 15th August 1947. In fact, Bhagat uses high imagination in his other novel *One Night @ the Call Centre* also in which the protagonists get a call from God and Lord Krishna himself approaches the writer-narrator, in the form of a beautiful girl. While the element of fantasy appeals to the young readers, the use of Gujarat mayhem as a backdrop could hook up older readers.

Ali has to be made interested in cricket through gifts of marbles because he is more interested in marbles. Besides, even though he strikes sixes, one after another, he easily gets tired after taking six balls. Ish is very serious about his mission. In order to get the boy trained by a visiting Australian cricketer, he even masquerades as the director of a reputed cricket goods company. Since Ish is a partner in the cricket goods shop along with the other two friends, Ali becomes the joint responsibility of the trio.

To complicate matters, Govind gets infatuated by Omi's sister as he gives her tuition in mathematics. This creates a parallel storyline which provides opportunity to the writer to throw in some sex scenes—a must for any popular novel. In fact, in *The 3 Mistakes of My Life*, Bhagat has thrown in an Australian beach scene (165-66), an indigenous maiden kissing scene (183) as also a passionate love scene (200-02). After all, popular fiction is normally "formulaic, commercial, sensational, melodramatic, and sentimental" (Genre Fiction), as it has to cater to mass market.

The infamous Godhara carnage in which some Muslim fanatics burnt a train carrying Hindu devotees forms an important plank of the plot. The horrendous event sets off large-scale communal clashes in the state. The voluntary zeal of the friends is now pitted against the Omi's maternal uncle—Bittu Mama—who criticizes the younger generation for not being politically conscious, and can only think of wreaking revenge on the Muslims for the Godhara carnage in which his son was also killed. Not impressed with his nephew's humanist leanings, he wants Ali's blood in retaliation for his son's murder. However, it is Omi, who has to pay with his blood while saving Ali, ironically at the hands of his Bittu Mama. So, the element of surprise is built into the plot.

The final drama played out in a bank building is full of suspense and thrill. The other friends Govind and Ish are also injured while saving Ali from the marauding crowd led by Bittu

Mama. The way he challenges Ali to the 'final' cricket game and then the full use made of the opportunity by Ali who bats with full power to hit Mama's temple is something the Bollywood film producers would love to include in commercial flicks. The Mama slumps as the ball hits him twice and is then done in finally by Ish. The detail of the attack with tridents and the ingenious manner in which Ali is saved easily brings to mind such scenes from Hindi films.

Towards the end of the novel, the remaining friends Govind and Ish even pool together an amount of five lakh rupees to get Ali's wrist surgery done in England. All this underlines the high idealism of the youth. In the end, the narrator gets his beloved Vidya after getting reconciled to his friend, but not before a stylistic move by the writer— something he has made in each one of his novels. If it was Lord Krishna appearing as a beautiful damsel in the train and getting a promise from him to write the story of his novel *One Night @ the Call Center*, in the present novel, Govind's email entices Bhagat, the writer, to go meet him in an Ahmedabad hospital and record his story in the first-person narrative. There are, thus, two narrators in the novel—Chetan Bhagat and Govind, both of whom use the first-person narrative. Such a feature also adds to the singularity of the novel.

The writer brings himself in the Prologue as also in the epilogue. Bhagat shows himself stationed in Singapore and states that he has received an anonymous email from a person in India who has popped sleeping pills to commit suicide because he has failed in love. The writer then dons the mantle of a detective, locates the sender and, towards the end of the novel, becomes instrumental in bringing about a rapprochement between a hospitalized Govind and Ish, thereby paving the way for union between Govind and his beloved Vidya who happens to be Ish's sister. Thus, from the beginning the curiosity of the reader is sought to be aroused. What follows is like a flashback in a film.

The reader's curiosity is aroused through the title also. Bhagat has a knack for selecting interesting titles for his works. The reader is naturally curious about which are the three mistakes he refers to in the title of the novel. These have to be gleaned from the text since references to them lie strewn all over. The first mistake of Govind, the narrator, as per his own admission, is investing his money in a shop in an upcoming mall which was totally destroyed by an earthquake (107). The second mistake was getting sexually involved with his best friend's sister (200) and the third one was moving a wee bit late in trying to save Ali due to which Ali received wrist injury (246).

III

The postmodern view of writing derides the notion of hierarchy with regard to literary and popular texts, but it should not lead us to deny any difference between the two. While a classic literary work presents the writer's vision transcending the bounds of the immediate and the superficial, and deals seriously with the various elements of novel, the popular category would make do with broad strokes only for the simple reason that the readers of popular fiction approach such a work to pass time only. The aim of a popular novel, therefore, is not to discuss any philosophy or impart any message to the world but to provide amusement to the reader while he journeys by bus or train or seeks diversion after a hectic working week.

The question naturally arises if such an absolute division between these black and white categories is possible. In this respect, the study of Stuart Hall's study of popular art can provide valuable guidance.[2] Referring to Hall's views as expressed in his famous work *The Popular Arts* (written jointly with Paddy Whannel[3]), James Procter comments,

> *The Popular Arts* refuses to use high culture as a yardstick to measure the success/failure of popular culture: 'the movies have their own special virtues but it is doubtful if these can be revealed when they are regarded only as stepping stones in a hierarchy of taste' (TPA: 37). It is pointless, Hall and Whannel might argue, to compare the music of Kylie Minogue and Mozart because 'different kinds of music offer different sorts of satisfaction.' (21)

Despite this insistence on using different parameters for classic and popular arts, they do recognize the importance of 'good' and 'bad' in popular culture. Whereas the former emerging out of folk art admits of personalization, the latter is inspired by mass art and gives in to stereotyping and formulae. Hall does not apply the criterion of sales to declare a work popular for its obvious capitalist underpinnings, but a popular work bringing in money is axiomatic in our times.

One cannot really do with total abrogation of hierarchy even in popular cultural manifestations as the following observation with regard to the postmodern theorists Hall and Whannel suggests:

> In terms of film they distinguish between the tedium of Hollywood blockbusters like *Around the World in 80 Days* and a more sophisticated European cinema. In each case, the examples reveal a degree of elitism that would seem to contradict the authors' attempts to validate popular cultural forms elsewhere. [...] they go on to install new hierarchies: 'the best cinema – like the most advanced jazz—seems to push towards high art: average films or pop music are processed mass art' (TPA: 78). Hall and Whannel's earlier point that popular cultural forms should not be viewed as 'stepping stones in a hierarchy of taste' appears to have been forgotten here. (Procter 23)

What it means for us is that among all sorts of popular novels, the ones with a measure of canonical quality about them stand a chance of being distinguished from run-of-the-mill works. Hall's evaluation finds support in the ascendancy in esteem of popular novels in contemporary times. The Booker award for *The White Tiger* goes to prove the point that there could be better books within the domain of popular fiction. For the purpose of our study, it all boils down to this that a popular novel cannot retain its appeal over a long period of time and for a wider expanse of world if it is only buoyed by flippancy and fantasy. There has to be something of more permanent worth; at least a semblance of it is a prerequisite. So, Bhagat mixes raw wisdom with wit, the result is wisecracks like: "Who you are, what do you want versus what people expect of you. And how to keep what you want without pissing off people too much. Life is an optimisation problem, with tons of variables and constraints" (198). Some of the witty one-liners encapsulating common wisdom may remain etched in reader's mind after he/she has laid the novel aside, as for example, "If politicians fuel a fire, there is no fire brigade to check it" (71). For young male readers, the 'wild zone' of girl's mind is apt to arouse curiosity. Here are some specimens that cater to the readers' interest:

> A girl's 'nothing' usually means 'a lot'. (79);
>
> Girls talk in circles. Like an algebra problem, it takes a few steps to get them to the point. (89)

The philosophical observations would appeal better to the young mind if these seem to favour youth over age as in the following wisecrack:

> "Anyway, screw politics. My point is, that the clueless Sixties to Eighties generation is now old, and running the country. But the Nineties and the, what do they say..."
>
> "Zeroes."
>
> "Yeah, whatever. The Zeroes think different. But we are being run by old fogeys who never did anything worthwhile in their primetime. The Doordarshan generation is running the Star TV generation," Ish said. (75)

Humour is the pre-requisite of any good novel. It operates at the levels of utterance, appearance or behavioural pattern of a character or a situation. Normally, it is the wit that makes an utterance humourous but Bhagat presents humour sans wit as in the innocent question put by Ali: "Why do people run between the wickets to score runs?" (74). Similarly, the tricky situation in which the narrator Govind goes along with his girlfriend Vidya to a bookstore whose owner is known to him is funny enough to create peals of laughter. As is common in such a situation, the shopkeeper wants to know the credentials of the girl and her relationship with Govind but he cannot ask it straightaway. The narrator finally tells him pointing towards his companion, "Student, I take tuition," I whispered to satisfy his curiosity lest he gave up sleeping for the rest of his life" (85).

Talking of maths books, Govind muses: "Now if Resnick and Halliday are scary, M.L. Khanna is the Exorcist" (86). Bhagat finds humour in a romantic situation also:

> She opened her mouth and brought it close. Her lips were eight millimeters apart from mine.
>
> Soon the gap reduced to Zero. I don't know if I came towards her or she came towards me. The tiny distance made it difficult to ascertain who took the initiative. I felt something warm on my lips and realized that we have come too close, or maybe too far.
>
> We kissed again. The mosquitoes on our respective heads rejoined. (183-84)

In fact, it is Bhagat's brilliant wit which has also contributed to the popularity of his novels. If humour is an essential tool to make a novel popular, so is the use of language peppered with slang used principally by youth. Here are some examples:

> You, Ish and Omi are really close. Like you have known each other since you were sperm. (89)
>
> Sorry, I meant Ish and Omi are your best friends. But if you have to bitch...oops, rant about them, who do you do it with? (89)
>
> They (Australia) have twenty million people. We have one billion, growing at two per cent a year. Heck, we create an Australia every year. Still, they cream us. (124)

Add to this, Bhagat's stylistic one-upmanship in ending a serious description with anti-climactic under-statement or a humorous hyperbole: "I noticed her dress. She wore a new purple and white bandhini salwar kameez today. Her necklace had a purple teardrop pendant and matching ear rings. She had freshly bathed. Her hair smelt of a little bit of Dettol soap and well, her. Every girl has a wonderful smell right after a bath. I think they should bottle it and sell it" (181).

Talking of Australia, Bhagat has stuffed Australian colloquialism on pages 158-59. By a fluke of luck, the partners of the cricket shop have landed on Australian soil and so have to be conversant with the English spoken there. Thus, we learn that 'burl' for Australians means to try something and "As the day progressed, so did my Aussie vocabulary. 'Onya' was short for 'good on you', which meant well done. An easy ball was a 'piece of piss', while a good one 'packed a wallop'. The mosquitoes were 'mozzies', and soft drinks 'coldies'. When I took the loo break..." (158). Bhagat also tries his hand at neologism when Omi refers to Ali as 'stick insect' (74) or the 'lassi moustache' (99). Vidya seeks a 'back-up friend' in Govind so that she can vent her pent-up feelings about her close friend Garima (89).

It may be pointed out here that even in canonical literature, the use of light colloquial prose is admissible. E.M. Forster used the term 'popular tendency' for the phenomenon of the popular prose becoming an integral part of the creative artist's language. This popular tendency lends freshness and informality to the writer's medium of expression (Sharma 76). But the use of informal language all through the novel firmly places it in the category of popular novel. In the case of popular fiction, it becomes a necessity, for the readers of such novels are not necessarily grounded in the minutiae of literature. They come from all walks of life and are supposed to be conversant with common day-to-day language.

Chetan Bhagat, the 'biggest-selling English-language novelist in India's history' has actually blazed a trail. The baton of popular novel has passed through many a hand since and has spawned many variants. The enfant terrible Campus Novel has given birth to its father—Metro Reads or Quick-Reads, which target the young readers with little time but with plenty of penchant for reading. Like a commercial film, therefore, this particular novel by Bhagat has the usual ingredients—romance, sex, chicanery, suspense, secret conclaves, murders, etc. and yet it is a cut above the rest not only because Bhagat is a pioneer in the field of popular novel in India but also because adorned with various graces, his novels can be called 'good' popular novels as Stuart Hall would have it.

NOTES

1. Elizabeth Lowell, nee Ann Maxwell has written popular novels of all categories—romances, historical, science, mystery, etc. Her views on readership choices expressed in the article "Popular Fiction: Why we read it, why we write it" are interesting:

   People who believe that life's problems can be solved through intelligence and effort are often attracted to crime fiction, which centers around the logical solution of various problems. People who believe along with Shakespeare that there are more things on heaven and earth than we dream, are attracted to science fiction of various kinds.

People who believe that a good relationship between a man and a woman can be the core of life are attracted to romances. People who believe that absolute evil lurks just beneath the surface of the ordinary are attracted to horror. And so on.

2. Stuart Hall (born 1932), is a well-known cultural theorist who has lived and taught in the U.K. since 1951. Hall, along with Richard Hoggart and Raymond Williams, was one of the founding figures of the school of thought known as British Cultural Studies. Hall took over from Hoggart as director of the Centre for Contemporary Cultural Studies (CCCS) at Birmingham in 1968, and remained there until 1979. He is known for his insightful study of the popular culture, race relations, identity politics, etc.
3. Atholl Douglas (Paddy) Whannel (1922-1980) was a key figure in the British Film Institute's educational work throughout the 1960s. He went on to teach at Northwestern University, Illinois until his death in 1980. In 1964, he co-authored *The Popular Arts* with Stuart Hall, in which he showed his interest in popular (particularly Hollywood) film as a serious subject of study, at a time when this kind of cinema was still neglected by traditional British film criticism. (<http://en.wikipedia.org/wiki/Paddy_Whannel>)

WORKS CITED

Bhagat, Chetan. *Five Point Someone*. New Delhi: Rupa, 2004.

——. *One Night @ The Call Centre*. New Delhi: Rupa, 2005.

——. *The 3 Mistakes of My Life*. New Delhi: Rupa, 2008.

——. *2 States: The Story of My Marriage*. Delhi: Rupa, 2009.

Sharma, K.K. *Tradition in Modern Novel-Theory*. N.J.: Humanities Press, 1981.

Cuddon, J.A. *A Dictionary of Literary Terms and Literary Theory.* New Delhi: Maya Blackwell, 1998.

Genre Fiction, Wikipaedia, Wikimedia Foundation. 26 April 2011, Web 3 May 2011. <http://en.wikipedia.org/wiki/Genre_fiction>

Lowell, Elizabeth, 'Popular Fiction: Why we read it, why we write it' n.d. Web. 15 May 2011. <http://www.elizabethlowell.com/books.html>

Procter, James. *Stuart Hall*. New York: Routledge, 2004, First Indian Reprint, 2007.

8

Keki Daruwalla's *Swerving to Solitude*: Attacking Emergency with a Semi-Sheathed Sword

Acclaimed poet Keki Daruwalla's interest in history of remote past as also not so old is well known. It is this that has probably drawn him into novel writing even as his stories were always popular. He likes to juxtapose the political with the personal so that there is more than a single narrative in his fiction. His first novel *For Pepper and Christ* dealt with the early sea voyages to India by Europeans. The two major motives, hinted at in the title were doing business and spreading Christianity, which later got intertwined with struggle for power. His second novel *Ancestral Affairs* focussed, apart from the love life of a youth, on the period around Independence and the simultaneous Partition of the country. How the Junagadh state wavered before joining India and the role of the Dewan, a Parsi, is graphically portrayed. It must be said that apart from Amitav Ghosh, Daruwalla is the other important novelist in the genre of Indian English Fiction, who does meticulous research for his novels.

Swerving to Solitude: Letters to Mama takes up the history of India from the period of Emergency (1975) to Operation Bluestar (1984). The locale shifts from Delhi and Lucknow in India to Canada, US and Mexico, placing action during the period of the First World War. The story is told in the form of a monologue of a young, married woman Seema, though she addresses it to her dead mother! Obviously, there is no response, so it is safe to take it as a diary with a difference. For the lack of response, the novel can be compared to the Booker prize winner Aravind Adiga's novel *The White Tiger* in which the protagonist sends regular mails to the Chinese Prime Minister, of course, without any sign of getting a reply.

That should not in the least lead us to believe that the two are similar in other aspects too. Adiga's strategy, were it to be used today, would be outdated for the tremendous progress that China has made so that its premier would hardly need tips on business from an Indian! Besides, Balram Halwai of Adiga's novel is a village-grown semi-literate chauffeur who picks up the ways of the city capitalists fast enough and soon comes one up on them. Here, in the present novel, Seema comes out as an educated, ideologically committed person, though she does not fire shots like her mother did in her youth. Her conduct is unconventional and befits her intellectual integrity. This liberated woman can utter the word *lulu* (local term for genitals) publicly—something rare in Indian society (13). On the other hand, her constant reference to "Mama" brings out the child-like innocence in her, for she is supposed to be frank with her mother, and it goes to the credit of the novelist that both her innocence and fighting spirit of an ideologically committed journalist are juxtaposed in an artistic manner.

Emergency Period

The time is the infamous period of Emergency imposed by the then Prime Minister of India Indira Gandhi and the locale is Lucknow in the state of Uttar Pradesh (UP). Seema, wife of Nishant, an IAS officer, is a budding journalist with the *Lucknow Chronicle*. She is an outgoing, outspoken, Left-leaning intellectual type. Her friends Shilpa, Rabia, and Zaira make a mirthful company and in their private conversations make fun of Indira Gandhi and her actions. Seema is kind to her maid's hysteric daughter Elham whom she accommodates in her house so that she is not taken for a possessed girl and referred to some exorcist by her superstitious mother.

Seema's rebellious instinct shows itself when she has a two-night stint in jail (cooler) for slapping a policeman who had hit an innocent person in the street while he was watching the sealing of a Jan Sangh cadre Shambhu Nath Pandey's shop.

Alfred Hemmings (Alfie), known to her through her friend Shilpa, is a foreign journalist working in India for the *Christian Science Monitor* and has sympathy for the opposition parties. He later persuades Seema to take a packet containing money to Pandey.

The writer is able to bring alive the Emergency days by describing how the opposition parties and their sympathizers worked under that reign of terror; how even a lowly maid is picked up because her daughter, in a psychic state of mind, predicted jail for Indira Gandhi; how the journalist Alfie goes missing. It was the time when you became a celebrity if you were on the side of the government, like that sweet seller Anupam became. People were under strict surveillance and so the 'special branch' is alerted when Seema goes on a rickshaw to Pandey's house some distance away from her own, resulting in the visit of a cop to her house and the institution of a court case later.

We do read about people being rounded up for vasectomy operation during the Emergency period. How some of them run out of the operation van even as a fellow is undressed makes for a funny, even though grim reminder of those black days, but it is not a detailed exposure of the Emergency days as many others like Rohinton Mistry in *A Fine Balance* have done. Daruwalla and Mistry are on the same page, even though Daruwalla obliquely criticizes Mistry as a "second rate writer" referring to the novel *Such a Long Journey*, also dealing with the Emergency days. Many journalists, historians and other writers have written a lot on the Emergency.

Swerving to Solitude now shifts to the period after Indira lost elections and the new government was formed. But what does not change is the modus operandi of the bureaucracy at whatever level. While the upper echelons have a *bhaichara* or fellow-feeling based on region, the lower functionaries, here in the police department, continue with their brash and idiotic ways. So, the cops visit Seema to record her statement as to what she knew of Pandey. It is reported that he had murdered his wife and the suspicion is that he must have been involved with some other woman, meaning Seema.

There are comments on the working of the pressmen and women in the capital and about the demographics of the capital. Quite a few chapters centre around what happened in the Press Club or Seema's reminiscences of her Balbir Uncle and her mother's past as also the several mother-father tiffs. Daruwalla reminds you of Shashi Deshpande's rummaging through family history, albeit in an ironic vein.

International Politics

Structurally, the section captioned "Mother's Journal (1910-1920)" seems dispensable, as it deals with the history of Seema's parents and grandparents, but the personal history is intertwined with the history of the immigrants in the US, Canada, and Mexico during the heady days of India's freedom movement coinciding with the eruption and ending of the First World War. The tenuous link that this section has with the main narrative appears to be to locate Seema's revolutionary DNA in her family genes and so the journal ends with: "A minority always has to rule, the mass can't rule by itself. But it is the stir among the masses that brings about a revolution. Never lose faith in October 1917" (175).

Shail's father shifted to Mexico, where Shail became secretary to M.N. Roy as she was good at Spanish language. His meeting with a certain ammunition supplier becomes the albatross around her neck. As a loyal worker, she tries to shoot some attackers too. One fine day, Roy disappears. Later, she learns from someone that he had left for Soviet Russia which was then in the making. The Mexican politics with its protagonists Madero and Diaz is described: "The country seemed a cauldron with revolutionaries going around as bandits, and bandits going around as revolutionaries" (147). An attempt has been made to highlight Roy's role as he does not find wide mention in the history of the Communist movement, according to Daruwalla. In this, it is a "reflective historical novel", as Turner would say (Dhar 1999, 18), as he is trying to fill up the gaps—little known aspects of Roy's life—through innovative details.

For Roy, however, the Communist movement mattered more at the world level rather than in the confined space of India as is evident from his comment to Ramos in which he explains why he turned a Socialist: "I thought the good of mankind, which means the proletariat, is a better cause than the good only of Indians" (142). This is also confirmed by Balbir uncle's assessment of Roy: "Shail had followed her mentor MN, who had forgotten his country, or I should say for whom revolution came first and India next" (191). True, Roy's brief surfacing in Bombay as Dr Mohammad is described but nothing of his activities in India finds mention. This disputes the committed critic Manohar Shetty's view that the novel is the story of Left-wing politics in India and that Roy tried to get support of European leaders to "expel the British from India" (Shetty 2018).

Daruwalla, a former super-cop, could not have stayed away from weaving in spy operations and so it becomes an acutely international plot with the famed Mata Hari put to work, eliciting information in bed from the S.P. Special Branch of CID Calcutta, Jeffrey Denham who is under order to arrest Roy. Shail is now under scanner for having served Roy. The story undergoes a twist at this point as it is told in the form of letters of Seema's mother retrieved from a safe locker the key to which also comes to her like it would to a spy (after all her mother had been part of the secret movement!). From the letters, Seema learns that her mother had been imprisoned in America during the days of McCarthyism.

The Emergency period is infamous in history not only for draconian laws and authoritarianism but also for height of corruption. Back to present, Seema is now dragged to court to appear as a defence witness in the case of wife's murder by the Jan Sangh member and businessman Pandey. She admits in court that she spent two nights in jail for slapping a cop, which fact gets reported in press and becomes a sticking point in her family relationship. However, Seema hits upon some disturbing skeletons in his cupboard: he had swindled a hefty amount from a Swiss bank, where his former boss—a minister had stashed away ill-gotten wealth. Seema can now relate the acquisition of an old BMW and his gifting her the expensive Swarovski crystalware and Mallorcan pearl necklace. Seema, an idealist is not able to digest this and calls it quits. This is her "swerving to solitude". She is ready to lead life alone, even though the tumult within her is not expressed in as many words as if she did not want to hurt her mother! This is indeed a tribute to the innocence and the ingenuity of the individual who dares to take her own course in life.

Taking on History

The novel *Swerving to Solitude* deals with recent history. Now, the nexus between history and fiction is an old one having originated with novelists' attempt to be faithful to history. Walter Scott's novels have been praised even by the likes of Gyorgy Lukacs for their allegiance to history. However, scope always remains to fill in the gaps left unattended by historians, who are more obsessed with the political aspects of history and deal with the high and the mighty only. Yet, the novelist was, in the past, obliged to take up historical personages or events, without which the novel would not don the glamorous "historical" tag.

At the same time, the question arose as to which period could be considered history; it won't be prudent to include the present times in history, after all. The limitation of the time period advanced by literary historians like Avrom Fleishman as around fifty years before the writing of the novel was criticized as an arbitrary and artificial categorization. Joseph Turner's distinction between documented historical novel, the disguised historical novel, and the invented historical novel broadened the area on pragmatic bases (Dhar 1999, 14-18). When the novelists took the liberty to supplant actual personages with similar ones, theorists like F.J. Tickner reminded them: "The actual personages who appear in its pages must resemble, more or less closely, the real persons of history; the fictitious characters must behave, more or less, as if they had been living at the time" (Dhar 1999, 15). An advance was made when the focus shifted from historical personages to historical time and society at large. Keeping this as background, the novelist could coin characters other than the lofty Aristotelian ones.

In postmodern times, the hierarchy is sought to be obliterated in literature and the novelists now feel free to re-write totally history and historical figures. That is an extreme position and a fake one, for it then dons the term "historical" without basing details on any evidence. This becomes crucial when recent history—still fresh in public mind—is taken up. However, there are always differing perceptions even with regard to recent past also.

Daruwalla's novel is a "historical novel" in the sense that it has a historical background and there is clear mention of the historical figures like Indira Gandhi, even though Daruwalla avers in his first novel *For Pepper and Christ*, "A historical novel is neither history nor fiction" (2009, 4). He has located his characters in different time zones. While the international politics under the section titled Mother's Diary pertains to the period 1918-22, the rest of the novel is placed in the time zone 1975 onward. As a novelist, his choice is to study its historical impact on an ordinary individual in Indian society. His interest in world history is responsible for linking an individual to a historical figure; in this case protagonist Seema's mother to M.N. Roy.

Daruwalla's thoughts on history are revealed somewhat in the present novel through Seema who comments on the biographies of contemporary politicians as a literary writer would do:

> Have started wondering about people who are still alive and kicking, reading their biographies. It will be just that swatch of politics which will show in the life of a politico, elections won and lost, parties changed (no mention of barter money) and of course none of the mistresses will be named, and if it's a woman politician, then the studs in khadi. If one is writing about Mata Hari, it will just be her affairs and espionage. What about fits of anger and spasms of regret and interludes of love? (182-83)

Indeed, history writing is very selective in content. When it comes to the biography of a historical figure, what is left out in the context of a biography is probably life itself, as Seema points out at the end of this—what should be the longest sentence in the novel:

> What of a bad dream that turns your morning tea bitter and you don't want to even touch the paper, what of failure and dejection, looking back and ruminating on destiny and how one has drifted, for we drift like a fallen leaf in the wind, we need to respect the scratch and scrape of a dry leaf as it moves with a halo of dust around it, dust and leaf propelled by the wind, like sisters drifting into marriage; a night of love kept away from the world's eyes' the fear of acne, the guilt of squeezing a pimple; and distractions—even memory and thought are distractions, you sit down to write and think of the fate of the editor, or the smell that comes from the mouth of the sub sitting in the same cubicle as you; the gallop of blood in anger or in lust; the lighting of an incense stick, the pouring of milk in the dog's bowl, or the terrible regret in the office for having forgotten to pour the milk in the dog's bowl. (183)

Daruwalla is drifting towards Eliotean theory of poetic process here.[1] There is no doubt that the adaptation of history into fiction by a novelist is also a poetic enterprise. One needs poetic imagination to seek and illuminate vague truth, and so, a novelist presents life—like characters with the help of his powerful imagination.

In postcolonial fiction writing, however, the novelist finds himself in a dilemma. There are multiple stakeholders in any political situation and siding with one invites allegations of partiality and ideological commitment from the other. If a writer is ready to withstand such insinuations, he goes ahead and we get novels like Arundhati Roy's *The Ministry of Utmost Happiness*, which, going by Roy's political activist record and the major portion of the book reveals her sympathies for the terrorists fighting a proxy war for Pakistan in Kashmir (Batra 2017).

However, the angle of ideological inclination is something that still has a bearing on any writer, unless one is way above mundane considerations and judgments. The novel *Swerving to Solitude* does hint at Daruwalla's effort to steer clear of biases. It is obviously critical of the Emergency imposed by Indira Gandhi way back in 1975. But this is a known fact that the

Left parties were in cahoots with the government at that time, as is borne out by the confession of CPI leaders: "Forty years after it had supported the Emergency, the Communist Party of India (CPI) leadership has said it was a political mistake. While CPI general secretary S. Sudhakar Reddy said the party had failed to understand political reality by supporting the Emergency, veteran party leader Gurudas Dasgupta said it was 'a great political mistake'" (Singh 2015).

The Communist sympathy for Indira Gandhi could be due to the fact that Soviet Russia provided a model of governance during the Emergency and its spies had infiltrated the Indian establishment in a big way by bribing and even honey-trapping those who mattered, as the Mitrokhin Archive papers released to public some time ago showed (Bobb 2005). The press was denied freedom and strict censorship was imposed.[2] The Jan Sangh and RSS leaders as also other followers of the movement led by Jai Prakash Narayan were behind bars and their workers were hounded. According to a historian, "The Emergency was followed by arrest of over 10,000 opponents of the government. There were countrywide arrests of non-CPI opposition leaders and some Congressmen. The government also imposed pre-censorship of the news under the Emergency Proclamation" (Aggarwala 1985, 80). The officials put in charge of censorship would screen news minutely and issued from time to time a number of instructions to newspapers regarding what was to be published and what not. Journalist Kuldip Nayar's book *Emergency Retold* reproduces many such instructions verbatim (2016, 295-320). Even leaving blank space after censor had scissored certain news item was declared a crime (77).

Here, in the novel, if the protagonist Seema is Left-leaning, her antipathy to the Emergency regime is hardly justifiable from historical point of view. However, her action in saving a Jan Sangh functionary and helping him unconsciously suggests a measure of transcendentality to her—but just a measure—for the help is rendered without any idea of Pande's political affiliation. As an enlightened intellectual, Seema seems to be unconcerned about the social taboos and prejudices and has the gumption to take on the world. That is why she obliges Alfred and goes to deliver the packet to Pandey's house.

Daruwalla's aversion to present-day BJP leadership is evident in the form of a forecast from the minor character Elham, who, true to her name, has intuition or dreams which foretell the fate of Indira Gandhi. The latter's loss at hustings and her death are forecast by her leading to threat to her own life too. The novel concludes with one such dream which she is coaxed to share with Seema: "A huge man riding on a wild donkey, with a *barcha* in his hand, a *barcha* with three spearheads, with lots of followers also on wild asses, will be riding towards Delhi" (234). Here, the present Prime Minister is portrayed as leading a crowd of trident-wielding people on ass-backs, but Daruwalla desists from naming Narendra Modi. That is a fictionist's artistic privilege to keep the veil on and yet make intent clear!

Secondly, there is not much detail of the behind-the-scene machinations of politicians—Indira Gandhi's coterie,[3] for example, which helped her maintain the Emergency regime. This is in contrast to his earlier novel *Ancestral Affairs* in which politics at the highest level in the state of Junagadh has been depicted in great detail. The description of the events that unfold in the wake of the declaration of Partition is indeed absorbing and realistic in that novel. Daruwalla spent four years as a child in Junagadh and while writing the novel, he was privy to the then Commissioner of Junagadh's papers received from the latter's son as Daruwalla declares in the Acknowledgements' section of that book.

Daruwalla, a retired senior government official having worked with the Prime Minister's Office besides holding other important charges in the police department under the Home Ministry is witness to a lot and has the status of an insider. His ethnicity aligns him to an elite minority of India—the Parsi community. His poetic interests bring him closer to the ground so that he can empathize with ordinary people and provide the reader with insight into philosophical musings. Going by this yardstick, there appears no reason to believe that Daruwalla does not have knowledge of the goings-on at the highest level.

He could share more information about the way Emergency was imposed or perpetuated for 19 months but he has chosen not to step into that area.

Conclusion

As a novelist, Daruwalla is influenced by the novella form, so that in his novels, one can easily identify two distinguishable narratives brought together at some point. In *Ancestral Affairs*, it was the life story of a father and son, the former neck-deep in politics of Junagadh state and the latter knee-deep in youthful love. Here, in the present novel, the story of the daughter crosses the story of the mother as also the grandmother. Ironically, while the mother is a helper in the communist movement in Mexico, the daughter is at the receiving end of the Communist Party of India-supported Emergency regime in India.

On the whole, the novel is an artistic tour de force. Daruwalla's innovative style in making the protagonist address her dead mother has the advantage of her being truthful in a uniquely endearing way. Seema becomes a child when she writes the narrative for her mother: "The police call it embossing, Mama. So does the army. Ever heard the term?" (14) or "There has to be more to a family than just your name, Mama" (100). But she also abstains from using overmuch mushiness probably for fear of upsetting her mom! In this and elsewhere too, the writer has maintained a distance that is able to bring in a kind of alienation effect that Bertolt Brecht would have been jealous of.

The language of the novel is befittingly colloquial—something that comes as a surprise for readers of Daruwalla's short stories and even many poems couched in rather difficult English. The novelist uses Indianized English portmanteaus like "dialoguewala", words redolent of spoken English like "pheemale" (13), and coinages like "debussed", etc. A poet's rich fund of similes and metaphors is there for the readers to enjoy, as for example, "Dreams or hallucinations also come in series, like M.F. Husain's paintings on horses" (44), or "The Nation is a bank without guards, don't you see?" (144). The pen pictures with a touch of poetry are so haunting:

> Remember it was winter, grass yellowing, trees black-barked, a wisp of a ground mist that vanished soon. I was observing the scene, goat tracks scissoring away from the main road, pine needles soggy because of a shower, straggling shrubbery. In the town, I remember a dhaba cook slapping dough on an inverted griddle, a shuttered paan kiosk being opened lazily by a Tamboli in his dhoti, a chained Bhotia dog who did not bark at us, meaning driver and me, a goitered hill woman carrying fire wood on her head. (72)

The novel is full of witty wisecracks with symbolic undertone. When the protagonist, making an analogy of the captured house rats, comments that "Those who know they are boxed in deserve another chance. It is only those who are unaware of being trapped who don't deserve a thing" (77), we can sense Seema's rebellious nature. Also, Daruwalla's characteristic wit is reflected all over the novel: "The past has a habit of digging its way up like a rodent sometimes" (144). "His thoughts tumbling over each other like boulders in an avalanche" (153). A country becomes backward because of backward beliefs which sit on our shoulders like Baital on the shoulders of Vikramaditya" (185). Daruwalla takes a dig at the Parsi community too. They used to be fighters once, he says, now they only fight in courts! (203).

It is a lively narrative laced with humour that keeps the reader engaged. This novel balances the political and the personal in a charming manner. The narrative is indeed "nuanced with just the right measure of storytelling elements that highlight an engaging perspective on politics, history and human beings, in this order" (Puri 2018).

NOTES

1. T.S. Eliot wrote on the poetic process in his famous essay "The Metaphysical Poets": "When a poet's mind is perfectly equipped for its work, it is constantly amalgamating disparate experience; the ordinary mind's experience is chaotic, irregular and fragmentary. The latter falls in love, or reads Spinoza and these two experiences have nothing to do with each other, or with the noise of the typewriter or the smell of cooking; in the mind of the poet the experiences are always forming new wholes" (1951, 287).

2. Regarding censorship, writer Nayantara Sahgal noted: "The censors in New Delhi and the state capitals whose job it is to black out news and opinions inconvenient to the government—and they cover the whole territory of newspapers, magazines, commentary, fiction, theatre and films—may be dispensed with once the emergency is lifted, but control of all media will continue. Radio and television are government monopoly in any case, and in the past Mrs. Gandhi has used them blatantly to promote herself and her party and distort happenings in India. Now a single news agency, *Samachar*, feeds the press in India with official handouts. Respected editors have been thrown out of their jobs and replaced by sycophants, and newspaper management, already government manipulated will soon be its complete tool in what the minister for information and broadcasting picturesquely describes as re-structuring and entire newspaper industry so as to make accountable to the people" (1997, 141).

   Eminent author Shashi Tharoor, now a Congress leader, has to his credit the following criticism in his allegorical novel *The Great Indian Novel*: "Duryodhani censored the press, stifled public debate, and placed restrictions even on the reporting of the speeches of the few opposition stalwarts left in the House to criticize the new laws she was bulldozing through parliament like the steel-rimmed Chakras of an invincible juggernaut" (1989, 372).

3. Indira Gandhi's coterie, also called "'Kitchen Cabinet' was the expanded version of the 'Back-Benchers Club', formed during the Shastri years. Her Kitchen Cabinet, a wheel within the wheel, comprised of Dinesh Singh, I.K. Gujral, Nandhini Satpati and Ali Ahmed. This 'Nucleus of Power' assisted and advised the Prime Minister Indira Gandhi's crucial decision making" (Miller 2016).

   Regarding the coterie of Sanjay Gandhi (Indira Gandhi's son and extra-constitutional authority during the Emergency period), John Dayal (2015), co-author of a book on Emergency observes in an online article: "Sanjay Gandhi never occupied any office in government when his mother imposed the Emergency. He was not a Member of Parliament at that time. And though several members of the Youth Congress became part of his coterie, and threw their weight about, the people 'obeying' his orders were cabinet ministers, senior bureaucrats, ranking police officers. Among them were ministers such as Vidya Charan Shukla, in charge of Information and Broadcasting; Om Mehta, the junior minister for Home Affairs; Jagmohan, the vice chairman of the Delhi Development Authority; PS Bhinder, a top functionary of Delhi Police; Municipal Commissioner B.R. Tamta; and the governors, chief ministers and chief secretaries of several states" (2015).

REFERENCES

Adiga, Aravind. *The White Tiger*. New Delhi: Harper Collins, 2018.

Aggarawala, Satish C. *Legacy of Indira Gandhi*. New Delhi: Socialist Age Publishers, 1985.

Batra, Jagdish. "A Politico-literary Response to Terrorism: A Study of Arundhati Roy's *The Ministry of Utmost Happiness*", *Humanities and Social Sciences Review*, Vol. 7, No. 2 (Dec. 2017). <www.universitypublications.net/hssr/0702/index.html>

Bobb, Dilip. "Book on KGB unveils Russian agency's ops in India during Cold War, political storm ensues." *India Today*. 3 Oct., 2005. <https://www.indiatoday.in/magazine/nation/story/20051003-mitrokhin-archive-kgb-operations-in-india-during-cold-war-786931-2005-10-03>

Daruwalla, Keki N. *For Christ and Pepper*. New Delhi: Penguin, 2009.

——. *Ancestral Affairs*. Noida: HarperCollins, 2015.

——. *Swerving to Solitude: Letters to Mama*. London: Simon & Schuster, 2018.

Dayal, John. "What drove Sanjay Gandhi and his coterie during the Emergency". *Scroll.in* 26 June, 2015 <https://scroll.in/article/735576/what-drove-sanjay-gandhi-and-his-coterie-during-the-emergency>

Dhar, T.N. *History-Fiction Interface in Indian English Novel*. New Delhi, Prestige, 1999.

Eliot, T.S. *Selected Essays*. London: Faber & Faber, 1951, reprint 1986.

Miller, Diane Cynthiya. "Indira Gandhi: First Woman Prime Minister (1966-1971)". AIDCC 18.11.16. <http://www.indiancommunities.org/2016/11/18/indira-gandhi-first-woman-prime-minister-1966-1971/>

Mistry, Rohinton. *Such a Long Journey*. London: Faber & Faber, 1992.

——. *A Fine Balance*. London: Faber & Faber, 1995.

Nayar, Kuldip. *Emergency Retold*. New Delhi: Konark, 1977, Fourth Impression 2016.

Puri, Suparna-Saraswati. "Facts, fiction & a heady concoction". Review of *Swerving to Solitude. The Sunday Tribune*, 2 December 2018, p. 10.

Roy, Arundhati. *The Ministry of Utmost Happiness*. New Delhi: Penguin, 2017.

Sahgal, Nayantara. *Point of View: A Personal Response to life, Literature and Politics*. New Delhi: Prestige Books, 1997.

Shetty, Manohar. "Lessons from history". Review of *Swerving to Solitude*. Literary Review, *The Hindu*. 28 October 2018.

Singh, Shiv Sahay. "Supporting Emergency was a Mistake: CPI Leaders". *The Hindu*, National. 27 June, 2015. <https://www.thehindu.com/news/national/supporting-emergency-was-a-mistake-cpi-leaders/article7359292.ece>

Tharoor, Shashi. *The Great Indian Novel*. New Delhi: Penguin, 1989.

9

Jhumpa Lahiri's *The Lowland*: Exploring Dark Recesses of Mind

Jhumpa Lahiri's second novel *The Lowland* is a deeply disturbing novel that was shortlisted for the Man Booker prize. It is an epical story covering sixty years in the lives of four generations of a Bengali family located in two continents—India and America. Also it is a saga of love that survives for a surprisingly long period of time after the death of the beloved. The novel presents the predicament of dashed hopes of parents left behind in India, problematic family ties in America and above all, a contrast between an idealist frame of mind and a practical one. While it is a powerful novel that tries to capture the confused undercurrents of mind of its principal characters, it fails to account for the problems it raises, most of all the moral question. The novel has double foci—the rise of Naxalite movement in India and the life of Indian characters in the US. For this purpose, some critics treat it as a political novel but far more than the cursory treatment of the political events, the major focus shifts to the minds of key characters who are placed in the US even as they retain family links in India.

The novel derives its title from a geographical feature near Udayan's house in Tollygunge area of Calcutta. At this place, water got accumulated during rainy season. The vegetation called water hyacinth would cover the water and because of its dense growth, the surface would give the semblance of solid ground covered with green leaves. That, of course, was an illusion. This seems to hint at the illusive calm prevailing in society which may camouflage tumult and turbulence underneath. In another way, the title misleads the reader into believing it to be only a locale-specific work, which it is to some extent, but more than that, it gives a peep into the muddy and dark recesses of mind. This area also has two ponds which signify two brothers who resemble each other in looks but who are poles apart in their thoughts and life graphs.

Even though the novel starts with and substantially lingers over the lives of male characters, it misleads one into believing it to be hero-centric novel. Coupled with her remarkable treatment of male protagonist Gogol and a pervasive male point of view in Lahiri's first novel *The Namesake*, the impression grows upon the reader that *The Lowland* too undertakes a deep study of male mind. Instead, Lahiri goes whole hog into drawing powerful female characters, viz. Gauri and Bela in the present novel. The central issue to be probed in this piece is why the two behave the way they do.

In comparison to *The Lowland*, Lahiri's first novel *The Namesake* succeeded in accounting for the wayward ways of Moushumi. From a reserved and shy girl at school to an unrepentant flirt post-college, the obedient Bengali girl had been thoroughly Americanized under the pressure of host culture. It happened the same way with Gogol, who faced acute frustration due to his name because of taunts from his fellow students until the moment his father revealed the secret even as the actual acceptance happened only after his father's death. In *The Lowland*, while Bela's character is understandable, her mother Gauri's remains highly complicated and incomprehensible. She had seen her husband being shot at a distance by the cops. Had it made her insensitive to human feelings? We are not given a peep into her mind. The novel gives more of externals, which again is a mirage-like impression created by a master story-teller.

Brothers

The novel starts with snippets of shared life experiences of two teenage brothers Subhash and Udayan. The period is of 1960s and the location is Calcutta. Born fifteen months apart, these children of Bengali parents settled in Calcutta are immensely friendly with each other. Their various peccadilloes like transgressing the bounds of an elite club to steal a golf ball or watching glamorous actresses at the film studio are realistically portrayed. Both the children are interested in science and conduct experiments at home. They also set right home appliances. In the streets of Tollygunge, they wander before dusk and in the hyacinth-strewn pond they play for hours on end. Udayan is always in his elder brother's sight. That is in keeping with their parents' instruction "not to lose sight of one another" (10). We have two young brothers having identical features and voice but very different in their worldview—Subhash is conformist who goes along with society and its ways, on the other hand Udayan is a restless soul.

As they grow up, Udayan, the impulsive and somewhat troublesome child for parents, feels attracted towards Naxalite movement—a brand of communism inspired by Mao-Tse Tung of China—which preached a violent end to capitalist class. So committed is Udayan to the ideology that he would risk his all—his married life, his pregnant wife, his brother and parents—to work for the party. However, Subhash is not interested in this ideology. Even when he is taken by his brother to attend meetings, he feels ill at ease and remains politically inactive.

Gauri is the female protagonist in the novel. She comes in contact with Udayan through her brother Manish. Their house is near the college where Udayan is studying Physics. Subhash, on the other hand, goes to the Rhode Island in USA to study Chemistry. Rhode Island, incidentally is the area where the writer Jhumpa Lahiri spent most of her unmarried life. The novelty of the place, lifestyle and culture overwhelm Subhash even as he fails to find any linkage between what he finds in his host country and back home in the country of his birth. He comes to India after learning about the killing of his brother at the hands of the police. It is here that he thinks seriously about re-settling Udayan's wife Gauri who is pregnant. Much against the wishes of his parents, he marries Gauri and takes her to the States to usher her into a new life (186). He believes she would be able to forget Udayan's tragedy and find meaning in life but he is proved wrong. Even when he took her as wife, she seemed lost in herself and was rather doubtful about the outcome of Subhash's proposal. He had to assure her that he would not go against her wishes and that she would be free to lead her own kind of life. In the US, bringing her round to a wife's ways was a painfully long, and finally an unsuccessful affair.

Gauri

The part of the story dealing with Gauri's life in America is a journey from her silent, inchoate state to an Americanized libertine. What it misses out on is the signpost of Subhash's wife; the train seems to have sped past this station. Finally, when they are able to unite physically, it is almost a one-sided affair and Gauri's response remains uncertain. Later, she plunges herself into study of philosophy rather than taking up any radical role of a political activist as her late husband Udayan had been. She has a rather single-track mind that remains obsessed with academics to the extent that she forsakes her daughter, Bela, whom she had begotten with Udayan.

The novel records Gauri's escape into a thoroughly academic world when she suddenly walked out on her second husband one day leaving behind her child from her first husband. The novelist does not give the reader a glimpse into her consciousness. Her thinking is interpreted by the writer. The objective third person narrative has its plus points but when a psychological issue of this type is under scanner, the intimate inscape portrayal of the character involved in the form of interior monologue becomes a necessity. As it is, one has to gather it all from Gauri's tangible actions only. Gauri is portrayed as a free-willed person who wishes to abjure the self-cultivated obsession of sanctifying Udayan's memory through abstinence:

> She slept with him [Subhash] because it had become more of an effort not to. She wanted to terminate the expectations she'd begun to sense from him. Also to extinguish Udayan's ghost. To smother *what haunted her.*
>
> Nothing in their lovemaking had reminded her of Udayan, so that in the end, the fact that they had been brothers was not so strange. There was the focus of seeking pleasure and the numbing effect, once they were finished, removing all specific

> thoughts from her brain. It ushered in the solid, dreamless sleep that otherwise eluded her. (Emphasis added 161)

Granted that she started living life at the Lawrentian plane of physicality, what was it that haunted her mentally that the above lines indicate? Did she consider herself responsible for her husband's murder? Were these the pangs of conscience over marrying her dead husband's brother on being approached by him? The writer resorts to the artist's prerogative of avoiding a direct answer. An explanation could be that Subhash's parents had not been able to reconcile to this decision and Gauri was deep in grief over Udayan's murder and yielded to Subhash's altruistic step but later rued her decision. If this were the case, there was no point in taking to lovers freely in America after having deserted her second husband. Was it also the 'numbing effect' she found in Subhash's company that worked as intoxicant to forget the moral question she faced? But what of the child she got from Udayan? If she was deep in love with the memory of her dead husband, Bela should have been a precious legacy for her. How could she forsake her?

Subhash, on the other hand, devoted himself wholeheartedly to bringing up Bela, playing the dual role of mother and father to her. When Bela wants a babysitter for her daughter, Subhash disagrees; he would rather himself look after her. Gauri's reaction is to be noted here: "And so she felt antagonized by a man who did nothing to antagonize her, and by Bela, who did not even know the meaning of the word" (164). This is a quizzical streak in Gauri's character which hints at jealousy of a mother who had failed to tend to her daughter properly.

Gauri, it would be seen, was unemotional, as when Bela threw tantrum one day and would not go to school. She grasped her hand tightly and dragged her to the school bus. It is suggested that the bloody scenes of Calcutta had steeled her: "I watched your father killed before my eyes, she might have said" (170). Is it the same callousness that enables her to walk over her living husband? If yes, then it sits ill with her touted emotional attachment with her dead husband. She was least bothered about Subhash's sensitivity when she decided to give herself a new look. On the other hand, on seeing a middle-aged man, she feels attracted which shows her lack of moral scruples—something indicated as the reason for her lack of union with Subhash, who had done so much for her.

Gauri wanted to be independent. For that matter, she started leaving Bela for a short jaunt to the store around the corner. This short furlough expanded to many minutes of absence from home, leaving child Bela to fend for herself. When Subhash found her missing one day, he was shaken and "it took Subhash, who was standing at the window, his back to the room, several minutes before he turned around" (175). He could sense the insensitivity in Gauri's character. "The wide berth for herself that she had been seeking in their marriage, he now willingly gave. He no longer wanted to touch her in bed, he no longer brought up the possibility of a second child" (176). The gulf between the two was widening fast now.

One can believe that this changed attitude was not entirely due to the past traumatic experience; perhaps the American individualism pervading the society of their adopted land had given a fillip to it. Things would have been different in case she had stayed on in India. Ironically, she leaves home when Subhash and Bela are in India on a short visit following his father's death. Gauri had stayed back apparently due to her dissertation work. Walking over her husband is not the only thing that throws in bold relief the streak of insensitivity in Gauri's character, the novelist traces it in her life till many years later also. Leaving her daughter Bela and not even thinking of her for many years is something which does not easily appeal to mind.

The writer seems to have yielded to what is termed as the character growing out of the mould cast by the writer. Gauri's moral dilemma does not stay for long. That is despite her study and teaching of philosophy about mind and time, and about Plato and Descartes. The writer admits: "Her ideology was isolated from practice, neutered by its long tenure in the academy long ago, she had wanted her work to be in deference to Udayan but by now it was a betrayal of everything he had believed in all the ways he had influenced and inspired her, shrewdly cultivated for her own intellectual gain" (234). Can we say the time is a great healer or that heart follows its own drumbeats so that the conflict between mind and heart or thoughts and emotions is endlessly playout out in life?

As a researcher and later as a professor, she does not uphold or teach any revolutionary ideals. Gauri takes to American ways instead. She gets hair cut according to the fashion prevailing there, throws away her saris and attempts to lose herself in the study of philosophy. Ironically, feeling of isolation comforts her as the writer mentions: "Isolation offered its own form of companionship: the reliable silence of her rooms, the steadfast tranquility of the evenings" (165). She enjoys sexual freedom and "juggled lovers" (237), though she does not allow them to complicate her life through conception, a fiercely freedom-loving woman that she is. She also has lesbian liaison with her graduate student Lorna. Clearly, the high moral ground is no longer available to Gauri when the novelist examines "moral conundrums inherent in violent revolution" (Seaman). Despite the passage of so many years, Gauri does not think of seeing her daughter. She has developed craze for unbridled freedom. According to a critic:

> Her life had always been stretched to the extremities by choice or circumstances. While her elder sisters led a normal life with her parents, she was brought up in her grandparents' house and she felt a sense of autonomy. Later, she had felt audacious eloping with Udayan, flaunting conventions. With Udayan's death, she felt, the ligaments that had held her life together had perished. Now her impulsive and calculated decision to be Subhash's wife, to flee to America with him, and with that action also to flee from Tollygunge, to forget everything her life had been, she felt even more extreme. (Pius 7)

Bela

Contrary to Gauri, her daughter Bela is an intellectual type who would use knowledge for the betterment of the marginalized people. She had done her major in environmental science and her senior thesis was on the effect of pesticides in a local river.

Instead of studying further at the graduate level, she chooses her own path. She rejects, like her father Udayan did, a comfortable family life and at twenty-one, she joins not a revolutionary group but the Peace Corps. She works on the farm—irrigating field, harvesting crop, cleaning animal pens, etc. She moves from one farm to the other across different states in America. She does not mind if she is paid a pittance or just provided food and shelter as compensation. She is virtually a nomad but when she visits home, she tries to apply green technology to areas of daily life.

Bela's description of self is interesting. She tells Drew, the farmer for whom she falls finally, that "she'd been created by two people who'd loved one another, she'd been raised by two who never did" (299). Bela is initially angry towards Subhash, her foster father, as she believes him to be responsible for driving out her mother and not trying to win her back. The revelation about the identity of Bela's father happens quite late. When Subhash's father dies, he and Bela journey to Calcutta, where Subhash's mother, Bijoli, nearly reveals that Udayan is Bela's father. When Bela asks about Udayan, Subhash tells a lie that Udayan is her uncle who is no more. The turnaround comes when she becomes pregnant and envisioning complications ahead, Subhash tells her about her real father, viz. Udayan. On learning that Subhash is not her real father, Bela is devastated.

Bela keeps in touch with people including Subhash on her own terms though she appreciates Subhash's parenting. This is borne out later, when she becomes an unwed mother but does not care to be in touch with the father of the child. On being asked about the reason, she says, "The father was not a part of her life, not aware of her condition. He was simply someone Bela had known, with whom she had been involved. She did not want to inform him because "he's not the kind of father I want for my child [...]. He's nothing like you," she tells Subhash (263).

By the time Bela is thirty-three and Subhash sixty years old, Gauri visits her abandoned family. The shame—something unexplained in the novel—"that had flooded her veins was permanent. She would never be free from that. Ultimately, she had come seeking Bela. She'd come to ask about Bela's life, to ask Subhash if she might contact her now. To ask if there was a phone number, an address to which she might write. To ask if Bela might be open to this, before it was too late" (306-07). Subhash was away with Elise, whom he had married lately, for a walk. Meghna, Bela's young daughter was there along with her mother who was doing household chores. As expected, she got a mouthful from Bela.

It was the encounter of two women who fiercely guarded their freedom, which meant self-sufficiency, meaning as much truck with fellow beings as was adequate for self-fulfilment and sexual satisfaction. Is that possible? It is a teaser. The difference existed in that whereas Bela had chosen a vocation which directly served the downtrodden and the marginalized, Gauri had grown into a smug intellectual given to academic pursuits. Does Lahiri place active social work above passive intellectualism? Another teaser. Bela could appreciate parental emotions and desired to give to her daughter the same care and love which she had not got from her mother.

Therefore as Gauri entered, the first salvo fired by Bela was a poser: "Why have you come here?" (312) and asked her to get out! Gauri did try to explain but Bela would have none of it. She said she knew about Udayan, meaning she did not find the reason of Gauri's callousness following Udayan's death a substantial excuse. "You're not my mother. You're nothing," she told her mother and added, "You're as dead to me as he is" (312-13).

The terse reception must have shaken Gauri, for she goes to Calcutta thereafter, as if on a pilgrimage for penance: "She was the sole accuser, the sole guardian of her guilt. Protected by Udayan, overlooked by the investigator, taken away by Subhash? Sentenced in the very act of being forgotten, punished by means of her release" (320). This summing up of her life will not convince many, for clearly it was she herself who had accused own conscience for not standing behind Udayan. She also remembered Bela's sarcastic assessment of her existence;

for her Gauri did not exist. She even told her daughter Meghna that Gauri is her great aunt, not her grandmother. So, it is also the tale of abjuring of parental responsibilities on the part of Gauri that offends Bela.

Gauri's tormented self had enveloped the entire family. Standing in Calcutta, she aspires for annihilation of remnants of self and contemplates suicide, to achieve "the bond of not existing" (320); to be one with Udayan in this way:

> She leaned forward. She saw the spot where she would fall. She recalled the thrill of meeting him, of being adored by him. The moment of losing him. The fury of learning how he'd implicated her. The ache of bringing Bela into the world, after he was gone.
>
> She opened her eyes. He was not there. (323)

These actions do not seem convincing, for if there was ever a moral question haunting her, it had faded over decades of her life in America. The pattern is akin to Hamlet's inaction for which T.S. Eliot had faulted Shakespeare and called the play "an artistic failure" (Eliot 1951). So, her late visits to Bela and to Calcutta fit ill with her unabashed material existence in America. Mercifully, the writer debunks her scruples and makes her return to Rhode Island. As a postscript, the novelist introduces Meghna's innocent query about Gauri along with Bela's assurance to Gauri that when "Meghna is older, when she and I are both ready, we can try to meet again" (325). The future must not be written down in stone, for who cannot change?

Understanding Gauri

The character of Gauri is full of dark recesses. In this regard, it would be fruitful to go through what motivated Lahiri to write this novel.

> Lahiri says the book is based on a tragic incident she first heard about in India, during one of her many visits while she was growing up. Two young brothers, who had become involved in a violent political movement, were executed just a few hundred yards from her grandparents' home in Calcutta. The young men's family was forced to watch as they were

> killed. "That was the scene that, when I first heard of it, when it was described to me, was so troubling and so haunted me—and ultimately inspired me to write the book, [...] I wanted to understand what it might have been like to witness something like that, and what the consequences would be of witnessing something like that...I mean, she's a 23-year-old woman. She's in love with her revolutionary husband. She watches him shot in cold blood. She discovers after the fact that she is carrying his child. How does one move on from that?" (Neary)

This is indeed a worthwhile issue that Lahiri has taken up. Visualizing Gauri's future in the US, in the aftermath of the tragic incident in India, is a macro form of what Ashima in *The Namesake* felt when she got the message on the telephone about the sudden death of her husband due to heart failure. He had gone there with the complaint of minor stomach problem and she never expected this to happen. Ashima's reaction is to be noted:

> Instead of answering, Ashima hangs up the phone as the woman is still speaking, pressing down the receiver as hard as she can into the cradle, keeping her hand there for a full minute, as if to smother the words she's just heard. [...] She begins to shiver violently, the house instantly feeling twenty degrees colder. She pulls her sari tightly around her shoulders, like a shawl. She gets up and walks systematically through the rooms of the house, turning on all the light switches, turning on the lamppost on the lawn and floodlight over the garage, as if she and Ashoke are expecting company. (*The Namesake* 169)

Going by this type of physical response to a crisis should be a temporary affair but then in case of Gauri, it goes on for too long and what is more, her deep-settled love along with the moral scruples attached to it get dissolved at times while at other times, these crop up, demanding the reader's suspension of disbelief.

One reductive argument that might fit in is that the twin characters of Bela and Gauri are illustrations of the twin elements—heredity and environment—in the theory of evolution.

In case of Gauri, we do not know of her lineage and the composition of DNA. All that we know is that she was witness to the horrendous act which took away her husband's life. This came as a climax to her earlier exposure to Naxalite environs of Calcutta, where she barely escaped getting victimized herself. Udayan's death was a big shock for her. Her transportation to USA and the consequent change of milieu did not bring her to the golden mean of life; instead she swung to the other extreme, getting thoroughly Americanized and living life as a free animal but not without periodic U-turns.

Gauri's scruples of loyalty to her late husband taper off over a period of time. When she starts sleeping with other lovers, it is definitely time for her to shed the masquerade. And yet she desists from patching up with Subhash and Bela and merrily goes on with her newly acquired American sense of fulfilment in life—something for which she is thankful to American environment. The only word that represents her nature vis-à-vis Subhash is selfish.

Bela, on the other hand, appears a mixed copy of her parents. There are hints thrown in by the writer "Behaving as Gauri used to do" (214). Heredity expresses itself in her altruistic mission to help the destitute just as her father Udayan was moved by the plight of the downtrodden in India and had taken to a radical path that appeared to him to be the only remedy in the Indian condition. She swims against the materialist current in America and feels impressed by an 18th century cult preaching celibacy and simple life, though she amends the celibacy injunction herself later on. That is her take on radicalism of her father joined to free-wheeling lifestyle of her mother. She has steely determination like her mother and refuses to have any truck with her mother Gauri or the nameless father of her child. Heredity, it may be mentioned, depends on the gene pool of quite a few generations; as such it becomes sometimes quizzical to link a particular trait to one's immediate parents.

However, if these characters could be strictly subsumed under either of the two rubrics, viz. heredity and environment, they would be flat and wooden. As it is, we find the characters growing and changing. We know that heredity and environment act together in different proportions. Great advances have been and continue to be made in unravelling the functioning of human mind in our times. Psychologists like William James, Sigmund Freud, Jacques Lacan, etc. have contributed greatly to our understanding of the subconscious that guides the conscious mind. And yet it presents an enigma. We believe now that human action may depend upon any immediate or past experience, thought, emotion, instinct—repressed or raw—stored in the unconscious. Therefore, writers today abstain from portraying fixed characters; they live moment to moment only. In *The Lowland*, Lahiri presents an interesting psychological case study. Indeed, one tends to agree with the *Washington Post* reviewer who comments: "The worlds of the familiar, the exotic, the best of human nature and the most selfish inhabit Jhumpa Lahiri's new novel, *The Lowland*" (Lothar).

Conclusion

In conclusion, it can be said that the novel *The Lowland* is another classic from Jhumpa Lahiri. She touches upon multiple themes like political violence, parenting woes, fractured relationships of brother from brother, husband from wife, mother from daughter torn asunder, and the struggle to appropriate the identity of a parent (Is Subhash or Udayan uncle or father/ Is Gauri grandmother or grand aunt?), etc. One can't call it a Greek tragedy where destiny totally controls lives, for here we find ample scope for individual choices which are indeed made by all the characters.

It is clear that rather than exploring the political problem, Lahiri's intent in this novel is the exploration of the dark recesses of mind of various characters. In this, while the reader can easily co-relate the thoughts and actions of characters like Udayan, Subhash, their parents, and even Bela, those of Gauri are simply intriguing. For most part, she is quiet or reticent and the reader has to figure out her thoughts from her actions—very much in the vein of Eliot's Objective Correlatives (Eliot 1951). Lahiri abstains from entering herself in the narrative or giving a hint about the real nature of a character. Her prose description is economical which is her signature style and is admittedly a valuable feature, for it "shows" rather than "telling" and thereby gives the reader ample opportunity to muse over these issues and take own decision.

The problem arises with regard to Gauri because her actions are not straight—her abundant love for Udayan which survived his death to the extent that she wanted to commit suicide but drew her steps back because "he was not there" (323), her reluctance in marrying Subhash, having married him her loathing of physical relationship, her aloofness from relatives including her own daughter from her beloved past husband Udayan, then going whole hog for relationships with others culminating in lesbian relationship with her student. Was that final step the reality about her nature. If so, why did she choose to marry Udayan, and then Subhash? The several occasions that provide opportunity for rapprochement between these characters at odd with each other are simply rebuffed. As Subhash develops love for Bela. Gauri distances herself from Bela. She behaved as if "she'd reversed their roles, as if Bela were a relative's child and not her own" (159).

Gauri's actions remind one of Virginia Woolf's famous quote: "Life is not a series of gig lamps symmetrically arranged; life is a luminous halo, a semitransparent envelope surrounding us from the beginning of consciousness to the end" (159), but even this luminous halo comprises several shades mixed in irregular proportions! We may dismiss this kind of portrayal of this character as being symbolic of the writer's own failure in appropriating the character because she was, after all, trying to understand the goings-on in the mind of such a character who faced real-life murder, or the portrayal grew out of the planned mould, or we may agree with T.S. Eliot when he makes obscurity an important feature of a poem—by extension of a literary work! Eliot admitted the use of obscurity as an important poetic feature and so avoided any direct expression of ideas in preference to impressions only, being an impressionist. He says, "I am no better qualified to say No! [to any interpretation] than is any other reader" (Eliot 1944). So, the jury is still out and the reader is the jury for *The Lowland*!

WORKS CITED

Eliot, T.S. *The Use of Poetry and the Use of Criticism*. Faber & Faber Ltd., 1944.

——. "Hamlet," *Selected Essays*. London: Faber and Faber, 1951, reprint 1986.

Lahiri, Jhumpa. *The Lowland*. NOIDA: Random, 2013.

——. *The Namesake*. NOIDA, India: HarperCollins, 2003, reprint 2012.

Lothar, Corrina. Book Review: *The Lowland*. *Washington Times*. 31 November 2013. <http://www.washingtontimes.com/news/2013/oct/31/book-review-the-Lowland/#ixzz2lwBISieE>

Neary, Lynn. Author Interviews. "Political Violence, Uneasy Silence Echo in Lahiri's 'Lowland'." *NPR*. 23 September 2013. <https://www.npr.org/2013/09/23/224404507/political-violence-uneasy-silence-echo-in-lahiris-lowland>

Pius, T.K. Jhumpa Lahiri's *The Lowland*: A Critical Analysis. *IOSR Journal of Humanities and Social Science*, Vol. 19.10 (2014), pp. 100-17.

Seaman, Donna. Litlovers. 'Lowland (Lahiri)—book reviews'. n.d. 28 November 2013. <http://www.litlovers.com/reading-guides/13-fiction/9392-lowland-lahiri?start=2>

Woolf, Virginia. "Modern Fiction" (1925). *Essays of Virginia Woolf*, Vol. 4 (1925-1928), ed. Andrew Mcneille. London: Hogarth Press, 1984, pp. 157-65.

10

Aravind Adiga's *The White Tiger*: Re-writing Canon!

The White Tiger indeed represents India as a cheap Bollywood movie would. Besides, it is also couched in the Bollywood type language, lacking a certain standard. It is not merely the lop-sided treatment of the Indian reality but also making an irrational rogue the hero of the novel that should and did raise hackles. Written in the form of a series of emails from the desk of "The White Tiger" described as "A Thinking Man and an Entrepreneur", for Wen Jiabao, Premier of the "Freedom-Loving Nation of China", these details at the beginning of Adiga's first novel arouse eyebrows. However, the initial surprise subsides when one notices that the character writing the epistles is a quirky driver, now running a taxi-service for the call-centre employees of Bangalore. The reason for the narrator Balram approaching him with the dark secrets of his heart is that Mr. Jiabao is visiting India to learn a thing or two about entrepreneurship and Balram has volunteered on his own to enlighten him in this regard as if China was in need of it!

Leaving aside the flimsy excuse for finding a fantastic addressee, the one outstanding feature of the novel is the portrayal of the mindscape of the semi-literate chauffeur Balram, in a befitting language, focalizing suitably the narrative to denote the age of the protagonist at various points of time. He is supposed to represent the nameless poor Indian who resents the audacious display of riches around him. Based in a metropolitan city, he retains his links with his native village, though Balram takes a cue from the evil ways of the prosperous and murders his master for the sake of money.

The first chapter uses the props provided by a police look-out poster for Balram. So, his village in the district of Bodh-Gaya, his own dress, the thirty-six million (Adiga confuses lakhs for millions but then for the foreign readers it might be helpful!) plus deities worshipped here, the colour-blind, bungling police personnel, etc. come in for mention. Also he tells us, via his epistles addressed to Jiabao that he got his nick-name "The White Tiger" because he was good at studies but then the corrupt school inspector pocketed his scholarship money and he was forced to work at a tea-stall as a "human spider" (reminiscent of Indra Sinha's "Animal" in *Animal's People*). It was here that he learnt the lesson of chicanery and dishonesty. Later, he migrated to Dhanbad and learnt driving car. He is a pastmaster in sycophancy which quality stands him in good stead when he hunts for a job. He shifts to Delhi where he gets the job of a driver in the house of a wealthy businessman identified as "the Stork" who belonged to his village. When asked how much he expected by way of salary, he shows his gift of the glib thus:

> "Absolutely nothing, sir. You're like a father and mother to me, and how can I ask for money from my parents?"
> "Eight hundred rupees a month," he said.
> "No, sir, please—it's too much. Give me half of that, it's enough. More than enough."
> "If we keep you beyond two months, it'll go to one thousand five hundred."
> Looking suitably devastated, I accepted the money from him. (66)

The White Tiger can be looked upon as a *bildungsroman* of sorts, in which Balram Halwai alias Munna learns the evil ways of the world. In Delhi, he drives his master Ashok and his Christian wife "Pinky Madam" around the city. Ashok studied in America where he got married to her. Occasionally, Ashok's father (the Stork) and his elder brother Mukesh (Mongoose) come to Delhi. The Stork is into coal business in Dhanbad and

Ashok has to liaise with government offices and ministers in Delhi.

Balram learns how the other drivers work, from one identified as "Vitiligo-lips," also a driver. On a night of drunken revelry, Pinky Madam drives the car rashly and crushes a child under its wheels. When she comes to senses, she wants to go and see the injured whereas the Stork and others are against it for obvious reasons. The Stork and the Mongoose persuade Ashok to foist the blame for the accident on Balram and get papers signed by him, though the need to use them does not arise. However, the incident sits heavy on her conscience and she leaves for America from where she divorces Ashok.

Sometime after this incident, Ashok renews his friendship with his ex-flame. He also bribes the minister concerned often through a middleman whom he treats to prostitutes, in order to get his work done. These corrupt ways of his master shock Balram so that he loses all sense of professional ethics and morality. One day, finding his master with his red bag full of money meant for a minister, he murders him and flees with his bag and his identity to Bangalore, where he establishes himself as a taxi service provider with a fleet of twenty-six vehicles. Experience has taught him how to avoid the long arm of the law. This is what he calls the real face of entrepreneurship in India. Every rich and successful man has killed someone else, according to him. As if the Chinese with their bloody history of the last six decades need to know it or they must be super-clean in honest ways!

Cynical Realism

Adiga claims to portray reality (Walia) and for this purpose divides India into an area of Darkness and the other area of Light. Adiga quite graphically describes the flip side of life here. One comes across problems almost everywhere, like no electricity or drinking water, inadequate sewage, health and public transportation system. We find in *The White Tiger*, descriptions of abysmal healthcare facility responsible for the death of the protagonist's father (49), dowry-seekers wanting to "screw" the girl's family (51), doctors being fleeced by "The

Great Socialist" and so compensating for their losses by working in private hospitals while signing the attendance register in government hospitals (97-98), etc. In his native village, while Balram's granny eyes his income, in the city, his friend Vitiligo-Lips him to keep mum about his secret (265).

This money-driven relationship is taken to extreme by Adiga. Nobody would believe the episode where the menfolk return home after a long stay far away from home to earn livelihood and the first thing that women at home do is that instead of welcoming them back, "pounced [on them] like wild cats on a slab of flesh. There was fighting and wailing and shrieking. My uncles would resist and manage to keep some of their money, but my father got peeled and skinned every time" (26). Anyone who knows about life in India would confirm the strong familial links in which such episodes are most unlikely to happen. Critics observe that "Adiga fails to project any sort of human relationship in India and what comes out in effect is a sort of cynical anthropology. The people in Darkness are rendered as puppets pulled by the string of an urge for money..." (Dhawan and Santwana 448).

The novel suffers from many other flaws too. That Balram journeys around and stays in different Bangalore hotels for four weeks along with the boy Dharam and the red bag full of cash, without anyone noticing it, is unrealistic. Once in Bangalore, he can distinguish IBM from Hewlett Packard when he overhears conversation of software professionals! Soon he learns to use computer and develops the confidence and the acumen to converse with the Prime Minister of an enemy nation—all this is rather high flight of writer's fancy. Generalizing and stereotyping is the general bane of this novel; the writer just refuses to look at the positive aspects of Indian life. Even in the case of women from the neighbouring country Nepal, stereotyping them as prostitutes is bad in taste and was in fact, objected to by certain Nepalese writers (Sarkar).

Having gone through the litany of woes, it would be interesting to know the solutions offered by the novelist. The protagonist is no great scholar and his analysis of problems is quite simplistic: "To sum up—in the old days there were one thousand castes and destinies in India. These days, there are just two castes: Men with Big Bellies, and Men with Small Bellies" (64). If only one could write off castes in such a simple fashion, India would indeed be a paradise! For him, the servants are like the chicken in the rooster coop which they do not think of leaving even though they have miserable existence there (174-5). He thinks millions of men and women are trapped effectively in the trap because of the family system (176)! Apart from these intellectual nuggets, the convoluted logic of the protagonist can be seen when after privileging beauty to spirituality, he waxes eloquent: "The moment you recognize what is beautiful in this world, you stop being a slave. To hell with the Naxals and their guns shipped from China. If you taught every poor boy how to paint, that would be the end of the rich in India" (276). Elsewhere, his wisecracks like "White men will be finished within my lifetime" (305) amuse the reader. One could shrug off these simplistic statements as a dramatic requirement, uttered as these are by an illiterate driver, but then, the writer's own views articulated in an interview given to Nona Walia are hardly different: "There are only two real outlets for their [India's underclass] entrepreneurial drive: crime or politics." These days, when the two have joined hands, it means only one avenue!

What one gathers from the study of the novel is that the writer has very superficial knowledge not only of India but also of the old version of Marxist philosophy which forms the bedrock of his words of wisdom. Apart from his professions about the economic nature of most problems in India (Dhawan and Haldar 445), Adiga makes his protagonist mock gods, as for example, describing Hanuman as "an image of saffron-coloured creature, half man half money"—words which no villagers will use for a god. As to why he is worshipped, Adiga reveals the secret—because he is "a shining example of how to serve your masters with absolute fidelity, love and devotion. These are the kinds of gods they have foisted on us, Mr. Jiabao" (19). Are these really foisted? Probably, in his flow of thoughts, Adiga has taken India for China where everything is foisted by the State. Another example of how the anti-religious views of Adiga are mouthed by his protagonist: "The next day I went to a roadside temple in Gurgaon. I put a rupee before the two resident pairs of divine arses (sic)..." (187). Such trivialization of Hindu spiritual icons can only hurt the sentiments of devout Hindu readers—something Adiga could have done without.

Critiquing Style

Talking of the character, Adiga's Balram tells Jiabao "the autobiography of a "Half-Baked Indian" (10), but elsewhere he shows high confidence, as when he writes off America as "yesterday" and himself as "tomorrow" (6). He believes Indians take to technology like "ducks to water" (12) and divides India in two parts—an "India of Light", and an "India of Darkness." Since he is telling it to a foreigner, there is ample scope for him to revel in the Indian trait of verbosity with regard to everything—the rate card at the liquor shop, beggars selling items on road-crossings, a sticker pasted on a rickshaw and so on. He becomes an online tourist guide introducing everything Indian to the Chinese Premier and the text becomes an overlong dramatic monologue that occasionally notes the listener's response.

This semi-literate chauffeur has picked up a few nuggets of knowledge, which are reductive in nature, to say the least. There are ample specimens of it strewn all over in the novel, as for example, he believes there are three nations in the world that never let themselves be ruled by foreigners: China, Afghanistan and Abyssinia! (5). He judges the West in similar vein: "Our erstwhile master, the white-skinned man, has wasted himself through buggery, mobile phone usage, and drug abuse" (6). There are four poets he admires: Iqbal, Rumi, Mirza Ghalib and the fourth one he "has forgotten" etc. That is rather too much to know for this rustic character and speaks volumes about the realistic craftsmanship of Adiga!

The writer seems to be confused about portraying the character of Balram. He is an illiterate person but he is able to name the poets as also tell us about the "minimum height and weight standards set by the United Nations and other organizations" (19) for the village children! It seems portraying a character in a novel is made quite easy. One has only to show the protagonist as a dumb fellow and write whatever one wishes to in whichever part of the novel!

Applying the standard of realism to the major action of the protagonist, one would simply say that in murdering his master is nothing less than savagery. His murmurs of regret afterwards show an eccentric and unstable character. From the detail given about Ashok, one finds that he treated Balram all along in a humane manner. There should, therefore, have been a stronger and more convincing motive behind this action. Apart from the artistic failure of lacking in substantial motive that seems the obverse of the situation in Shakespeare's *Hamlet* which Eliot declared as an artistic failure,[1] the act is highly unethical as also unrealistic as by no account does Balram represent an ordinary rustic or urban Indian youth.

So far as the style of *The White Tiger* is concerned, this novel is no match to the works of other celebrated authors like Salman Rushdie or Kiran Desai. In comparison, the prose style of Adiga is bland and the language does not display any richness. Different literary embellishments like imagery, metaphors have to be discovered with some effort. The writer has a valid excuse in that the protagonist is a semi-literate village bumpkin who cannot be expected to show command of language in the first person narrative. But within these constraints, writers have worked wonders. Raja Rao's *Kanthapura* is one such example. However, the novel does have an ironic undertone: "The poor dream all their lives of getting enough to eat and looking like the rich. And what do the rich dream of? Losing weight and looking like the poor" (225). Also, there are a few instances of surrealism, as for example, Balram having a conversation with self through the buffalo:

> "Your brother Kishan was beaten to death. Happy?"
> It was like experiencing a nightmare in the minutes before you wake up; you know it's a dream but you can't wake up just yet.
> "Your aunt Luttu was raped and then beaten to death. Happy? Your grandmother Kusum was kicked to death. Happy?"
> The buffalo glared at me.

> "Shame!" it said, and then it took a big step forward the cart passed by, full of dead skinned faces, which seemed to me at that moment the faces of my own family. (256)

Similarly, the dialogue between puddles of paan-spits (246), although introduced in the vein of the lamp posts' remarks in Eliot's "Rhapsody on a Windy Night" (Eliot 1969, 24) is no match to the latter and appears like an add-on only. Even so, these features can be counted on the finger-tips. Such usage demands adequate supportive description. When the narrator seeks promise from the city, in expressionistic mode, to drown the fat politico, he fails to work up the agitation to an intensity justifying this punishment.

Debating Canonization

Booker as also Pulitzer have been the most prestigious awards in the field of literature. Awarding it to a novel like *The White Tiger* recognizes in the eyes of the jury at least the worth of the novel and canonizes it in a way. For quite sometime now, the criterion for the Booker has undergone change which is regrettable. M.H. Abrams notes about the canon of literature: "Another demand that is frequently voiced is that the standard canon be stripped of its elitism and its 'hierarchism'—that is, its built-in discriminations between high art and lower art—in order to include such cultural products as Hollywood movies, television serials, popular songs and *fiction written for a mass audience*" (43 italics mine). Now, if it has to be mass readership as the criterion, then there were many other writers like Chetan Bhagat who have been selling books in millions. Why take up a writer like Adiga who had just published his book! But demanding "abolition of standard canon" would also abolish the value of Booker or any award that means to judge on the basis of established literary standards.

A brief look at the other novels that got the Booker in the field of Indian English Literature vis-a-vis *The White Tiger* will show the difference. A novel by its very design is riveted to a set of problems which reach a climax and then the denouement. In case of novels dealing with socio-political scene, any number of problems can come a novelist's way.

Rushdie's *Midnight's Children* too talks about the post-partition history of India and underlines the fissiparous tendencies at work but how artistically it is tied to the body of the protagonist. As an Indian writer, he was the first to hoist the flag of postmodern fiction alongside use of magic realism, whatever their merits or demerits. Besides, his famous 'chutnification' of language with his vast knowledge of world literature is a treat for the reader. Prof. Deena rightly remarks: "Rushdie has become an important and prophetic voice in the complex postmodern world of the 21st century. His life, lectures, and works will continue to sound the trumpet of freedom, democracy, creativity, love and intellectual pursuit" (Deena 16).

Arundhati Roy, in her novel *The God of Small Things*, highlights the plight of the subaltern in a state ruled by a political party that arrogates to itself the status of sole champion of the underdog. Her language has had a pioneering effect in fiction writing. Kiran Desai in her novel *The Inheritance of Loss* lays bare the working of separatist political parties and the impact that these have on the lives of the young people. Quite artistically in her signature snapshot-description, she interweaves this narrative with the other narrative of a subaltern struggling to find a place in the postmodern society of America. Pulitzer winner Jhumpa Lahiri, in her novel *The Namesake*, very subtly and beautifully maps the sensation of being torn between American and being Indian in the lives of the diasporic Ashoke family.

We know about the behind the scene manoeuvres in deciding awards carried out by lobbies of publishers, literary agents, advertising companies, and so on and the motive is to publicize a work through hook or crook. If a controversy erupts as in the case of *The White Tiger*, so much the better for sales!

Neo-Orientalism

What probably caught the eye of the jury was something that has been increasingly seen in the novels dealing with Indian themes written by the diasporic outsiders. Sir Simon Jenkins, the former chairman of the Booker prize jury, put it quite bluntly: "Indian writers in English face a peculiar problem—they write about India but their readership is mostly in other countries. Because of this paradox they create an image of India that is exotic and doesn't show the real India. I worry about this. If people create an image of India on the basis of what they see in Bollywood movies, it would be a very odd India. That's why a work of fiction can't really create the true picture of India."

In this respect, this dystopian novel is hardly different from the stereotyped fiction that is produced by the majority of westerners or the West-inspired Indians because such a work gives a kind of sadistic pleasure to the imperialist mind which has not been able to free itself of colonial hangover and refuses to reconcile to the fact that the ex-colonized can rule themselves. The ex-colonizers wish to be reassured that India remains backward, in sync with the Orient portrayed by the western writers. Such a fictional work, therefore, has a fair chance of winning international awards instituted by westerners.

There are any number of writers settled abroad who thrive on the depiction of ugly India in their works *a la* Orientalist portrayal which has come to be known as Neo-Orientalism (Lau & Dwivedi), for it comes from Indians themselves. Adiga was himself raised in Australia; later he studied in England and worked in the U.S.A. His visits to India as the correspondent of the Times do not make him an insider simply because he has reported India; he has not experienced it. So, *The White Tiger* is an outsider's rather than insider's viewpoint.

Conclusion

It would only be a prejudiced mind possessed by a certain ideology who may look upon the novel as a realistic story. How is it possible that in a vast country like India, only wrong things and actions take place and there is nothing positive that the author can talk about. It shows a deeper agenda as has been pointed out above. Also, a double-faced murderer falls in the category of anti-hero that has no place in a canon comprising of classics. "The canon is the result of the concurrence of a great many (often unexpressed) norms and standards, and among these, one crucial factor has been the high intellectual and artistic quality of the canonical works themselves, and their attested power to enlighten and give delight, and to appeal to widely shared human concerns and values" (Abrams 43). Such a fictional work has no value from the point of view of Indian poetics either, which considers literature as the body of knowledge for the benefit of mankind (*hiten saha sahitam, tasya bhavah saahityam*) (Shastri and Goswami 2).

By a strange coincidence, when *The White Tiger* got the Man Booker Prize, the same year, the Booker of Bookers was awarded to Salman Rushdie's, *Midnight's Children* which recognized the canonical merit of Rushdie's novel in relation to other Booker winning works over the last forty years. A classic is one that has a widespread appeal over time and space and *Midnight's Children* fits the bill. Rushdie's magnum opus is certainly not appreciative of post-independence India but its artistic merit has lent it weight. Juxtaposed with it, *The White Tiger* appears a puny work that presents a misleading picture of India and its young generation. Though unintended, it seemed as if the award committee were trying to reassure the literary world of their concern for canonical quality even though a novel from the non-canonical category had been awarded the prize!

NOTE

1. T.S. Eliot, in his much-quoted essay "Hamlet" notes that the play lacks objective co-relative that is "a set of objects, a situation, a chain of events which shall be the formula of that particular emotion such that when the eternal facts, which must terminate in sensory experience, are given, the emotion is immediately evoked" (145). Here in this novel, the action of revenge takes place but the motive is not powerful enough.

WORKS CITED

Abrams, M.H. & Geoffrey Galt Harpham. *A Handbook of Literary Terms*. New Delhi: Cengage, 2009.

Adiga, Aravind. *The White Tiger*. New Delhi: HarperCollins, 2008, Ninth Impression, 2009.

Deena, Seodial Frank, Ed. "Introduction," *Salman Rushdie's Global Philosophy: Critical Essays*. New Delhi: Prestige, 2014.

Desai, Kiran. *The Inheritance of Loss*. New Delhi: Penguin, 2006.

Dhawan, R.K. and Santwana Haldar. "Aravind Adiga's *The White Tiger*: A Study in Dalit Discourse," *Exploring Fourth World Literatures*, ed. Raja Sekha Patteti. New Delhi, Prestige, 2011.

Eliot, T.S. *Selected Essays*. London: Faber and Faber, 1951, Reprint 1986.

——. *Collected Poems*. London: Faber and Faber, 1969.

Jenkins, Sir Simon. "Novels tell exotic tales from India." *Sunday Times of India*. 16 Oct. 2009, Capital ed.: p. 8. Print.

Lahiri, Jhumpa. *The Namesake*. New Delhi: Harper Collins, 2003.

Lao, Lisa & Om Prakash Dwivedi. *Re-Orientalism and Indian Writing in English*. Hampshire, UK: Palgrave Macmillan, 2014.

Rao, Raja. *Kanthapura*. New Delhi: Oxford, 1938, Reprint 1989.

Roy, Arundhati. *The God of Small Things*. New Delhi: Penguin, 1997.

Rushdie, Salman. *Midnight's Children*. London: Vintage, 1981, Reprint 2012.

Sarkar, Sudeshna. "Nepal sees red over White Tiger". *Sunday Tribune* 23 Oct. 2009, Spectrum sec.: p. 5. Print.

Shastri, Omprakash & Sharanbihari Goswami. *Sameeksha Tattva*. Delhi: Hindi Sahitya Sansar, 1967.

Walia, Nona. "I tried to tell a very real story about India". *Sunday Times of India* 16 Oct. 2009, Capital ed.: p. 11. Print.

11

Tishani Doshi's *The Pleasure Seekers*: Exploring Limits of Acculturation

India-born Tishani Doshi is a talented poet and novelist besides being a performing artist. She has published three collections of poetry and an equal number of novels so far. Her debut anthology of poems was *Countries of the Body* which won the Forward Poetry Prize in 2006. Her other book *Fountainville* (2013) has as its theme the surrogacy business in which pregnant women are shown cocooned in a house, much like hens waiting to lay eggs, till the time they are ready to give the gift of a baby to a stranger. Doshi's novel *Small Days and Nights* (2019) portrays a narrator of mixed origin who visits her dead mother's house in Pondicherry where she is called upon to deal with some family skeletons.

Her first novel *The Pleasure Seekers* is indeed special as it has elicited rave reviews from the likes of Salman Rushdie, whose comment—"A captivating, delightful novel" as also another comment—"has a grace and gentle comedy of its own" (*Sunday Times*) adorn the back page of the book as blurbs. The novel has a poetic touch about it and reminds one of Chitra Banerjee Divakaruni's *The Mistress of Spices*, whose enigmatic and oracular character Tilottama has parallel with Ba in the present novel. Another aspect that makes this novel unique is its autobiographical character, but still, it has not drawn much the attention of academy that it deserves.

The Pleasure Seekers is a novel that deals with the transculturation or the lack of it of young females with similar, though at a reduced scale, side-shows of two males. The story of the novel starts in the year 1968 when the protagonist Babo Patel belonging to a Gujarati family of Madras (now Chennai) in India arrives in London. This was the time when, as the writer reminds us, Russia and Warsaw Pact forces invaded Czechoslovakia which proved to be a turning point for the Communist Block. Symbolically, the Patel family's deeply conservative character was also set to be shaken, the seeds of which were being sown now.

More than that, the period reminds one of the migrations of a wave of Indians, particularly the young professionals to the US and Europe in search of greener pastures, and a little later, of the skilled and unskilled workers from Kerala to the Gulf countries. Also, in the 1970s, Gujaratis from East Africa (Kenya, Tanzania, Mozambique, South Africa, etc.) re-migrated (the first migration from India took place in 1890s) now as Commonwealth citizens to UK after nationalist sentiments rose there following freedom from colonial powers. So, these migrations and re-migrations encouraged the young Babo to aspire to study abroad.

Globalization, as a defining feature of the contemporary postmodern world, has thrown open new vistas in every field of human activity. Crossing seas to work in another part of the world has become so common. But it was not always like this. Remember Mahatma Gandhi who was reluctantly permitted by his mother to go to South Africa after he had undertaken certain vows. So, here too, Babo, the eldest son is allowed to go to England to study engineering on the condition that he would observe faithfully the Jain code of strictly vegetarian food and abstinence from liquor, which however, he violates at the first available opportunity in London and takes meat as also liquor. So much for the sanctity attached to one's word that has come about since Gandhi's days.

Now, whether it was the first batch of the indentured labourers called *girmitiyas*, who were forcibly sent by the British rulers of India to work in far off lands like Guyana, Surinam,

Mauritius, etc. or the latest migration of computer professionals to different parts of the world, one thing that emerges as a common feature is that they have to work in a multicultural environment and proper adjustment holds the key to a happy life. One must agree that the environment in alien land is much different from the multicultural environment that one might find in India which is also considered by some as a multicultural country but there are common roots of many a sub-culture here and besides, the common experiences as a nation creates the awareness among people of being part of a single society with common destiny.

In this society is introduced a British *bahu* (bride) who weds her Gujarati beau Babo Patel coming from a Jain family. The Jains form a prosperous trading community which constitutes only 0.4% of India's total population and has much in common with the majority Hindus in terms of religious philosophy and practices. The bride in question is Sian who comes from the rural belt of England, from a village with the queer sounding name Nercwys. Both met in London where Babo was studying for his engineering degree and Sian was working as a temporary staff in an office.

There has been a great outpouring of fiction giving vent to the anxiety, culture shock, maladjustment, nostalgia, etc. of the 'desi' (native Indian) trying to settle down in any European country or in the US. Surely, the experience of a European settling down in India, and on top of that, as a housewife in a traditional family should arouse the interest of readers. There were earlier accounts of failure of such a settlement as in the case of the German immigrant in India, Ruth Prawer Jhabvala, the writer of the Booker-winning novel *Heat and Dust*, who, after spending twenty-five years in India assessed India as intolerable because of poverty, backwardness, class-division, etc. (Ghoshal, 2003), but that is an old story. Since then, much water has flowed down the Ganga, as they say, and we have had happier accounts of the union of the East and the West as in the case of the other German-Indian writer Roswitha Joshi, whose autobiographical novel *Indian Dreams* (2000) speaks of marital bliss enjoyed by Norma with her husband Akash.

That the story of *The Pleasure Seekers* has an autobiographical touch is surely suggested as the writer has a Welsh mother and a Gujarati father, corresponding respectively to the characters Sian and Babo in the novel. Subconsciously, it seems, Doshi has not been able to wean herself away from the real life graph with its myriad vicissitudes, so that the plot of the novel too becomes meandering, sticking at times to incidents she would love to harp upon, like the sibling-rivalry, or taking a long jump at other time when she is rather shy of revealing something, like the gap between the period of childhood of the sisters Mayuri and Bean and the stage when Mayuri starts dating a boyfriend.

Babo's Adaptation

Coming to the acculturation process of different characters, we find that in England, Babo is assigned to the care of Bhupen Jain's family. Bhupen is an old friend of Babo's father Prem Kumar Jain and had been living in London for a long time. He guides Babo well with regard to the do's and don'ts of daily life in London. Despite this patronage, Babo flouts the Jain code of food. This is his first step towards integration with the host society, and the need for integration arose because he got romantically involved with an English girl Sian. For his acculturation in England, which is a stage in the progress towards adaptation of the culture of the host society. Acculturation is a process of learning and imbibing language, mannerism, beliefs, practices, value system, etc. starting with lifestyle components like food, dress, entertainment modes, etc. of the new society to which immigrants have been introduced. These elements bring about the much-needed adjustment with the host society, it is felt. The adjustment, however, can take many forms and the simplest and a rather reductionist view is presented by the four stages outlined by John Berry, which are, moving from the best to the worst: Assimilation, Integration, Separation and Marginalization (John, 1997). These stages depend on various factors like the inclination, resources, social conditions, and mental make-up of the immigrant and the policies formulated by the government of the host country. Babo is here as a temporary migrant, though post-relationship with Sian, he dreams of settling down in England. For the present, he needs to adapt himself to the English way of life and then gradually seek deeper integration or assimilation, as circumstances might call upon him to do.

For his acculturation in English society, which has shades of racial discrimination, even though the state policy is of integration, Babo does not need any grounding in English language as he is proficient in it except, of course, for perfect pronunciation, but behavioural acculturation demands change in dietary habits, and of course, in social manners. Again, as psychologists aver: "Language and behavioral acculturation occur immediately after immigrants' arrival in the new country, as they struggle with communicating in the new language and adapting to behavioral norms and expectations in the new society. However, other aspects of cultural change such as identity or values are thought to come later" (Birman and Poff 2010, 29). So, Babo's taking plunge straightaway into Western food is in line with this acculturation process.

It may be noted that early research in popular culture has proceeded on the presumption that acculturation travels one-way only—to assimilate the immigrant in host society where he acquires the new culture after shedding his linkage to culture back home. But it stands revised now, as the critics outline the contrast: "Thus, immigrants may either continue to retain their culture in a separatist or traditionalist stance or assimilate into the new society. However, [...] Berry (1980) suggests [...] immigrants may also choose to acculturate to both cultures, resulting in integration or biculturalism; or become disconnected from either culture, resulting in marginality" (Birman and Poff 2010, 29). After all, we are dealing with human material!

So, while acculturation in terms of social manners is a pragmatic step, in the private space of home, his hosts, the Bhupen Jain family has not been able to shun the Indian cultural mindset, so they intimate Prem about Babo's rendezvous with the English girl which alarms the people back home so much so that Babo is summoned home on the pretext of his mother being seriously ill. The charade is off when he reaches home in

Madras where he is presented with the fait accompli to marry the Gujarati girl Falguni selected earlier by the family with his consent. Understandably, the parents are shattered because, as is customary in Indian society, the families of both the boy and the girl were involved. The cause of additional concern for Prem Kumar is that Babo wants to settle in England with his English wife.

Sian's Transculturation

While those who go by the rulebook apply the term 'acculturation' to a diasporic community as a whole or a group thereof, the term preferred for the individual entering an alien society through the route of wedlock, is transculturation—a term coined in 1940 by the Cuban anthropologist Fernando Ortiz. He first introduced it as a "methodological tool meant to synthesize the extensive and detailed analysis on the development of Cuban society and culture in his book *Cuban Counterpoint: Tobacco and Sugar* published in 1940" (Cote 2010, 123). The meaning in both cases—acculturation and transculturation is almost similar—to acquaint oneself with the social and cultural mores of the host culture and to adapt oneself to it. The extent of integration in such cases varies from person to person as also the context—how receptive is the host culture; and how adaptive is the immigrant, but whereas acculturation suggests an ongoing process, transculturation suggests transformation. In case of marriage, the urgency and inclination to get assimilated for life becomes a serious concern.

Fearing the addition of a foreigner to their close-knit family, a condition is laid down by Prem Kumar that the couple would have to stay with them in Madras for a minimum two-year period, before they could be allowed to settle wherever they liked. The Indian code of patriarchal family is accepted and followed sincerely by Babo as an obedient son. Sian, after initial doubts, also cooperates and comes over to India to be Babo's bride. As a newly-wed, she has to contend with her husband's family which has besides Prem Kumar, his wife Trishala, two daughters Dolly and Meenal described as 'unibrows', and another son Chotu who remains *chotu* (literally, a younger child) and his real name is not given.

In the extended (from the Western viewpoint) family of Babo Patel is also his grandmother, lovingly referred to as Ba, who lives in Ganga Bazar village of Bhuj, Gujarat. It is an interesting character portrayed by Doshi. The wizened old lady has oracular intuition: "Ba could smell the lingering camphor from the marriage pyre, the sickening smell of leftover vegetable oil, dying jasmine. She could smell Dolly's tears and Trishala's sulphuric gunpowder anxiety hanging like a shroud over everything" (167), describes Doshi in her poetic prose. It is here that Babo and Bean's marriage ceremony takes place. Ba is the head of the family, besides her house is like a farmhouse which is convenient for such get-togethers. She provides counselling as well as refuge to Babo and Bean when later, each of them turns up at her door to get advice and spend time away from the humdrum of Madras, even though Ganga Bazar is quite far-off from Madras. Her words are mysterious as those of a prophet. When her grandson visits her with Sian, she advises them: "Look to the sky every day—for the sun and the moon signify eternal devotion of husband and wife, look to the sea—for love flows deep and you must be prepared to flow deeper; journey like the fish and the birds—because it is only those who agree to their own return who can participate in the divinity of the world" (80-81). Undoubtedly, Doshi's language outpaces all other fictional elements in this novel.

Sian's transculturation involving several rites of passage that will turn her from a Western girl to an Indian *bahu*, but as Sam and Berry's study (2010) observes the process of acculturation is much simpler and easier in case of an immigrant who migrates for marriage or employment as compared to other categories of immigrants where one has to migrate perforce, as for example, refugees. According to these researchers, the comparative ratio of ease of acculturation in these two cases is 2:1 (Sam and Berry 2010, 480).

Sian's responses can be gleaned from her lived experience in the extended Gujarati family of patriarch Prem Kumar and the neighbourhood. Sian is trained to put on a sari, cut vegetables sitting on kitchen floor like her mother-in-law does. In her room, Jain religious symbols and icons are displayed. She is taken along when the family members visit the local Jain temple. Their children Mayuri and Bean are also initiated into Jain rituals so that at the time of Chotu's death, both sisters are seen counting the prayer beads. Sian is the focus of all sorts of efforts to acculturate her into Indian life. At times, she resents overmuch attention given to her. It is only after Meenal's marriage and her first delivery that the family diverts attention from Sian, who also witnesses with a sense of wonder the hefty Gujarati weddings, when each one of her sisters-in-law departs from home as a bride with a rich trousseau.

It is not merely the family with which Sian engages herself so well, it is also with the Madras society at large. The children, while riding the car through Madras notice the poor and the sick, but then Sian does not exhibit any Orientalist feelings the way the writer of *Heat and Dust* did. Here, Sian takes her children to Andhra Mahila Sabha school where she teaches free of charge, the children belonging to underprivileged section of society (140). Sian also takes to charity work through the Overseas Women's Club. Visiting mental patients in hospitals, she is moved over their plight.

In the immediate neighbourhood, Sian makes friends with a Parsi widow, who introduces her to The Garden of Redemption, a spiritual community headed by a spiritualist Manna who helps her come to terms with life whenever she is anxious. Manna too speaks life lessons in a mystical language: "If we understand our own births and deaths, we'll know what to erase and what to put forward" (158). These social and spiritual activities help Sian immensely to understand and be a part of the Indian society.

Now, as Weichold comments, "Moving from one culture to another is a major life transition often accompanied by unique stressors (e.g. disruption of social ties) impacting on individuals' developmental pathways" (Weichold 2010, 1). Sian's anxiety as to whether she is on the right track is set at rest as she is able to compare her notes as a foreigner wedded to an Indian, with

Derlene Malhotra nee Adams from Tennesse, USA; or with Janet Krishnamurti nee Miller from Plymouth. Twice-a-week, these three families met at the Madras Gymkhana Club—a remnant of colonial days—for drinks and discussions. She was warned of the overbearing mother-in-law with whom she would have to put up till one of them died. There was not going to be any respite the Western way—putting the aged people in the Age-care homes! But she had resolved to make her marriage a success and believed that her husband would outlive her. She had even decided what to do if ever in life she was left alone.

A lot of space is given to the rearing up of children who interiorize Indian and Western manners (Sian and Babo having "time alone" in bedroom as children waited outside), food (served on the eve of Bean's departure) and entertainment (Gymkhana gatherings of OWC), etc. Of course, there is a kind of competition between sisters as is normal in any family where girls are of almost equal age. Bean gets cues to develop urges and model life from Mayuri just as Chotu gets from elder brother Babo.

Sian's Family

While Sian's married life progresses well in India, her family back in England nourishes puzzlement as they never in their wildest dreams ever thought of having an Indian son-in-law. Sian's mother gets the opportunity to see at first hand how her daughter is braving it out in India, when she visits India on the occasion of marriage of her granddaughter—long after her daughter had migrated to India. For Sian's mother, the world has not globalized, so to say. For her, travel is not that easy and frequent as it is for any youngster. Hence, her concern for the welfare of her daughter is more acute, and also let's say, blown up.

We are also given a glimpse of the extended family of Sian—her mother Nerys, father Bryn; her two brothers—Huw and Owen; her paternal aunt El who lives nearby. Often, the two families meet up on special occasions. The aunt is described in a slang-laden language:

> Aunty Eleri, who relished other people's problems like honey in her thumbs, thought Sian was in over her head. Poor Aunty El, who'd come by for a cup of tea with her dog, Gwythur, whose eyes nearly fell out of the back of her head when she saw Sian standing here, pleased as pie. Her brother's last chick who sh'd heard had a place in London and was making big city money, had given all that up and was now saying, "Didn't Mam tell you, Aunty El? I'm going to India to get married." (72)

Sian visits her home in England following her father's death. She remembers him, as would every diasporic; his words to her not to forget the family which she had not abided by and had allowed the concern for her original family to fade. "She had packed it all away in the bottom drawer of her heart and began a beginning halfway across the world" (155). But then, she believed that she had learnt the "secret of surviving in a foreign country. It had something to do with love" (154). Thoughts like these indicate a measure of assimilation in the Indian culture which bespeaks perfect transculturation.

On the other hand, when Babo went to his in-laws' house in England to condole the death of his father-in-law, he expected to be received by the entire village folk at the railway station—something common in an Indian village, however, to his dismay, it was only his brother-in-law Owen who came to receive him. Here he displayed lack of acculturation revealing the Indian trait but this streak helped him win over the village community by being helpful to them on many occasions.

Bean's Failed Acculturation

Sian, though herself a totally acculturated Indian, was concerned about her children, since being of mixed race they might invite derisive or adverse comments in England, even if in India, they were treated as privileged children. The 300 years of colonialism have instituted the "adoration of white skin" (95) in India, as the writer rightly observes. If we consider the situation of the Anglo-Indian community in India, we find that after independence of the country, many people belonging to this category stayed on in India, even though most migrated to England or to other Commonwealth nations like Canada and Australia. But it is not merely due to their British links that they have enjoyed privileged status, many Anglo-Indians have distinguished themselves in fields like military, sports, education, literature, etc. India also had a sizeable Portuguese-Goan population. Confining, however for the sake of this study, to the Anglo-Indians, we focus on the sister-duo Mayuri and Bean.

Acculturation or transculturation of youth is surprisingly not so comfortable if they are 'mixed race' children. This term was preferred in a survey conducted in London over others like 'biracial', 'half-breed', 'half-caste', or 'hybrid' which were considered offensive by the young people having parents from different races (Aspinall 2008, 5). There are several instances where they face the identity issue. In this case, Mayuri and Bean happen to be Anglo-Indians and the writer uses the term "hybrids" for them (235). Bean is alarmed when she hears Selvi describe Shyam Malhotra (son of Derlene) as the ugliest child observing that "Sometimes all this mixing gives bad results" (133)! That is the viewpoint of an ordinary person indeed.

The fact that Part Three of the book captioned "Levisham to Ganga Bazaar (1996-2001)" traces Bean's journey to England twenty-two years after her father Babo's, suggests the importance that the author attaches to her life graph which revolves around her period of biological and psychological maturation from adolescence to youth, and her attempt at imbibing, culturally speaking, the totally individualistic Western approach to life, that is focused on experiencing pleasure. As to why Bean decided to go to England is unclear to her patents. Her boyfriend Michael Mendoza had gone to Australia with his divorced mother.

> Perhaps it's inevitable, Babo thought, that our children suffer a similar displacement; that in order to understand the pattern of their lives here, they must go elsewhere. [...] Part of it must have had to do with the boredom of college life, where for four years Bean went and came home with a dull look in her eyes, with no new boyfriend or best friend

> of note, and a degree in English literature which she didn't know what to do with. (236)

Her restless soul probably yearned for more adventure "like Dick Whittington and his cat, on a quest to conquer the city of London" and more definitely "to find love: the kind of love Babo and Sian had found in London" (238).

Bean goes to England and while staying there, she, for once, is much appreciative of the orderliness, punctuality, and decorum in the functioning of public facilities like the trains, "nothing like India with all its abundance of chaos and noise," she comments (250). But then, the same Bean was upset with the rules followed in the Bhupen Jain household! The Jain family had indeed absorbed some of the orderliness of English society but it seems, she expected the Indian lifestyle there. This hybrid approach is an indicator of her imperfect acculturation in future in the English society.

Bean's mental make-up contrasts well with her sister's. We do not learn about any problem in Mayuri's wedded life. That shows her adaptability to a multicultural setting as she is wedded to a Parsi boy in India. Bean, on the other hand, tries and for a good period of time, appears to be well-soaked in the Western culture. London is a place where identity is re-fashioned or not fashioned at all. When Bean visits Uncle Huw and Aunty Carole in Brighton, her cousins Gareth and Ed "paraded her around town as the exotic cousin visiting from India" (247). In a white village, such a response is understandable, but in metropolitan London, with its large multiracial population, no such reaction is expected. Of course, we hear of episodes of racial discrimination about which Bhupen had cautioned both his Indian guests.

So, Bean takes to the openness of western society as a fish takes to water. While working at Stonewell, she happens to have a glimpse, through the glass wall of her office, of a smart man—a Spanish working in an adjoining architect's office and is instantly bewitched by him, As luck would have it, she also happens to meet Javier in person one day and their friendly relationship begins which soon leads them to the bedroom.

Later, she learns that this man is married and has three children also, but despite the sane advice from her friend Allegra to stop seeing him, she fondly hopes to win him over forever!

Not only this, she also has physical relations with a number of people—a Brazilian dancer, a Nigerian investment banker, a Greek musician, a Russian scientist, an English actor, a Canadian rock-climber, and so on (268). But surprisingly, after her failure to win over Javier, she is heartbroken and thinks of returning to India. Bean's failure in case of this relationship shows a lack somewhere. As a child, she was always outwitted by her elder sister Mayuri. So, she had entered into a sort of competition with her. It was in all fields from possessing toys, taking part in school activities or striking friendships. When Mayuri fell for a neighbourhood boy, Bean could not have lagged behind, so coming one up on her, she even got pregnant from her boyfriend! Even though Mayuri helped her with secret abortion, she did not learn any lesson. Instead, she felt as if a door had opened and there was no looking back on sexual adventures. The experience with the Spanish architect revealed to her the other side of physical relationship: it could also hook your heart!

Heart desires stability of home but Bean becomes an eternally rootless person even as wanting home all the time. There is the archetypal Indian grandma waiting for her and only she can help her "separate love from betrayal, anger from abandonment" (284). She had prophesied looking at a cobra coiled in the branches of jamun tree that "this last grandchild would be serious and quiet and would know the failure of flight" (140-41). The prophecy has come true!

Bean's journey to Bhuj to have second abortion does not have any closure. The home she was expected to return to lies in shambles due to the earthquake. She muses: "Is this my real life or is it just a prelude to something before I return...return to where? Why do I always feel like I'm visiting wherever I go? [...] One foot in, the other foot out" (248). Home, for a diasporic like Bean—she is a diasporic at heart—is just not there: *There is no such thing as home. Once you've forsaken it and stepped out of the circle, you can't ever re-enter and claim anything as yours.* How could you? When you've portioned yourself in such a way? It was always going to be like this: [...]. Hadn't Bean tried? Hadn't she gone away to recover parts of herself and failed? (278, italics in original).

Bean's 'parts' are indeed scattered. She has had behavioural acculturation but identity has not completely metamorphosed into British or European. Hence, the pull back. It is also suggested that having trouble fitting in with European peers, she rejects European identity and instead adopts what Birman and Trickett term as "reactive identification" (Birman and Poff 2010, 32) with her native Indian culture so that she flies back to India and finds solace in Ba's sanctuary.

According to a critic, the expatriate writer upholds family life in India because the writer faces xenophobia in the adopted country and has to glorify her land of birth (Bhattacharya 2012, 134), but the critic misses the fact that the writer is herself a biracial child and is settled in Madras and this is an autobiographical novel. Doshi herself remarked in an interview: "This is a novel that comes from life. It is a tender love story of desire, independence, choices...,". We are told that Tishani's father is Gujarati, and mother Welsh and the couple decided to stay in India and make their life here "at a time when most people would go to the West because that was the sensible economic choice" (Raj 2012).

Conclusion

The novel is a study of different types of acculturation processes. There is the adaptation or partial acculturation of Babo Patel in England; a total transculturation of Sian in India and the failed acculturation of Bean in England. There is the interesting difference in racial background. While Babo is Indian, Sian is British and Bean a bi-racial youth. Again, there are differences in terms of motives in going to another country. Babo goes as a temporary expatriate to study; Sian comes to India for marriage and family; and Bean goes for adventure and love. The comparison of the life graph of Sian with her daughter Bean's brings into focus the difference in terms of acculturation in a different land. While Sian is able to get assimilated in Indian society so well that she does not miss England much, her daughter Bean is a misfit and is always floundering. It has something to do with how much of the alien spirit one is able to imbibe without undergoing the clash with one's innate native sensibility and cultural moorings. After her failed affair with Javier, Bean is just not able to move on like a hard-boiled European. The acculturation is incomplete. Bean's indeed is an ambiguous persona.

The title of the novel provides a signpost to the mindscape of the protagonists in a reductionist manner. It has been taken from the Bible: "In the last days, men would be lovers of themselves [...] lovers of pleasure rather than lovers of God" (2 Timothy 3, 1-4). All characters, and indeed everybody in the world seeks pleasure. While Babo and Sian had their share of pleasure, they had to contend with myriad other problems which life brings along. They accepted them and so seem contented. Bean is not able to adjust with the shock of refusal by her lover. In this, "love is reflected upon deeply at the precipice of loss" (Shah). Bean's return is, at quite another plane, reminiscent of Biju's return in Kiran Desai's *The Inheritance of Loss*. In both cases, the protagonists return to their Indian moorings and family as the last resort and as losers.

Ba's crystal gazing in her mystical vein, *a la* oracles, provides a hazy view of things to come: "Mayuri is going to sink her roots deep. She will know what she is and what she wants, always. But this one, this Beena, she will change from earth to water to fire, again and again. She will want to move like water, forever taking a different shape but she will also long to stay still" (117-18). The house in Ganga Bazaar lies in rubble due to the earthquake. The immersion ritual performed earlier at Ba's house when she was bodily lowered into a well is a symbolic act denoting re-birth. Red garoli lizard (common house gecko) become almost a motif. A lizard hibernates for long winter period and then awakens. Also it re-creates its tail when it gets amputated, and so, serves as a symbol of regeneration. There is hope for a new beginning in the end.

REFERENCES

Aspinall, Peter J. (2008). "Ethnic Options of 'Mixed Race' People in Britain: A Report for UK

Census Agencies on references for Terminology and Classifications". University of Kent. <https://www.whatdotheyknow.com/request/213437/response/532699/attach/4/Aspinall%20 mixed%20race%20report%201.pdf>

Berry, John W. (1997). "Immigration, Acculturation, and Adaptation". *Applied Psychology*. 46 (1): 10. <https://iaap-journals.onlinelibrary.wiley.com/doi/abs/10.1111/j.1464-0597.1997.tb01087.x>

Bhattacharya, S. (2012). The Return of the Native, But Not Alone in Tishani Doshi's & Shilpi

Somaya Gowda's *Secret Daughter*. *Asiatic: IIUM Journal of English Language and Literature*, 6(1), 132-41. <https://journals.iium.edu.my/asiatic/index.php/ajell/article/view/242/224>

Birman, D. and M. Poff (2010). Acculturation Gaps and Family Adjustment. *Bulletin of the International Society for the Study of Behavioural Development*, No. 2 (58). University of Jena, Germany, 29-33. <https://issbd.org/resources/files/JBD_nov10.pdf>

Cote, J.F. (2010). From Transculturation to Hybridization: Redefining Culture in the Americas. *Transcultural Americas*. University of Ottawa Press, 121-47. <https://books.openedition.org/uop/363?lang=en>

Desai, Kiran (2006). *The Inheritance of Loss*. Delhi: Orient. New Delhi: Penguin.

Divakaruni, Chitra Banerjee (1998). *The Mistress of Spices*, ed. 2005. London: Random Black Swan.

Doshi, T. (2010). *The Pleasure Seekers*, ed. 2011. London: Bloomsbury.

Ghoshal, S. (2013). Between the Lines: Love and Loathing in India. *Mint*. 5 April 2013. <https://www.livemint.com/Opinion/lXBpWIbBxKPT3M561CK9pN/BETWEEN-THE-LINES-Love-and-loathing-in-India.html>

Joshi, Roswitha (2010). *Indian Dreams: A Novel*. New Delhi: UBS.

Raj, Anand (2020) Tishani Doshi: "There is something mysterious about writing", *Friday* (People & Profiles). 4 May 2020. <https://fridaymagazine.ae/life-culture/people-profiles/tishani-doshi-there-is-something-mysterious-about-writin-1.2307797>

Sam, D.L. and Berry, J.W. (1 July 2010). Acculturation: When Individuals and Groups of Different Cultural Backgrounds Meet. *Perspectives on Psychological Science*. 5(4): 472-81. <https://journals.sagepub.com/doi/10.1177/1745691610373075>

Shah, Ranvir (2010). Different Avatars of Love. *The Hindu*. 14 October 2010. <https://www.thehindu.com/books/Different-avatars-of-love/article15780046.ece>

Weichold, Karina (2010). Introduction to Mobility, Migration, and Acculturation. *Bulletin of the International Society for the Study of Behavioural Development*, No. 2 (58). University of Jena, Germany. <https://issbd.org/resources/files/JBD_nov10.pdf>

12

Ashok Banker's *Siege of Mithila*: An Anglo-Indian Reading of Ramayana

Ever since the visual media was thrown open to private players by the government, a number of channels dedicated to religious programmes have come up. This has meant an increased interest in religion and the occult. In keeping with this trend, writers have also increasingly taken to writing on themes related to these subjects. Fictionalization or re-telling of myths, therefore, has become a lucrative venture. Such an endeavour cannot be faulted on artistic grounds, but tampering with a text considered sacred by a large number of people calls for caution. If a writer does not share the sensitivity of a believer, his treatment of such texts may even dent the acculturation process of the young generation.

Ashok Banker, a prolific writer and commentator, started his career as a journalist but soon turned to writing fiction. His short fictional trilogy *The Iron Bra*, *Murder & Champagne*, and *Ten Dead Admen*, published in 1993, was based upon crime. Soon he started writing thrillers, turning finally to myths like the Ramayana and the Mahabharata. He has brought out a series of fictional works based on Ramayana which are claimed to be international best-sellers. These include *Siege of Mithila* (2003), *Prince of Ayodhya* (2003), *Demons of Chitrakoot* (2003), *Armies of Hanuman* (2005), *Bridge of Rama* (2005), *King of Ayodhya* (2006) and *Gods of War* (2009). Banker has the gift of imagination and an eloquent prose style. This paper looks at the strategies employed by him in fictionalizing the Ramayana in his book *Siege of Mithila* and the impact it may have on the acculturation process that goes on incessantly in any society.

Plot Structure

The story of Ramayana re-told in the present book starts with the student life of Rama and Lakshman and runs up to their marriage. Both the brothers are shown studying at the Sidha Ashram which is headed by the 5000-year-old Guru Vishwamitra. The first chapter shows Rama being woken through a psychic message from the Adi-Shakti who takes him to the nearby Bhayanak Van. As to what transpires there is nowhere revealed in the book. Soon thereafter, Bejoo, the captain of the army formation called Vajra Kshatriyas arrives to deliver the message that both the brothers are wanted at Ayodhya. The Guru, who has come to know through his telepathic powers that the king of Asuras—Ravana means to attack the Aryavarta nation, leads a big contingent of Brahmin acolytes and Vajra Kshatriya warriors. Meanwhile at Ayodhya, Ravana has already planted Manthara as his spy. She performs devilish magic rites to invoke her lord Ravana and to transform a serving girl into the queen Kaikeyi who is deputed to murder Dasaratha.

Ravana also infuses life into Bheria, a dead soldier of Bejoo's army unit. This 'twice-lifer' is then made to go to Ayodhya to possess Dasaratha's body and pass orders on his sons Bharat and Shatrughan to proceed with the entire Ayodhya army to two different destinations so that Ayodhya is left deenceless and Ravana can seize it. Bheria actually succeeds in his mission but the situation is finally handled by Guru Vasishtha who defeats Ravana's design.

Sita is no demure princess; she is depicted as a warrior who, along with a female bodyguard Nakhudi disguised as soldiers, goes about in the Dandak-Van and Bhayanak-Van forests scouting for the security of Mithila, and is accosted by bandits, from which predicament she is delivered by, who else, Rama! The sage had deliberately taken a detour to touch Mithila en route because he knew Ravana would first attack Mithila. On the way, Rama rescues Ahalya who had been condemned to be a stone by her husband a long long ago. At Mithila, the defences are low due to the spiritual proclivities of the king Janak.

The *Swayamvar* is marred by the appearance of Ravana in camouflage who is able to meet the condition set down for the *Swayamvar* (later shown to be partial) and claim Sita. When Janak resists, he holds him by the throat at which Sita begs for her father's life and agrees to be Ravana's wife. However, the situation is saved by the two brothers and then Sita is won by Rama. Ravana disappears but not before warning of seizing Mithila by the evening and then raping the kingdom and its princess Sita! Both the brothers are in the vanguard to defend Mithila against the invading Rakshas hordes with the help of the Brahmastra provided by their Guru. It is a mantra rather than an armament, which they have just to read to make the hordes disappear. Banker's Ramayana—part two—ends on this happy note.

Fantastic Realism

Needless to add here that the writer has also contributed his mite to fantasizing the details like the 7.5 lac strong Ayodhya army, 7000-year-old Guru Vasishta (255), etc. Guru Vishwamitra, the 5000-year-old seer, walks so fast while leading the inmates of his ashram that others fall far behind. When brought to his notice, he slackens his pace so that others can catch up with him. The power of the gurus is so great that they can be compared to gods. Banker's portrayal of state of affairs places the sages at the head of administration. Guru Vasishta chalks out the plan to tackle the invading army of Asuras. He has the foreknowledge of aggressors' designs and movements and can order the Prime Minister Sumantra and the princes to march forth. He is aware of his power, therefore, he can tell King Janak, "I decree that this very night your great and virtuous city shall be given the fruit of its immense spiritual labourers. You shall resist this approaching Asura horde and defend Mithila with great honour and valour" (481). The Guru has the mantra-power (which Banker calls Brahmin power) with which the entire army of Asuras can be made to disappear in thin air. It hardly leaves any leeway for the king or the army to act.

Banker has gone ahead with what he calls 'retelling' of the Ramayana myth with a lot of additions and subtractions from his side. Rama, while studying at Guru Vishwamitra's ashram is taken away to the jungle by the Goddess Shakti, who appears naked to Rama. The explanation given by her is that one sees her as one wishes. She tells her name in this way:

> The people of Eric the Norseman named me Frejya. The Inuits of the land that is always clothed in ice call me Sedna. In the land of Nipon, I am known as Amateras of the Sun. In Greece, Demeer of the Corn. In Egypt, they know me as Isis of the River. In times past and future, I have been and will be known as Tara, Coatlicue, Ishtar, Artemis and Shakti. (7-8)

What emerges from the reading of this book is the vision of a world which was mired in magic and sorcery and in which mantra was used even by Ravana to appear in the midst of wooers at Sita Swayamvar at king Janak's court. He also had the power to appear before his devotees (Manthara, for instance) when they propitiated him like a god through sacrifice and mantras (270)! Ravana can hurt and heal his devotees. He can even enter Dasaratha's body to mislead latter's sons Bharat and Shatrughan (250)!

The serving girl is turned by Manthara into a Kaikeyi clone, who is then sent to poison Dasaratha as the famed 'vish-kanyas' of the middle-ages did. But while cradling the Maharaja's face between her 'blouse-encased breasts', she "opened her jaws, revealing two enormous serpentine fangs" (132)! Then, "With one final heart-chilling hiss, Kaikeyi raised her head and fell on Dasaratha with the fury of a predator in heat. Her mouth closed over Dasaratha's neck" (133). A female Dracula indeed! Manthara is portrayed as a very powerful sorcerer who throws even her queen Sumitra into her secret chamber the walls of which move with the chanting of mantras. And Sumitra outsmarts the dai ma through a fancy-dress act that makes her look like the goddess Shakti! (406)

Apart from the fictional depiction of the age, the skewed portrayal of the personalities of those times denigrates certain great figures. The great sages like Guru Vasishta are said to perform sorcery and exorcism (283). There is the depiction of the city of Mithila—a virtual Utopia, which is ruled by a spiritualist king Janak. The city is low on defences but high on gambling halls, blouseless beauties, polygamy and polyandry, etc. (411)! Surprisingly, Guru Vasishta is said to have used 'sorcery' to remove the veil of Sita in the jungle. And Sita wanted to "scream out loud and run away from these gawking, gaping people" (308). She rightly admonishes them, "And the rest of you, if you want entertainment, go find the nearest tavern or dance hall! This isn't a free show provided for your amusement" (308). If Vasishta has the Brahmin power, Ravana also has great Asura power; he can even cause nightmares to sleeping Sita and disorient Rama (472).

This mythical-magical world is made to co-exist with some realistic details of human behavior and the selection of details is done with the objective of making the narrative spicy. At places however, this approach lends an unexpected colour to characters. Rama and Lakshman are not deities but mortals and so the 'boy-meet-girl' pattern is adopted for their meeting:

> Sita's eyes sought him out. He nodded briefly at her. She turned away abruptly, ignoring the gesture.
>
> Lakshman came up beside him. He spoke softly in Rama's right ear, 'Looks like someone's still sore as a mule at being outed, brother. Watch out for her back-kick!'
>
> Rama dug his elbow into Lakshman's ribs. (353)

For the lovers of thrillers, the scene in which Rama goes down the pit of Vasuki to bring to life Ahalya is a perfect piece with horrendous Vetaals (phantoms) fighting with the two brothers and even Sita who also cuts down four-five of them (401). Banker is adept at painting amazons also as is borne out by his thrillers written before he took to the epics.

There is also the element of erotica to further add spice to the narrative. Prior to the *Swayamvar*, when they meet in the jungle, Lakshman speaks to Sita in this way, "I hear Mithila virgins have fine figures too! You really know to provoke a man's imagination"..."I'll be dreaming all night of naked virgins prancing down the raj-marg!" (274). Further, Sita is portrayed as a girl who is rather fussy about her match. "It was not the first swayamvara conducted for the rajkumari. She was notorious for turning down suitors by the hundreds" (412).

Ignorance

The writer could have at least taken the trouble of finding out the relevance and meaning of the mantra that he puts in the mouth of young students of the Sidh Ashram 'Om Hari Swaha' (147) as if this were the Sanskrit equivalent of 'Amen' said at the end of prayer. Guru Vasishta is made to proclaim this very word when he finishes his speech and the congregation too responds with 'Swaha' (282)! The normal ending in such cases is 'iti' meaning 'the end'.

Instead of the word 'brahmachari' for the students, Banker uses 'Brahmacharya' (150). The 'Chandravansh' is translated as the 'moonwood throne'. Seers are addressed as 'Mahadev'! One of his inventions is the reference to Vasishth Purana (111), but knowledgeable scholars deny the existence of such a work. There is the *Yoga Vasishta* though. Similarly, the invocation 'Jai Mata Di' (400) sits ill at ease with the description of mythical times. No king of the stature of Janak would request Guru Vasishta to 'say a Mantra'. Out of ignorance does the author interpret 'Indra-prastha' as the abode of god Indra and situates it in Swarga Lok (477)!

A special mention must be made of Banker's obsession with the Jat clan to which Sita's female bodyguard Nakhudi belongs. She has a 'gutturual Jat accent' (14). Even Lakshman cracks a caste-based joke: "I think there's a law that says even Jat newborn babes have to be at least six feet tall" (261)!

The structure of the novel is based upon intrigues so much so that it can be termed as a novel of intrigues with the only other competing element being a world of magic. The writer has made good use of the elements of novel such as suspense, climax-building and other narratological devices to turn the epical story into a fictionalized novel. There is no gainsaying the fact that Banker has felicity of expression. His narrative has a rare flow and ease which he combines with a rich vocabulary. Here is a specimen:

> Only now that he knew it was a woman he had caught, not a man, did he understand that unexpected softness and the vehemence with which she had resisted his touch. Everything, her sweating overly, her nervousness at certain questions, her blustering arrogance at others, made sense now. It even added to her personality as he had come to perceive it: the witty, sharp-tongued roving sword-for-hire Janaki Kumar was not entirely fictional. It was just that he was a she with an extraordinary lack of the coy artifice that most noble-born Arya women usually affected. (341)

Western Outlook

In his preface, Banker says that he chose to re-tell the myth in a 'modern idiom', i.e. "an amalgam of English-Hindi, Urdu-Sanskrit, and various other terms from Indian languages" (xxii-xxiii), and sure there are words like 'samosas, jalebis and rabadi' (124) which an ailing Dasaratha covets. Elsewhere, one freely comes across words such as rakshas, rajkumar, yojana, shakti, aatma, daiimaa, raj-marg, etc. but the effect sometimes is ludicrous, as for example, the queen Kaikeyi uses 'powders and creams' (128). She also calls the king 'Dasa' lovingly just as Kartikeya becomes 'Kattu' (28).

Clearly, there is a Western cultural nuance that pervades *Siege of Mithila*. Take for instance, 'the order of Bheriya' (63) of the Vajra Kshatriya (army unit) invented by him, which "wore the sigil and helm of the great grey wolf as his [armyman's] chosen totem" (63). Even in the use of language, the Western touch cannot be missed as is seen in the following remark made by Ravana to his sister Supanakha (sic): "I thought I made myself clear the last time we spoke...I was wrong" (58). Similarly, "The brahmin-in-training executed a deep bow and a namaskar while retreating backwards to avoid showing them [Rama and Lakshman] his back" (119). The conge that the writer has in mind seems to have been mixed up with the salaam that entered with the Muslim rule only. The Urdu terminology confirms it further: "Many of his former colleagues in the PF battalion he commanded, the *Purana Wafadars*—so named because they were veterans of the Last Asura War" (158 italics mine).

The modern idiom for Banker means foisting all types of modern ailments and lifestyle aberrations on the mythical period. Thus, the saints discovered cure for diabetics (72) and Manthara's serving girl offers to please her mistress in the lesbian style (84). The serving girl-turned-Kaikeyi goes about naked, 'brushing against the guards' (86) but the guards would only think that the queen had taken more of 'soma than she could hold' (86). Captain Bejoo of Ayodhya army "spat a mouthful of blood-red tobacco-stained paan juice every now and then to the side, evoking irritated stares from the nearest Brahmins who disapproved of tobacco consumption in any form" (278). The Kshatriya were enjoying 'roast meat' when the two disguised women met them in the wood (298). Elsewhere, Bejoo, the Vajra captain, "would have paid a hundred rupees for some soma or even some cheap local wine" (286). This brilliant leader of the army has little respect for the Brahmin community.

Sita and Nakhudi, disguised as soldiers, are taken to be travelling Kshatriyas willing to work for any master for money. Now, the concept of mercenaries is a Western one and there is hardly any similar evidence available in respect of ancient India. The Kshatriyas, represented by Kartikeya, brother of Vinayaka, is fond of smoking Ganja and having 'Ganja dreams' (26). The choice of names is not without a trace of disdain for the Hindu deities, even though the author claims to have profound reverence for the Hindu pantheon. Perhaps, in his obsession with the modern idiom, the author has slipped into depiction of a modern scene.

Life on this earth is ordained by destiny—this is the philosophy of life in Banker's work. Incidentally, this is also one of the several life philosophies propounded in ancient Indian texts. Nevertheless, this philosophy finds better affinity with the ancient Greek and Roman faith systems in which destiny is the only guiding force behind the actions of gods and humans. It is a westernized myth, or one might christen it Anglo-Indian myth if one were to take a hint from the personal profile of the author (See Note). The following description of the fake Kaikeyi, created by Manthara's magic, meeting a convalescent Dasaratha amply proves it:

> She leaned over him suddenly, her hair falling like a dark shower over his chest and face. Dasaratha jerked back, startled, but there was nowhere to go. His head pressed against the pillows and bolsters on which he had been propped up. Kaikeyi moved her face closer to his, and before Sumitra fully realized what was happening, the Second Queen had grasped the maharaja in her embrace and was showering him with passionate kisses. (129)

Upon this, Sumitra taunts Kaikeyi with the following words: "What have you been surviving on? Wine and song?" (130). With the fake Kaikeyi, the author seems to have created a fake culture of those times as well!

Even though Banker exhibits tremendous reverence for Hinduism in his preface when he says that his intention to relate the Rama tale 'respectfully yet realistically' (xxii), the fact is that his fictionalization has had a contrary effect. The emphasis shifts from the clash of forces of *dharma* and their adversaries, a value-reading of the myth as understood by the devotees of Hinduism, to the material aspect of gaining victory by one race over the other as the following lines make it clear: "A direct assault on Lanka was beyond the contemplation of any mortal army. And yet, as long as Lanka remained in the grasp of the demon lord, the Arya nations could not hope to explore and settle the subcontinent safely" (143). To be fair to the author, Banker depicts the Asuras as savages and the Aryans (described as Aryas in the book) as men of principles (305) so much so that King Janak forbids the killing of Ravana even though the latter had tried to kill the former (460).

Conclusion

In an interview,[1] Banker states that he took to re-writing the Ramayana and the Mahabharat to *survive* and not *escape* from his disorderly life (italics mine). But the impression that one gets after finishing his work is that it could be something different. This reminds one of the act of re-reading, which the psychologist Harold Bloom calls 'misreading' often resorted to by young poets against the 'father-figure' of earlier poets, for whom they have no match but whose good-will they seize upon to prop themselves. Of the various categories of 'misreading', Bloom's 'Clinamen' or the 'correction' variety befits the present case (71-98). This is a mode through which the new or young poet uses irony to show how the ancient poet was accurate up to a point bur then lost the track. The suggestion is that the original poem ought to have taken a different route as exemplified by the new poet.

Banker has taken substantial liberty with the myth written by a great sage of ancient India to turn it into an exciting novel but it has not been without inflicting violence on the underlying idealizing intent of a text considered sacred by masses. The novel might appeal to those who do not think much of its cultural linkage, as for example, the readers in the West, and the writer must mint money on this count, but he cannot evade responsibility for the damage that this trivialization of deities and scriptures will cause to the cultural discourse which constructs the subject—the young subject belonging to the next generation, for whom Rama and Krishna may not mean the ideals of a race but only cardboard characters.

NOTE

1. My mother was an Anglo-Indian (please don't use the term "East Indian") and her mother, my grandmother, was Dutch-Irish-Scots. My grandma, in addition to being of foreign descent, was brought up by nuns in a convent school in Sri Lanka, and came to India in her twenties, first staying at Chennai (then called Madras) and later Mumbai (Bombay). She met and married a Goan Catholic, and had three kids in Byculla. My mother grew up there and was a very precocious girl, quitting school, rebelling, modeling (quite successfully), and generally being a much talked-about young woman of the time. She met my biological father, a US-and-Canada returned Gujarati Hindu who drove a Jaguar (brought back from the US), the son of rich parents, and they married three months later, when she was still only 16. It was a disaster; they split up, and she came

back to Byculla to live with her mother, where she had me... (I) descended into writing as a means of survival, not escape. I wanted to record what I was going through because I never thought I would make it out alive. (Excerpt from the interview given to Richard Marcus)

WORKS CITED

Banker, Ashok (2003). *Siege of Mithila*. New Delhi: Penguin, 2005.

Bloom, Harold. *A Map of Misreading*. New York: Oxford University Press, 2003.

Marcus, Richard, 'Interview: Ashok Banker', *BC Blogcritics*. Technorati, Inc./Technorati Media/Technorati.com/Blogcritics. 19 August 2005. Web. 8 January 2012 <http://blogcritics.org/books/article/interview-ashok-banker-part-one/two/#ixzz1isrIv0Ae>